THE
MANUFACTURING
FRONTIER

MARGARET WALSH

THE MANUFACTURING FRONTIER

Pioneer Industry
in Antebellum Wisconsin
1830–1860

MADISON
STATE HISTORICAL SOCIETY OF WISCONSIN
1972

INTRODUCTION

Manufacturing
and the Frontier of Settlement

MANY HISTORIANS HAVE WRITTEN about the early rural and agricultural west of the American prairies and plains. The growth, and the significance, of this western farming frontier for American development are well known. The existence of the mining frontier, the lumbering frontier, the cattlemen's frontier, and even the military frontier have likewise received their share of attention.[1] But it has not readily been acknowledged that the several new phases of population expansion also witnessed the development of an urban and a manufacturing frontier, that towns were laid out and settlement was begun contemporaneously with the cultivation of land, and that craftsmen and manufacturers were shortly thereafter making their goods for sale to pioneer settlers, whether in the town or on the farm.[2] The growth of manufacturing in early western society has been ignored too long. Man-

---

[1] The books which have "frontier" in their title or subtitle are legion. The original and basic work is Frederick Jackson Turner, *The Frontier in American History* (New York, 1921). Turner used the word to mean the existence of an area of "free land" which had a population of under two persons per square mile. He also interpreted "frontier" to mean the westernmost line of settlement in American development or the hither edge of civilization. In addition, other historians have described the frontier as a process whereby the land was settled in an economic succession of stages; or as a given place at a given time. In this study "frontier" is used metaphorically to stand for early development, more particularly the time span of the first two or three decades of settlement. As such it is not a specific population density — indeed many parts of Wisconsin did not have a population density of under two persons per square mile for more than two or three years — nor a process, but rather a flexible period of initial activity.

[2] Two notable exceptions are Richard C. Wade, *The Urban Frontier* (Cambridge, 1959), and James D. Norris, *Frontier Iron: The Maramec Iron Works, 1826–1876* (Madison, 1964). More generally see Harvey S. Perloff, *et al.*, *Regions, Resources and Economic Growth* (Baltimore, 1960), esp. 109–121.

ufacturing did play an important role on the frontier.[3] It was not the dominant economic activity, but it did contribute in more ways and with greater force than has hitherto been acknowledged.

Industrial activities in the mid-nineteenth century have traditionally been associated with New England and the Middle Atlantic states. Indeed these Eastern regions did provide the major share of the nation's aggregate manufacturing output, contributing 68 per cent when measured by value added in 1860.[4] Yet the newer Western states could not be discounted solely because they were the country's "grain belt." In 1860 these newer states — Ohio, Indiana, Michigan, Illinois, Wisconsin, Iowa, Minnesota, Nebraska, Missouri, Kansas and Kentucky — produced 18.6 per cent of the United States' manufacturing output. (Table 1.)

[3] Manufacturing is an economic activity which has had no fixed bounds. A current definition of the function is: "that range of productive operations entailing a change in the form of material goods and into which natural resources enter only through the provision of a site. . . ." Such a definition eliminates primary and tertiary activities — transportation, merchandising, service functions, and agricultural, forestry, mining, and construction operations — and thus restricts manufacturing to the fabrication of goods by hand, by machinery, or by any other agency. Mid-nineteenth-century definitions were less sophisticated and thus often included other economic processes. Then the term manufacturing applied not only to making things by hand and by machine, in households, shops, mills and factories, but also applied to many other economic activities. In this respect the terms manufacturing and industry were often interchangeable. The important criterion was whether or not a man was contributing to the industrial economy, so that the region might become self-sufficient, or might even produce a surplus. In this study, "manufacturing" falls within the mid-nineteenth-century framework and means any economic function which either produced some articles or which altered or processed some natural or semi-finished goods. For a wider discussion on the historical and present definitions of the term see R.E. Gallman, "Value Added by Agriculture, Mining and Manufacturing in the United States, 1840–1880" (unpublished Ph.D dissertation, University of Pennsylvania, 1956); Brooke Hindle, *Technology in Early America* (Chapel Hill, 1966), 67–82; R.A. Esterlin, "Estimates of Manufacturing Activity" in E.S. Lee, *et al.*, *Population Redistribution and Economic Growth in the United States, 1870–1950, Vol. 1* (Philadelphia, 1957), 638–652; S.D. North, "Manufactures in the Federal Census," *Publications of the American Economic Association*, New Series, No. 2 (March, 1889), 269–275; Nathan Rosenberg (ed.), *The American System of Manufactures* (Edinburgh, 1969); and *Twelfth Census, 1900: Manufactures*, Vol. VII, 34–40.

[4] Manufacturing activities will be measured by means of the construct "value added by manufacture" unless otherwise stated. This construct gives the approximate value created in the process of manufacturing by deducting from the gross product the cost of materials consumed, the fuel used, and other costs incurred in manufacturing the finished product. It therefore provides the most satisfactory census measure of the relative importance of given industries for any country.

This contribution was achieved mainly through the primary processing industries — lumber planed and sawed, flour and grist milling, brewing, leather tanned and curried, and meat packing — industries whose existence have for the most part been ignored, or have been dismissed as being merely "pre-industrial," even though they were of major importance.[5] (Table 2.)

[5] Victor S. Clark, *The History of Manufactures In The United States* (New York, 1949 edition), does deal with the processing industries in his encyclopedic interpretation of the development of manufacturing in the United States. Three other historians have specifically written about manufacturing in the early Middle West and have thus had to pay marked attention to the processing industries. See Elmer A. Riley, *The Development of Chicago and Vicinity As a Manufacturing Center Prior to 1880* (Chicago, 1911); Isaac Lippincott, *A History of Manufactures in the Ohio Valley to the Year 1860* (New York, 1914); and Louis C. Hunter, *Studies in the Economic History of the Ohio Valley: Seasonal Aspects of Industry and Commerce Before the Age of Big Business* (Northampton, Mass., 1935). A more recent study which pointed to the importance of the processing industries is Albert Fishlow, *American Railroads and The Transformation of The American Economy* (Cambridge, 1965), 226–228, but this was merely as one of the dynamic sequences to the expansion of the railroad.

TABLE 1

MANUFACTURING IN THE UNITED STATES IN 1860, BY REGIONS
(In Current $000,000's.)

Region	Number of Establishments	Capital Invested	Number of Hands Employed	Value of Product	Value Added
New England	20,671 (14.7)*	257.5 (25.5)	391,836 (29.9)	468.6 (24.8)	223.1 (26.1)
Middle Atlantic	53,287 (37.9)	435.1 (43.1)	546,243 (41.7)	802.3 (42.5)	358.2 (41.9)
Western	36,785 (26.2)	194.2 (19.2)	209,909 (16.0)	384.6 (20.4)	159.0 (18.6)
Southern	20,631 (14.7)	96.0 (9.5)	110,721 (8.5)	155.5 (8.2)	69.0 (8.1)
Pacific	8,777 (6.3)	23.4 (2.3)	50,204 (3.8)	71.2 (3.8)	42.7 (5.0)
Territories	282 (0.2)	3.7 (0.4)	2,333 (0.2)	3.5 (0.2)	2.3 (0.3)
United States	140,433 (100)	1,009.9 (100)	1,311,246 (100)	1,885.9 (100)	854.3 (100)

[SOURCE: *Eighth Census, 1860, Manufactures,* Vol. III, p. 725.]
*The figures in parentheses are the percentage contribution of each region to the national manufacturing total.

The newer West can not be eliminated from any comprehensive picture of the industrial landscape, because its pioneering economy was altered by innovations and improvements in transportation and technology. There was no clear-cut dichotomy between an industrial East and an agrarian West. The existence of new and relatively quick modes of access to other parts of the country, using first the seasonal water routes and then the year-round railroad, meant that the frontier no longer needed to be a series of self-sufficient communities, nor did it have to go through cumulative stages of growth. A more complex process of economic growth ensured the co-existence of several kinds of economic activity.

The Middle West at midcentury could produce those goods and services for which it was well endowed, namely agricultural

TABLE 2

LEADING INDUSTRIES IN THE UNITED STATES, 1850 AND 1860
(By Value Added, in Current $000's, and by Percentage
Contribution to the National Aggregate. Ranked in Order
in 1850 and Ranked in Parentheses in 1860.)

Industry	1850	Per Cent of Total	1860	Per Cent of Total
1. Lumber, planed and sawed	30,927	6.7	53,570 (2)	6.3
2. Boots and Shoes	30,119	6.5	49,161 (3)	5.8
3. Cottons	27,724	6.0	54,671 (1)	6.4
4. Flour and Grist Mills	23,020	5.0	40,083 (4)	4.7
5. Clothiers and Tailors	22,581	4.9	36,681 (5)	4.3
6. Iron Manufactures	22,004	4.7	35,689 (6)	4.2
7. Machinery	16,631	3.6	32,566 (7)	3.8
8. Woolens	14,936	3.2	25,032 (9)	2.9
9. Leather	14,837	3.2	22,786 (11)	2.6
10. Cabinet Ware	11,574	2.5	13,451 (15)	1.6
United States	463,982		854,257	

[SOURCE: *Seventh Census, 1850,* and *Eighth Census, 1860, Manufactures,* Vol. III.]

goods, lumber and mineral resources, and export them at a competitive price with respect to most other areas. In return the
region could import the goods in which it was deficient. It was
possible to enter the commercial economy of the national market
almost immediately and there was no need to develop gradually
in stages. Manufacturers did not have to await the arrival of
other economic entrepreneurs; they could move with the westward line of expansion, or at least very close to that line.

These manufacturers were eager to seize the advantages of a
good supply of natural resources and agricultural crops, together
with access to transportation. They then could act as intermediary
links between the resource sector and the consuming sector of the
economy by processing local products in mills and shops.[6] These
industrial plants varied in size from the village sawmill or gristmill to the large lumber mill or the city flour mill, but collectively
they introduced industrialization to the interior of the country
in a natural and automatic way by spreading technology and by
taking advantage of new forms of transport.

Though processing industries were of major importance in
shaping the industrial character of the West, they were not the
only branches of manufacturing established in that region. (Table
3.) Some entrepreneurs, who had a larger capital backing or were
more innovative, preferred to build plants producing iron goods
and machinery, especially agricultural machinery. Others, using
capital obtained by retailing, established manufactories catered
to the popular consumer demand for ready-made goods. Still
others, operating on a smaller budget, established craft shops.
Although these artisans were no longer protected by the high cost
of transporting manufactured goods from the East, as had been
their counterparts in the trans-Allegheny West prior to 1830, they

---

[6] Processing industries are those branches of manufacturing which are basically
"first-stage resource users" in the sense that they refine or process a natural
resource — namely agricultural produce, minerals or lumber — either for the
custom trade or for local or regional trade. Some of these processed goods are
consumed in their finished form; for example, flour, beer or packed meat. Others
are fabricated in a "second stage," as, for example, tanned leather is turned into
boots, shoes, or harnesses, and lumber into furniture or barrels. The key to processing is the first stage or immediate work done on natural resources. When
the "second stage" is involved, then the classification "processing" is applied only
to those branches of manufacturing whose backward linkages to the raw material
are more important than their forward linkages to the consumer.

still managed to contribute a share, declining though it might be, to the region's aggregate manufacturing economy.

Manufacturing growth on the frontier of Western settlement around midcentury was thus a composite of new and old kinds of industrial organization. The larger mills and the factories were entering the regional or even the national market. The manufactories were catering to a Western urban demand. The smaller mills were supplying local and neighborhood needs. The craft shops were gradually closing down under the impact of mass-produced goods, but were still numerically significant. Even the family system of home manufactures had not entirely disappeared. The Midwest was in a transitional period of industrial development and was passing through a variety of stages simultaneously. There was no complete breakdown of the earlier processes of manufacturing under the impact of modern techniques. Yet neither was there predominance by the traditional household manufacturing. Overall, the various forms and types of antebellum manufacturing contributed to stimulating the growth and diversifica-

TABLE 3

MANUFACTURES IN THE WESTERN STATES IN 1860,
SELECTED INDUSTRIES

(By Value Added, in Current $'s.)

Industry	United States	Western States	Western States As Percentage of United States
Agricultural Implements	11,961,791	6,279,616	52.49
Blacksmiths	8,224,176	2,051,679	24.94
Cooperage	7,238,018	3,016,947	36.68
Flour and Meal	40,083,056	18,018,704	44.95
Liquors (Malt)	11,313,610	4,395,878	38.85
Leather	22,785,715	3,141,605	13.78
Lumber planed and sawed	53,569,942	19,957,259	37.25
Provisions	7,091,809	3,802,003	53.61

[SOURCE: *Eighth Census, 1860, Manufactures*, Vol. III.]

tion of Western economic activities, thereby creating an underlying foundation for the more rapid industrialization of the region after the Civil War.

Wisconsin belonged to the Western frontier of the mid-nineteenth century. Located partly within the fertile prairie belt of the Old Northwest and partly within the Great Lakes lumber belt, and bounded by the navigable waterways of the Mississippi River and lakes Michigan and Superior, Wisconsin became a territory in 1836. Within a few years the remaining Indians were dispossessed, and increasing numbers of American-born migrants, mainly from the Northern states, and foreign-born migrants from Europe moved to the new lands, first occupying the good agricultural parts of the southeast and then fanning out in a northwesterly direction. Alongside the lead miners, farmers, and land speculators came lumbermen, blacksmiths, shoemakers, millers, machinists, and numerous other artisans and businessmen who sought work in the emerging villages and towns. By 1850, two years after Wisconsin attained statehood, the population had reached 305,566, and the goods produced in manufacturing establishments were valued at $8,984,533. Wisconsin was making rapid progress in the "mechanic arts." Taking advantage of plentiful natural resources and increasing farm outputs, and utilizing new transportation and technological facilities, the mills, shops, manufactories, and factories of Wisconsin were already partaking in a growing market specialization. This study attempts to analyze that process of industrial growth and change on the frontier.

* * * * *

In preparing this study I have received valuable advice and assistance from many people. For their co-operation, I should like to thank the staff of the State Historical Society of Wisconsin; the staff of the Manuscripts Division of the Baker Library in the Harvard Business School; the staff of the Social Systems Research Institute in the University of Wisconsin; and the Public Relations Managers of Dun & Bradstreet Inc., and of the J.I. Case Company. For their help and encouragement I should like to thank my colleagues at the University of Wisconsin, the State Historical Society of Wisconsin, the University of Keele, and the University of Birmingham. I should also like to thank the Ford Foundation Fund for financing the computer program on the census data, and the University of Wisconsin Graduate School for financing computer time. I am grateful as well to Professor Frederick Merk for his many useful comments. And most of all I am indebted to Professor Eric E. Lampard, whose timely advice and suggestions have guided this study in its development and final form.

MARGARET WALSH

Birmingham, England
March 1, 1972

CONTENTS

TABLES

MAPS

CHAPTER ONE

Early Development
of Wisconsin's Industrial Resources

"IF GOD HAD DESIGNED WISCONSIN to be chiefly a manufacturing
state instead of agricultural which she claims to be and is, it is
difficult to see more than one particular in which He could have
endowed her more richly for that purpose."[1]

Similar themes advertising the magnificent opportunities for
industrial development were constantly reiterated in Wisconsin
newspapers, commercial magazines, and official reports of the
late 1850's and early 1860's. Contemporary business leaders and
public officials believed that Wisconsin was designed, if not destined, to take a high rank among the manufacturing states of the
Union. Although these industrial advocates were mainly concerned to develop a local autarkic economy at the expense of the
older Eastern states, and thus prevent the loss of valuable money
supplies, still their eulogizing was not without foundation. The
potential for Wisconsin maufacturing was noteworthy. The state
possessed abundant and varied raw materials in the form of minerals, timber, and agricultural produce. Water power from its
many rivers was available in large quantity. Transportation facilities provided by inland waterways and, in the middle and late
1850's, by railroads were easily accessible; and finally Wisconsin
was well located with respect to the great markets.[2]

---

[1] Wisconsin State Agricultural Society, *Transactions*, 7 (1861–68), 50. (Hereinafter cited as WSAS *Trans.*)

[2] *Milwaukee Sentinel*, May 15, 1849; July 14, 1860; *Hunt's Merchants' Magazine*,
10 (1844), 554; WSAS *Trans.* 6 (1860), 61, 77–78; *Wisconsin Farmer*, 13 (1861), 50;
14 (1862), 61; State of Wisconsin, *Governor's Annual Message*, 1861, 13; John
Gregory, *Industrial Resources of Wisconsin* (Milwaukee, 1855).

Wisconsin's mineral deposits, especially of lead and iron, were among the important sources of the state's wealth. The most substantial known mineral concentration in the mid-nineteenth century was the lead region, which, in Wisconsin, consisted of the southwestern counties of Grant, Iowa, and Lafayette, some of Green, and the western portions of Dane county. (Map 1.) Being located entirely in the "driftless area," with the mineral-bearing rock exposed, this region was an early hive of industrial activity. The first mining operations of any size began around 1826 and for two decades the number of miners and the output of ore increased, reaching a peak production of 54,494,850 pounds in 1845. The Upper Mississippi Valley, in fact, became the nation's chief lead-producing area.[3]

Iron mining in antebellum Wisconsin was relatively undeveloped. The great beds of the Lake Superior region within Wisconsin remained untouched and virtually unnoted. To contemporaries, the most important deposit of iron, which was being worked in small amounts in the 1850's, was that of Iron Ridge in Dodge and Washington counties. Containing 51 per cent metallic ore, the extent of this mineral body was estimated at 27,255,000 tons. The largest known deposit of iron in Wisconsin was that in the Black River Falls region of Jackson County, where 55,000,000 tons of ore were estimated to contain between 45 and 48 per cent metallic ore. Here an enterprising German firm had erected a blast furnace in the late 1850's, for the manufacture of pig iron. Other iron resources included the brown hematite of Sauk County, Iron Mountain in Crawford County, and the bog ores extensively diffused throughout the marshes of Wisconsin, especially in the southeastern counties. Indeed contemporaries thought that, with the exception of Michigan and

---

[3] For more details on lead mining see Joseph Schafer, *The Wisconsin Lead Region* (Madison, 1932); T.C. Chamberlin, *Geology of Wisconsin, Survey of 1873–79,* 1 (Madison, 1883), 636–665; James A. Lake, *Law and Mineral Wealth: The Legal Profile of the Wisconsin Mining Industry* (Madison, 1962); Selma L. Schubring, "A Statistical Study of Lead and Zinc Mining in Wisconsin," Wisconsin Academy of Sciences, Arts and Letters, *Transactions,* 22 (1926) 9–99 [hereinafter cited as WASAL *Trans.*]; State of Wisconsin, Assembly, 5 Legis., 1852, 10 Legis., 1858, *Reports* of the Commmittee on Mining and Smelting; State of Wisconsin, Assembly, 7 Legis., 1854, 7 Legis., 1855, *Geological Reports; Hunt's Merchants' Magazine* 40 (1859), 244, quoting the *Galena Advertiser.*

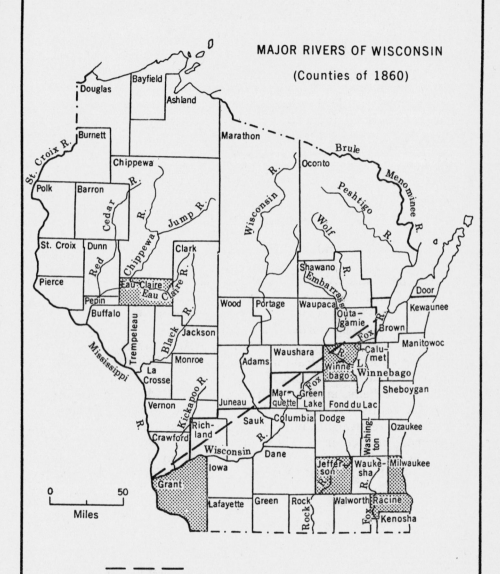

MAP 1

MAJOR RIVERS OF WISCONSIN

(Counties of 1860)

Northern-Southern Wisconsin boundary

Sample counties

Northern-Southern Wisconsin boundary
following county boundaries

3

Ohio, probably no state in the Northwest compared with Wisconsin in the abundance and redness of its iron ores.[4]

Zinc mining, before the Civil War, was in a very experimental stage, and insofar as it was carried out at all, was done so in conjunction with lead mining.[5] Though the zinc resources were clearly recognized, there appeared to be some doubt as to whether these ores could be obtained in sufficient quantity to justify economical manufacture. The copper deposits, especially those of the southwest, had mainly been exploited in the early settlement of Wisconsin.[6] At Milwaukee and at the other sites on the shore of Lake Michigan, stratified beds of clay furnished excellent material for cream-colored bricks. Also scattered throughout the state were such resources as building stone, crushed stone, sand, gravel, limestone, and marble, all of which were useful for construction purposes.[7]

Not only was Wisconsin's soil underlaid with the "richest mineral wealth," but the soil itself was "rich to a proverb," making the state the "wonder of the age."[8] Wisconsin was situated too far west and too far north to fall within the corn-belt proper, but the soils were naturally adaptable for wheat cultivation, and the prairie sections were ideal for wheat growing.[9] Being settled later than other parts of the Old Northwest, at a time when improvements were being made in transportation and when the demand for breadstuffs was rising both at home and abroad, Wisconsin farmers were straightway able to raise wheat for a commercial market. Production of wheat in Wisconsin rose from 212,116 bushels in 1839–40 to 4,286,131 bushels in 1849–50 and to 15,657,458 bushels in 1859–60.[10] Per capita production of wheat

[4] WSAS *Trans.*, 4 (1856) 357, 361; State of Wisconsin, Assembly 10 Legis., 1858, *Geological Report*, 22–47.

[5] Frederick Merk, *Economic History of Wisconsin During the Civil War Decade* (Madison, 1916), 114; Schubring, 10–11; WSAS *Trans.*, 6 (1860), 27.

[6] Merk, 121–122; WSAS *Trans.*, 6 (1860), 59; *Niles National Register*, 51 (1837), 307, mentions copper mining but gives no statistics.

[7] WSAS *Trans.*, 6 (1860), 199–217.

[8] *Niles' National Register*, 61 (1841), 63, citing *Milwaukee Courier*.

[9] John G. Thompson, *The Rise and Decline of Wheat Growing in Wisconsin* (Madison, 1909); E.E. Lampard, *The Rise of the Dairy Industry in Wisconsin: A Study in Agricultural Change, 1820–1920* (Madison, 1963), 23–32.

[10] *Sixth Census, 1840, Compendium*, 344; *Seventh Census, 1850*, 931; *Eighth Census, 1860, Agriculture*, Vol. II, 167–168.

shot up from 14.03 bushels in 1849 to 20.18 in 1859.[11] Wheat was the major crop which offered the farmer a decent cash return, and that crop was truly "king" of the state's agricultural economy.

Other crops cultivated in Wisconsin — corn, oats, barley, wool, and tobacco — served mainly for local consumption either directly or indirectly, as did the small amount of dairy and cattle production. Corn outputs rose from 379,359 bushels in 1839–40 to 7,517,300 bushels in 1859–60; oats from 406,514 bushels to 11,059,260 in the same years; and barley from 11,062 bushels to 707,307. Wool increased from 6,777 pounds in 1839–40 to 1,011,933 pounds in 1859–60; tobacco from 115 pounds to 87,340 pounds in the same year.[12] Several of these crops provided raw materials for the processing industries, and overall farm production encouraged the growth of an agricultural machinery industry.

In addition to mineral wealth and fertile soil, Wisconsin was endowed with magnificent lumber resources. Probably most of the state's 35 million acres contained important stands of timber. In the southern part of Wisconsin, the timber was mainly hardwood, notably oak, which was cut down to clear the land for agriculture and used for houses and fencing. The "true forest" lay almost entirely north of a line drawn from Manitowoc to Portage and then to the falls of the St. Croix River. This was not a homogeneous region. In the south there was a stretch of hardwoods about thirty to thirty-five miles wide, containing only about 5 per cent pine. North of this stretch was a belt of mixed hardwoods and conifers, about equally divided in quantity. Finally, along the headwaters of the Wolf, Menominee, Wisconsin, Chippewa, Black, and St. Croix rivers, there stood a valuable tract of conifers.[13] In the antebellum era, when the pride of the Wisconsin forest was the white pine, which was a light-weight

[11] Thompson, 180–191.

[12] Sixth Census, 1840, Compendium, 344; Eighth Census, 1860, Agriculture, Vol. II, 167–168.

[13] George W. Hotchkiss, History of the Lumber and Forest Industry of the Northwest (Chicago, 1898), 22; Robert F. Fries, Empire in Pine: The Story of Lumbering in Wisconsin (Madison, 1951), 6; Filbert Roth, On the Forestry Conditions of Northern Wisconsin (Madison, 1898), 10–12; Bernhardt J. Kleven, "Wisconsin Lumber Industry" (unpublished Ph.D. thesis, University of Minnesota, 1941), chapter one; J. Willard Hurst, Law and Economic Growth: The Legal History of the Lumber Industry in Wisconsin, 1836–1915 (Cambridge, 1964), 1–3.

wood and easy to work, the forest resources of Wisconsin were considered to be inexhaustible.

The state also possessed ample natural motive power for processing these resources into semi-manufactured or manufactured goods.[14] The rivers and streams of Wisconsin were deemed adequate to drive any quantity of antebellum machinery, and they were well distributed throughout the state. In northern Wisconsin the rivers were plentiful and their rapid flows were capable of generating large quantities of power. In southern Wisconsin the rivers were noteworthy for their wide and uniform distribution rather than for their size, but they still provided sufficient motive power.[15]

If the resources of Wisconsin provided a bountiful factor endowment for antebellum manufacturing, then the accessible markets, broken down into more specific factors — local population concentrations, transportation, the constraints of capital scarcity, technology, and entrepreneurial initiative — determined the forms and size of the firms and the scale of their operations.[16]

[14] Waterpower was the most common source of power in antebellum United States. See Peter Temin, "Steam and Waterpower in the Early Nineteenth Century," *Journal of Economic History*, 26 (1966), 204; Nathan Rosenberg (ed.), *The American System of Manufactures: Report (1855)* (Edinburgh, 1969), 24–25; Allen H. Fenichel, "Growth and Diffusion of Power in Manufacturing, 1838–1919," in *Output, Employment and Productivity in the United States after 1800, Studies in Income and Wealth*, Vol. 30 (Princeton, 1966), 444.

[15] Gregory, John, 98; Leonard S. Smith, *The Water Powers of Wisconsin* (Madison, 1908).

[16] General theoretical studies of the location of industrial activity place great emphasis on transportation and production costs in determining the location of manufacturing. See Edgar M. Hoover, *The Location of Economic Activity* (New York, 1948); Alfred Weber, *Theory of the Location of Industries* (trans. C.J. Friedrich; Chicago, 1929); and Walter Isard, *Location and Space Economy: A General Theory Relating to Industrial Location, Market Areas, Land Use, Trade and Urban Structure* (New York, 1956). By contrast, August Losch, *The Economics of Location* (trans. William H. Woglum; New York, Science Editions, 1967), stresses the market and the interdependence of economic activity. All seem to be concerned with the location of the larger firm. Melvin L. Greenhut, *Plant Location in Theory and in Practice: The Economics of Space* (Chapel Hill, 1956), who specifically concentrates on the location pattern of smaller firms, found that personal considerations such as business contacts or environmental preferences were important in determining site selection of manufacturing plants. Douglass C. North, "Location Theory and Regional Economic Growth," *Journal of Political Economy*, 62 (1955), 243–258, attempts to place the principles of location within a framework of American regional development.

In a frontier situation, accessible markets might be considered to be synonymous with local population distribution and agglomeration. A cursory examination of Wisconsin supports such an observation, for the southern part of the state had the highest proportion of both Wisconsin's population and manufacturing output. In 1840 those counties south of a line drawn from Green Bay to the Mississippi River contained 85.2 per cent of the territorial aggregate population of 30,945; in 1850 the percentage was 93.1 out of a total population of 305,391; and in 1860 it was 82.7 per cent of a total of 775,881 persons. In similar fashion the southern half of Wisconsin contained a high proportion of the state's manufacturing. By 1850 the southern counties contributed 91.6 per cent of the aggregate value added of $3,797,970; while in 1860 the south produced 83.5 per cent of the total value added of $11,323,017. It might thus be reasoned that population agglomerations created their own demand for locally produced goods and served as hinterland centers, thereby stimulating manufacturing.

The relationship of manufacturing growth and population distribution seemed relatively close. A simple linear correlation and regression analysis on the variables manufacturing by value added and population, both by county, showed that in 1850 the r coefficient was .73 and r^2 ratio was .527; in 1860 the r coefficient was .69 and the r^2 ratio was .478. Interpreting the r^2 ratio as the proportion of the total variation in one variable explained by the other variable, manufacturing had a positive relationship with population of .53 in 1850 and .48 in 1860, thus suggesting that population was a major factor in determining manufacturing growth and distribution.

However, on a more sophisticated level, using a multiple correlation and regression analysis, population does not appear to be such an important factor in influencing manufacturing development. With value added by manufacturing as the dependent variable and value of home manufactures, population, cash value of farms, capital invested, area, and total liabilities and net worth of banks, all by county, as the independent variables, population had only a .110 partial correlation with manufacturing in 1850 and .401 in 1860. This partial correlation is a measure of the variation explained in value added, by population, after all the other variables have explained all they could, or having controlled for the other variables.[17] In this, it appears that population, at least statistically, was not of such great significance in influencing the pattern of Wisconsin manufacturing.[18]

This multiple correlation and regression analysis reinforced the necessity of examining other market factors that might be significant in encouraging the growth of Wisconsin industry. Of these factors, transportation assumed an important role. Wisconsin was pioneered at a time when transportation facilities were being transformed by the advent of the railroad. Yet even before the construction of railroads in the 1850's, most settled areas of Wisconsin were able to reach outside markets. In the southwestern lead region and the western part of Wisconsin, the Mississippi and its tributaries gave access to New Orleans, and thence to the Eastern cities. In the eastern and central parts of Wisconsin, the Wisconsin and Fox rivers and the Great Lakes provided a water route to the East coast. To be sure, towns which were not directly located on water routes had problems of getting beyond local markets, but the plank roads provided some, albeit inefficient, means of access to wider areas, and the railroads were swift to follow in their wake in the 1850's.[19] (Map 2.) By the end of 1860, 806 miles of track had been constructed in Wisconsin, linking the southern part of the state to the Midwestern and Eastern markets and bringing more of the Wisconsin frontier within a regional, if not a national distributional framework.[20]

[17] Banking statistics were not available for 1850 as banking was not made legal in Wisconsin until 1853. It would be desirable to include transportation (railroad mileage per county) as another variable, but these figures were not ascertainable.

[18] Statistically the intervention of another partial of high explanation value — .909 capital invested — may account for the low partial value of population.

[19] State Highway Commission of Wisconsin, *A History of Wisconsin Highway Development, 1835–1945* (Madison, 1947), 228–230, cites the dates of the chartering of plank roads in Wisconsin. The majority of these roads were chartered between 1848 and 1854, but there were not as many plank roads built as were chartered. The information on the actual construction of plank roads is very scattered and thin. It can be found mainly in newspapers, commercial journals and city directories. There is also a little information in William L. Bolton, "Plank Roads of Wisconsin" (unpublished B.L. thesis, University of Wisconsin, 1897).

[20] For details on the construction and abandonment of each railroad in Wisconsin, with information on the cumulative mileage at the end of each significant year, see James P. Kaysen, *The Railroads of Wisconsin, 1827–1937* (Boston, 1937). For more general information on the development of the railroad network in

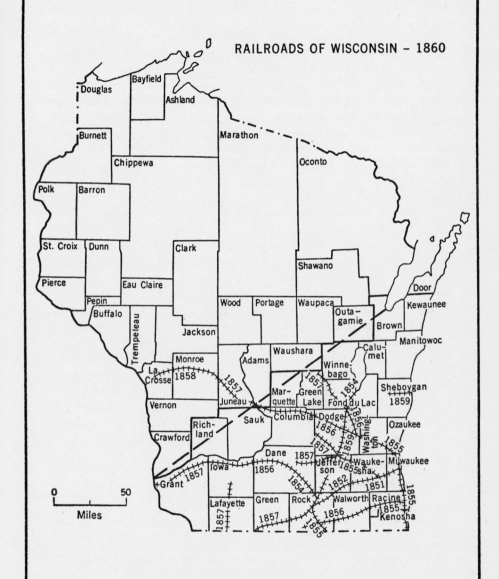

MAP 2

RAILROADS OF WISCONSIN – 1860

Railroads shown are those constructed and in use by 1860.

9

Granted local population agglomerations and an adequate transportation network, then the critical problem in establishing manufactures on the market side appeared to be the constraints of capital scarcity. Capital in this sense fell into two parts — labor availability and financial resources. Of these two, the supply of money was the more significant. Labor on the frontier might be scarce and more expensive than in the East, but many of the small-scale processing industries could use seasonal labor, especially in the winter, and many of the products processed directly from natural resources required little labor, or at least little skilled labor.

Financial assets, either in cash or credit, were essential if a manufacturing establishment aimed to serve more than a local clientele. In the early development of Wisconsin in the 1840's, capital was high priced and tended to migrate to the traditionally more profitable venture of land speculation, and later, in the 1850's, to railroad construction rather than to the more hazardous and unfamiliar manufacturing enterprises. Furthermore financial conditions in Wisconsin itself were not conducive to safe undertakings let alone to speculative business activities. Before 1853, short-term borrowing was hindered by the constitutional prohibition of banking, which was itself an inheritance from the crisis of 1837.[21] Then four years later the Panic of '57 and the ensuing depression shook and partially destroyed the foundations which had been laid, particularly among medium-sized establishments which had a few thousand dollars at stake.[22]

Wisconsin, see Frank N. Elliot, "The Causes and Growth of Railroad Regulation in Wisconsin, 1848–76" (unpublished Ph.D. dissertation, University of Wisconsin, 1956); Robert S. Hunt, *Law and Locomotives: The Impact of the Railroad on Wisconsin Law in the Nineteenth Century* (Madison, 1958); and Herbert W. Rice, "The Early History of the Chicago, Milwaukee and St. Paul Company" (unpublished Ph.D. dissertation, University of Iowa, 1939).

[21] For a discussion of the early development or nondevelopment of banking in Wisconsin see Theodore A. Andersen, *A Century of Banking in Wisconsin* (Madison, 1954), and Leonard B. Kreuger, *History of Commercial Banking in Wisconsin* (Madison, 1933).

[22] An examination of the firms located in the six sample counties suggests that the large entrepreneurs who came to Wisconsin either with money or with good credit facilities were able to survive the depression. They had considerable trouble in obtaining payments for their products and in purchasing supplies of raw materials, but they struggled through. The very small one-, two-, or perhaps three-man shop with only a few hundred dollars invested in plant and usually

Local financial resources were not readily available to the in-cipient manufacturer. Most of the $15,331,933 worth of Wiscon-sin banking assets in 1860 were used for short-term commercial paper, probably to finance agricultural, transportation, and urban developments, while much of the $17,167,500 worth of capital in manufacturing in 1860 was invested by outside entrepreneurs.[23] In many cases the operators of larger industrial establishments were either wealthy or had access to the resources of relatives or Eastern friends. The more exceptional "Horatio Alger" appeared to work upward by a gradual expansion of his business based on his own reputation rather than on borrowed capital. Many small-er firms had their financial security tied up in the local real es-tate and personal property of their owner-operators. The very small craftsmen had little security on which to borrow.[24] Bank-ing assets were probably more an index of general economic de-velopment than of the availability of money for loans to manu-facturers.

Within this financial context it becomes apparent that the role of the entrepreneur was decisive. It was only the more ad-venturous and farsighted "economic man" who risked his capital in setting up manufacturing operations in the new West.[25] But

---

with little or no machinery often succumbed to economic pressures. However, such men were not long in re-entering business on a very small scale since their investment level was also very low. The medium-sized firms with a few thousand dollars invested in plant and machinery were unable to withstand the tight financial strain and collapsed, but their founders' meager fortunes had been ruined and they were often unable to obtain sufficient financial assets to re-enter the manufacturing stratum with their former standing.

[23] There is no information on the short-term loan policies of Wisconsin banks in the 1850's. The semi-annual reports of the Bank Commissioner merely state the amount of money which any given bank had in loans. This statement is therefore tentative.

[24] These statements on the sources of capital for manufacturing are based on a study of sample firms in the counties of Dane, Eau Claire, Chippewa, Jefferson, Grant, Milwaukee, Racine, and Winnebago, as reported in the Dun and Bradstreet Mercantile Credit Reports, 1844–1861, in the Baker Library, Harvard Business School. (Hereinafter cited as D. & B.) It should be noted that these reports are cited as Dun & Bradstreet reports for convenience and ready identification pur-poses only. The reports were actually created by the predecessor companies of Lewis Tappan & Co., Tappan & Douglass, B. Douglass, or R.G. Dun & Co.

[25] "Economic Man," or the entrepreneur who can best use available information to build up an economic activity in the optimum location, can be either an Inno-vator, an Adopter, or an Adapter. For the subtle distinctions between these "actors," see the literature on Game Theory in Economic Geography; for example,

even he might not be fully venturesome. Adapters and adopters had often learned their trades in the East and thus had either business connections or a plentiful supply of money. Alternatively they might be able to borrow cash from friends and relatives, through various promotional schemes, or simply by advertising in Eastern newspapers. These entrepreneurs usually adopted manufacturing enterprises with which they had some familiarity, or adapted familiar processes to fit the western environment.[26] Such manufacturers might run less risk in investing money in the processing branches, particularly lumbering, but even there the returns might be marginal.[27]

The innovator, setting up a new production function, was less sure of success and was thereby a rarer phenomenon of the frontier. He might come from two backgrounds. A businessman by origin and endowed with capital, he might venture into an unfamiliar or new line of manufacturing. He might thus be considered an adapter in that he was adapting his skills and assets

Julian Wolpert, "The Decision Process in Spatial Context," Association of American Geographers, *Annals*, 54 (1964), 537–558; Peter R. Gould, "Man Against His Environment: A Game Theoretic Framework." Association of American Geographers, *Annals*, 53 (1963), 290–297; Walter Isard, "Game Theory, Location Theory and Industrial Agglomeration," *Papers and Proceedings of the Regional Science Association*, 18 (1967), 1–12; Benjamin H. Stevens, "An Application of Game Theory to a Problem in Location Strategy," *Papers and Proceedings of the Regional Science Association*, 7 (1961), 143–157; and Allan Pred, "Behavior and Location — Foundations for a Geographic and Dynamic Location Theory," *Lund Studies in Geography*, Series B, Human Geography, 7 (1967).

[26] In recent times Oscar Litterer, *Where Does Small Business Obtain Its Capital?* (Minneapolis, 1946) suggested that capital for small business enterprises is obtained from five sources: the entrepreneur himself; relatives and friends; business concerns; local and nearby capitalists; and the security market. It is probable that only the first three sources operated in the establishment of small manufacturing concerns or even larger manufacturing establishments in early Wisconsin. There is little evidence of the fourth in the activity of the Fire and Marine Insurance Company bank in Milwaukee (see Alice E. Smith, *George Smith's Money: A Scottish Investor in America* (Madison, 1966); and in the antebellum period there was very little of the fifth source anywhere in the country.

[27] Most of the large profits in the lumbering industry were made after the Civil War. For example, see Richard N. Current, *Pine Logs and Politics: A Life of Philetus Sawyer, 1816–1900* (Madison, 1950); Ralph Hidy, *et al., Timber and the Weyerhauser Story* (New York, 1963); Orrin H. Ingram, *Letters of a Pioneer: Early Lumbering Days* (Eau Claire, 1916); Arthur R. Reynolds, *The Daniel Shaw Lumber Company: A Case Study of the Wisconsin Lumbering Frontier* (New York, 1957); and Isaac Stephenson, *Recollections of a Long Life, 1829–1915* (Chicago, 1915).

to a new trade in a new environment. But he did innovate in the sense of chancing capital in an untested enterprise. The second type of innovator was the "interloper" — perhaps the antebellum Horatio Alger — who seized the opportunity of fluid economic conditions. This entrepreneur used his initiative to establish himself locally while the market was safe. He thus often developed a new branch of manufacturing, such as agricultural implements, though he might venture into the household-consumer branches or into iron products, provided that the market was initially sheltered from competition by high transport costs. Once having created a strong base, the innovator then expanded only if he could exploit a regional seller's market or if he took on a part-time retail function to supply extra capital for the transition to factory production. He thus had to be able to gauge the national market situation and utilize scarce resources to best advantage.[28]

Manufacturing progress in antebellum Wisconsin depended on the availability of local resources and the interaction of general market conditions. Institutional and special factors, or what might be called "fringe benefits," were of marginal, if indeed any, significance.[29] It was not until the late 1850's and early 1860's — about twenty-five years after initial settlement — that public policy took an active stand in fostering industrialization by lowering the interest rates and introducing tax rebates and credit regulations.[30]

Even when public interest in manufactures did develop it was purely local or at most state-oriented. The advocates of business had very little perception of the specialization of industry and of economies of scale on a regional or national level. The main objective was for the town, or the county, or perhaps the state to be "self-sufficient" and to stop importing goods from other parts since this "lost" valuable supplies of money abroad.

[28] In this context the "innovator" is similar to Schumpeter's concept. He is the "new man," the interloper or adventurer. See Joseph A. Schumpeter, *Business Cycles* (New York, 1939), 87–101.

[29] These factors include insurance rates, tax structure, climate as it affects operations, community attitudes, and personal facts with or without economic advantages. See Greenhut, *passim*.

[30] State of Wisconsin, *Messages of the Governor*, 1860–1863; scattered articles in the *Milwaukee Sentinel*, 1850–1861.

It was almost as if Western newcomers regarded the older Eastern states as a foreign country. Sometimes it might be possible or even wise to export manufactured goods, but a "self-sufficient," if not wholly autarkic economy was the prime reason for the establishment and advancement of local manufactures.[31] Entrepreneurs were thus not artificially advantaged. Though officials and journalists might laud the purchasing of locally produced manufactures — thus giving free advertising space — they did not promote the antebellum development of a manufacturing base which had a regional or a national threshold.[32] Manufacturers had themselves to rise above the parochialism of the local community.

Within the framework of available resources and market potential, the Wisconsin industrialists had achieved a great deal. In the short span of some twenty-five years since initial settlement, they had established several notable factories producing goods for a regional market and many diversified operations making articles for distribution throughout the state. Furthermore, scores of small mills and shops catered to neighborhood demands, and household manufacturing was scattered throughout the state.[33] Indeed, it might be said that despite the newness of the country,

[31] This is the common plea of underdeveloped countries with respect to more advanced countries, or underdeveloped regions with respect to more mature regions within the same country, and Wisconsin was no exception to the general rule. Reports and newspaper articles in the 1840's and 1850's were full of complaints that valuable money supplies were being drained out of Wisconsin to pay for Eastern goods, or that Wisconsin consumers had to pay the transport cost of goods brought in from outside.

[32] *Milwaukee Sentinel,* Sept. 10, 1839; July 27, 1841; Oct. 23, 1841; Oct. 12, 1859; July 16, 1860; WSAS *Trans.,* 4 (1854), 50; 6 (1860), 77–78; *Wisconsin Farmer,* 9 (1857), 164ff; 12 (1860), 99–100; 14 (1862), 61; 16 (1864), 47; *Racine Advocate,* July 2, 1856; State of Wisconsin, *Annual Governor's Message,* 1842 and 1861.

[33] The value of home manufactures in Wisconsin prior to 1860 was minute when compared to the manufacturing in establishments which produced articles to the annual value of $500 and over. In 1850 home manufactures were worth 0.5 per cent, namely $45,509, of the annual value of the product of mill and factory manufactures. In 1860, when the value of home manufactures was $128,563, the percentage had dropped to 0.44. Household manufacturing consisted of all those articles made in the home by members of the family, from raw materials produced largely on the farm where the manufacturing was carried out. They included baskets, bedspreads, brooms, carpeting, cloth, gloves, hats, mats, mittens, socks, yarn, and other miscellaneous goods. See Rolla M. Tryon, *Household Manufacturing in the United States, 1640–1860* (Chicago, 1917), 1; and *Census of the State of New York, 1855,* 328–329.

which had militated against the investment of capital in manufacturing, with the notable exception of lumber, and despite periodic economic crises and hard times, Wisconsin's pioneer manufacturing had flourished. Several diferent kinds of manufacturing had expanded both in output and variety so that by 1860, the total product was valued at nearly 30 million dollars.

Wisconsin's manufacturing was concentrated in primary processing, with secondary efforts in craft and household consumer products and in agricultural machinery and iron goods. In 1840, four years after achieving territorial status, Wisconsin displayed a very heavy predominance of manufacturing in mills — saw, grist, wool, and oil — namely 88 per cent of the total capital invested

TABLE 4

MANUFACTURING IN WISCONSIN, 1840
(In Current $'s.)

Industry	Value Added	Capital Invested	No. of Workers
Processing Industries			
Mills	350,993	561,650	850
Leather	11,800	9,002	13
Brick and Lime	6,527	n.r.	11
Houses	212,085	n.r.	644
Soap and Candles	n.r.	3,432	5
Liquors	n.r.	14,400	11
Household-Craft Consumer			
Furniture	6,945	5,740	29
Hats, Caps and Bonnets	61	10	n.r.
Mixed Manufactures	1,500	550	4
Agricultural Industries			
Wagons	2,600	325	8
Other Industries			
Machinery	716	n.r.	6
Printing	n.r.	10,300	24
Ships (built)	7,159	n.r.	n.r.
All other manufacturers	51,212	26,162	n.r.

[SOURCE: *Sixth Census, 1840, Compendium,* 347-353.]   n.r. = not reported

and 86 per cent of the hands employed. The remainder of the manufacturing, other than home manufactures, focused on house construction. Much smaller contributions were made in the production of liquors, furniture, wagons, and other manufactures. (Table 4 and Map 3.) Unfortunately the 1840 census did not make any distinction between the four kinds of mills, but probably the majority were sawmills and gristmills, both of which were essential in newly established communities. Obviously the Wisconsin manufacturing economy had not really had time to get on its feet, and such establishments as existed were concerned with the primary demands of food and shelter.

By 1850 Wisconsin manufacturing had a more complex face, but primary processing of raw materials counted heavily. About 40 per cent of the total value added by manufacture came from the milling of flour and lumber, with flour milling contributing the larger share. Construction materials made up for some 6 per cent of the state's aggregate value, again showing the influence of a new economy. Otherwise the products were distributed in relatively small proportions throughout the rest of the processing industries, the household-craft consumer group, the agricultural industries, and ironware products. (Table 5 and Map 4.)

A decade later, in 1860, a high proportion of the total value added by manufacture still continued to be in primary processing. Lumber and flour milling were again the major contributors, though now lumber was more important than flour and grist milling. Construction materials had declined in proportion to the total value, perhaps indicating a slight maturing of the economy. Blacksmithing and tinsmithing had also declined relatively, suggesting that these branches of the craft industries were dying out. Brewing and meat packing had increased in the processing group, but leather tanning and soap and candles had decreased relatively.[34] Agricultural machinery and iron products increased in absolute value, but maintained a stable position within the state's manufacturing economy. (Table 6 and Map 5.)

Manufacturing in antebellum Wisconsin focused on primary processing and was located mainly in the southern and more pop-

[34] Unfortunately the Census of 1850 failed to make a full count of meatpacking establishments. Hence it is impossible to ascertain the increase in this industry in the 1850's.

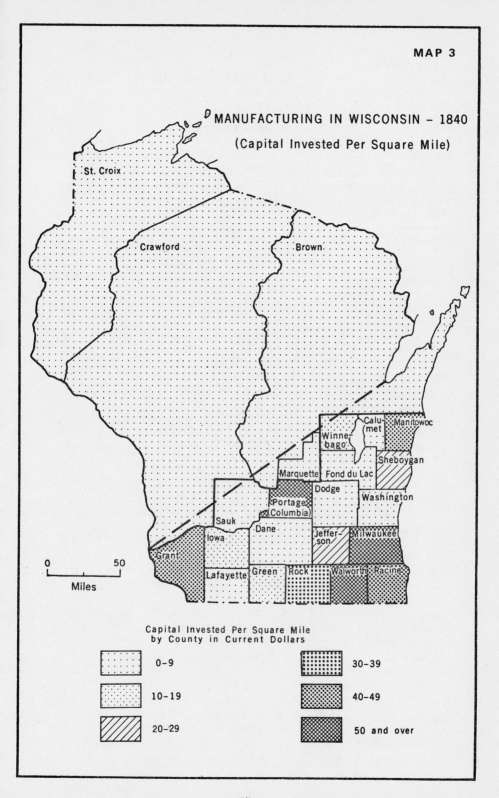

MAP 3

MANUFACTURING IN WISCONSIN – 1840
(Capital Invested Per Square Mile)

St. Croix

Crawford

Brown

Calu-
met

Manitowoc

Winne-
bago

Sheboygan

Marquette

Fond du Lac

Dodge

Washington

Portage
(Columbia)

Sauk

Dane

Jeffer-
son

Milwaukee

Iowa

Grant

Lafayette

Green

Rock

Walworth

Racine

0   50

Miles

Capital Invested Per Square Mile
by County in Current Dollars

0-9

30-39

10-19

40-49

20-29

50 and over

17

TABLE 5

MANUFACTURING IN WISCONSIN, 1850
(Value Added in Current $'s.)

Industry	Value Added	Per Cent of Total	No. of Workers	Per Cent of Total
Processing Industries				
Lumber*	622,426	16.40	1,540	24.72
Flour	953,453	25.10	406	6.51
Cooperage	69,998	1.84	170	2.73
Liquors	128,876	3.39	105	1.68
Leather	148,033	3.90	189	3.03
Construction Materials	204,854	5.39	601	9.64
Meat Packing	22,430	0.59	40	0.64
Wool	33,586	0.88	30	0.48
Minerals	154,545	4.07	264	4.24
Soap and Candles	62,447	1.64	30	0.48
Tobacco	23,228	0.61	45	0.72
Aggregate	2,423,876	63.81	3,420	54.87
Household-Craft Consumer				
Boots and Shoes	176,159	4.64	393	6.31
Clothing	114,694	3.02	432	6.94
Furniture	158,266	4.17	305	4.89
Blacksmiths	140,223	3.69	275	4.41
Confectionery	31,282	0.82	59	0.95
Tin, Copper, Etc.	80,063	2.11	141	2.26
Aggregate	700,687	18.45	1,605	25.76
Agricultural Industries				
Agricultural Impls.	157,960	4.16	221	3.56
Wagons	179,202	4.72	363	5.82
Aggregate	337,162	8.88	584	9.38
Other Industries				
Iron	191,997	5.06	315	5.05
Paper	31,873	0.84	79	1.27
Miscellaneous	112,375	2.96	229	3.67
Aggregate	336,245	8.86	623	9.99
Wisconsin	3,797,970	100.00	6,232	100.00

[SOURCE: Manuscript Census for the State of Wisconsin, 1850.]
* The industries are given in abbreviated format. For a full title for each classifica-
cation, see Appendix A.

ulous part of the state. But in actual manufacturing activities, there was a range of scale within the products and areas of Wisconsin which appear to indicate structural changes in industrial development. The character of manufacturing reflected several levels of development and accomplishment. Household manufacturing still existed side by side with the craft shop, the small mill, the larger mill, the manufactory, and the factory. This structural diversity stemmed basically from the evolutionary pattern of industrial growth, compounded by the breakdown of frontier conditions under the impact of technology, especially the technology of transportation.

In the early settlements of the late 1830's and 1840's and in areas further removed from transportation routes, manufacturing tended to be of a craft nature and was probably done in a small shop or mill. It was only in the more mature areas and those areas with access to waterways, roads, and railroads, that the larger mills and factories, serving a fairly wide hinterland, came into existence, alongside home manufacturing, craft shops, and small mills.

The breakdown in the scale of operation of manufacturing plants was never distinct within any given type of industry. The craftsman, the merchant-manufacturer, and the industrialist were co-existing contemporaries. Artisans such as carpenters, brickmakers, cabinetmakers, blacksmiths, wagonmakers, and tinners quite literally made their goods by hand for a custom trade. Merchant-manufacturers such as the clothier, the carriage maker, the boot- and shoemaker, and the stove manufacturer combined custom work with the retailing of ready-made goods. They were thus able to seize the expanding opportunities presented by wider trading horizons. Industrialists such as the flour miller, the agricultural implements manufacturer, the foundryman, the brewer, and the tanner produced their goods in a "factory" using machinery, and produced them for sale on a scale above that of the man doing piece-work or work-to-order.

However, the distinction between these types of manufacturers was not so much in the goods that they produced, for flour could be milled in a commercial mill or in a gristmill; clothes could be made for the custom trade or could be mass-produced; furniture could be individually styled or be "one-of-a-kind." Rather, the distinction lay in the size of the establishment and the result-

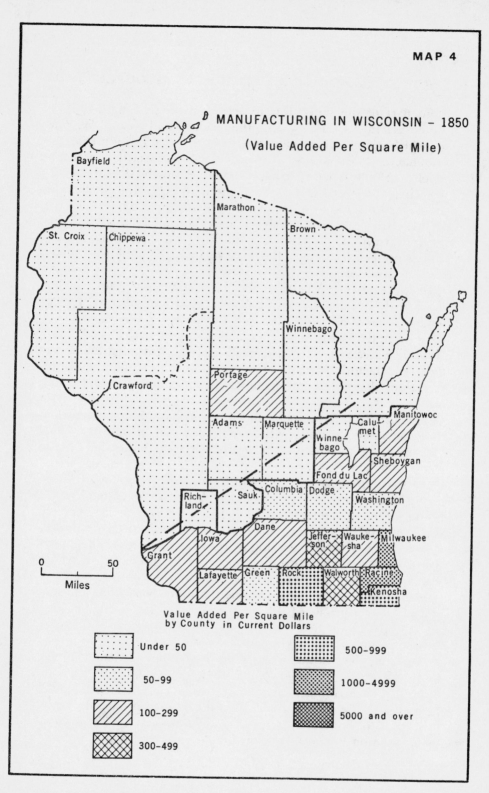

MAP 4

MANUFACTURING IN WISCONSIN – 1850

(Value Added Per Square Mile)

Value Added Per Square Mile
by County in Current Dollars

Under 50	500-999
50-99	1000-4999
100-299	5000 and over
300-499	

ing scale of organization. For example, there were basically three kinds of mills found in Wisconsin. The small gristmills, sawmills, and carding mills existed to serve the needs of the community, and might frequently operate on a custom basis. Their larger counterparts not only catered to the village or the town needs, but also entered the wider market and sold some of their flour, lumber, or wool "abroad." The still larger commercial mills were clearly much more interested in processing local resources for export outside the area.[35] The country or custom mill often had very little capital invested, perhaps a thousand dollars at most, and the owner did all the work himself, or with the help of one or two workers. In contrast, commercial mills, flour, lumber, or woolen, required a much larger capital, often used machinery, and employed more workers, both skilled and unskilled. The merchant-manufacturer occupied an intermediate position.[36]

Likewise there were three main kinds of clothing and footwear establishments. The tailor or the cobbler, who usually had a few hundred dollars invested in his shop, worked by himself or with an apprentice, and fashioned products by hand to suit the taste of the individual customer. He was the skilled artisan traditionally associated with pre-industrial labor conditions. The merchant-manufacturer, as the designation suggests, combined the functions of craftsman and merchant. The artisan himself could become a merchant-manufacturer if he sold imported ready-made goods alongside his own work, but such a change in status meant that the artisan had to acquire merchandising skills to avoid being displaced in the pattern of industrial evolution. This could be a difficult assignment. More often the merchant, familiar with the intricacies of catering to an unknown market, extended his trade backwards: he either employed a craftsman as a skilled wage-earner or took on an artisan partner who could look after

[35] A useful distinction between the size and operations of custom mills and commercial mills is made in Merle Curti, *et al.*, *The Making of an American Community: A Case Study of Democracy in a Frontier County* (Stanford, 1959), 237–238; Clarence H. Danhof notes the development of three types of gristmills — the small country mill engaged mainly in custom work, the country merchant mill, and the city merchant mill — in *Change in Agriculture: The Northern United States, 1820–1870* (Cambridge, 1969), 31.

[36] This distinction between the scale of operations can be drawn from a detailed study of the Manuscript Censuses for the State of Wisconsin, 1850 and 1860, Products of Industry, Schedule 5 (hereinafter cited as MCSW).

TABLE 6

MANUFACTURING IN WISCONSIN, 1860
(Value Added in Current $'s.)

Industry	Value Added	Per Cent of Total	No. of Workers	Per Cent of Total
Processing Industries				
Lumber	2,559,759	22.61	5,397	31.13
Flour	2,149,268	18.98	1,042	6.17
Cooperage	263,684	2.33	637	3.69
Liquors	556,892	5.02	470	2.72
Leather	303,808	2.68	432	2.50
Construction Materials	459,511	4.06	1,040	6.02
Meat Packing	205,968	1.82	200	1.16
Wool	82,429	0.73	130	0.75
Minerals	477,398	4.22	733	4.25
Soap & Candles	70,563	0.62	55	0.32
Tobacco	63,815	0.56	171	0.99
Aggregate	7,193,095	63.63	10,307	59.70
Household-Craft Consumer				
Boots and Shoes	488,790	4.32	1,153	6.68
Clothing	460,775	4.07	1,187	6.87
Furniture	415,665	3.67	627	3.63
Blacksmiths	114,831	1.01	231	1.34
Confectionery	74,525	0.66	104	0.60
Tin, Copper, etc.	148,614	1.31	271	1.57
Aggregate	1,703,200	15.04	3,573	20.69
Agricultural Industries				
Agricultural Impls.	474,784	4.18	632	3.66
Wagons	369,727	3.27	642	3.72
Aggregate	845,511	7.45	1,274	7.38
Other Industries				
Iron	596,506	5.27	582	3.37
Paper	291,660	2.57	432	2.50
Gas	56,927	0.50	75	0.41
Miscellaneous	627,118	5.54	1,023	5.95
Aggregate	1,572,211	13.88	2,112	12.23
Wisconsin	11,314,017	100.00	17,266	100.00

[SOURCE: Manuscript Census for the State of Wisconsin, 1860.]

the local custom trade.[37] The manufacturer in the ready-made clothing establishment and the shoe factory often employed twenty or more workers; in the former these are mainly women. These workers sometimes used machinery, and always practiced division of labor in producing a standard article for a larger, impersonal market.

The construct "average number of hands employed in each establishment in the different branches of manufacturing," though apparently critical to an understanding of the scale of operation, actually is of little help in distinguishing types of manufacturing organizations. (Table 7.) Only in iron in 1850, and in gas, iron, lumber, and clothing establishments in 1860, did the average number of hands employed exceed ten per firm. And only in gas manufacture were the majority of plants large. In lumber, clothing, and iron, the average number of workers, like many averages, was not a reality. In the lumber industry a relatively small number of very large logging operations raised the average of the more widespread local sawmill. In clothing, also, a few sweatshops, mainly in Milwaukee, again raised the state average, whereas the majority of such establishments were in fact small custom-tailoring and millinery shops.

Conversely, a small number of workers per firm does not necessarily imply that the industry was of a craft nature, as usually was the case with blacksmiths and tinsmiths. In the flour and gristmills, the average number of hands employed in 1850 was 3.4, and in 1860 it was 2.9. While small mills predominated, there was also a considerable number of commercial mills, especially in Milwaukee and southeastern Wisconsin. However, none of these mills, producing for export, employed more than twelve hands, suggesting that the larger flouring operations were to a certain degree mechanized and that an increase in the number of workers did not necessarily mean increased sophistication or increased output.

The measure "value added per worker" in the different branches of manufacturing in Wisconsin might indicate an increase in the scale of operation, at least in relation to the other

---

[37] For a very useful discussion of the role of the merchant-manufacturer, see Harvey A. Wooster, "Manufacturer and Artisan, 1790–1840," *Journal of Political Economy*, 34 (1926), 61–77.

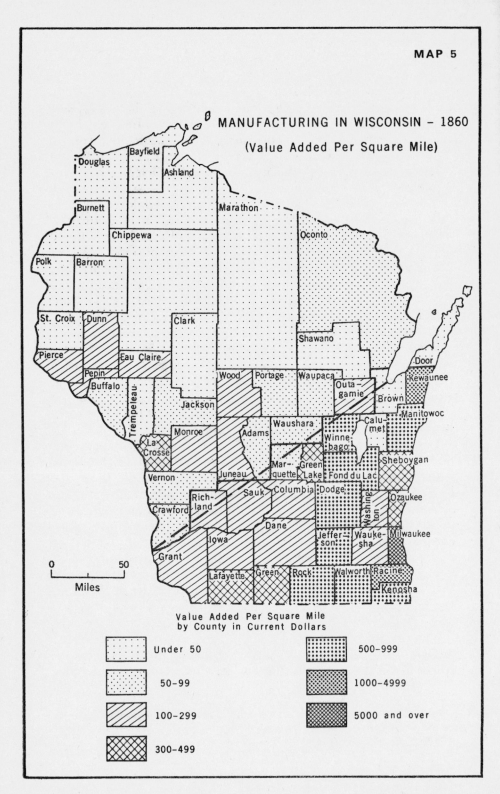

MAP 5

MANUFACTURING IN WISCONSIN – 1860

(Value Added Per Square Mile)

Value Added Per Square Mile
by County in Current Dollars

Under 50		500–999
50–99		1000–4999
100–299		5000 and over
300–499		

lines of manufacturing. This may well have been true of flour milling, liquors, and iron products, which were high in the state's ranking; but it was not true of soap- and candlemaking either in 1850 or 1860, or of wool manufacture in 1850. (Table 8.)

However, the measure reveals more about the status of Wisconsin manufacturing when refined on an intra-industry basis by county. For example, in 1850, in the category "lumber planed and sawed," the counties with the highest value added per worker were Rock ($876), Waukesha ($681), and Jefferson ($678) — all counties in the southeast, and not usually associated with Wisconsin's "Empire in Pine." This perhaps suggests that, other things being equal, the older settled regions were more produc-

TABLE 7

AVERAGE NUMBER OF WORKERS IN WISCONSIN MANUFACTURING ESTABLISHMENTS
BY INDUSTRY, 1850 AND 1860

(Ranked in Order in 1850 and Ranked in Parentheses in 1860.)

Industry	1850	1860
1. Iron	13.69	10.39 (4)
2. Clothing	8.30	10.59 (2)
3. Paper	6.58	6.64 (8)
4. Agricultural Implements	6.50	8.54 (6)
5. Construction Materials	6.13	6.88 (7)
6. Lumber	5.72	10.43 (3)
7. Meat Packing	5.72	2.94 (17)
8. Tobacco	5.62	8.55 (5)
9. Minerals	5.28	5.27 (10)
10. Boots and Shoes	5.10	3.85 (14)
11. Leather	4.60	3.37 (16)
12. Cooperage	4.47	4.36 (12)
13. Wagons	4.37	3.45 (15)
14. Furniture	4.35	4.78 (11)
15. Flour	3.41	2.85 (21)
16. Miscellaneous	3.31	4.22 (13)
17. Liquors	3.28	2.88 (19)
18. Confectionery	3.10	2.88 (20)
19. Wool	3.00	5.65 (9)
20. Soap and Candles	3.00	2.89 (18)
21. Tin, Copper, etc.	2.87	2.41 (22)
22. Blacksmiths	2.37	1.99 (23)
23. Gas	—	17.75 (1)
Wisconsin	4.84	5.44

[SOURCE: Manuscript Censuses for the State of Wisconsin, 1850 and 1860.]

tive in terms of labor input than the richly endowed regions of northern Wisconsin. A decade later, however, the situation in the lumber industry had changed markedly. The counties with the highest value added per worker were now Kewaunee ($1,917), Milwaukee ($883), Fond du Lac ($707), and Winnebago ($682). These counties, with the exception of Milwaukee, were situated in close proximity to the forested parts of northeastern Wisconsin — an area settled after the southeast, but having much better timber resources; and moreover, an area settled before the north-

TABLE 8

VALUE ADDED PER WORKER IN WISCONSIN,
BY INDUSTRY, 1850 AND 1860

(In Current $'s. Ranked in Order in 1850 and in Parentheses in 1860.)

Industry	1850	1860
1. Flour	2,348	1,967 (1)
2. Soap and Candles	2,081	1,283 (2)
3. Liquors	1,227	1,184 (3)
4. Wool	1,119	634 (13)
5. Leather	783	703 (9)
6. Agricultural Implements	715	751 (6)
7. Iron	610	1,025 (4)
8. Minerals	585	651 (12)
9. Tin, Copper, etc.	568	548 (16)
10. Meat Packing	561	1,030 (5)
11. Confectionery	530	717 (8)
12. Furniture	519	663 (11)
13. Tobacco	516	373 (23)
14. Blacksmiths	510	497 (17)
15. Wagons	494	576 (15)
16. Miscellaneous	491	615 (14)
17. Boots and Shoes	448	424 (20)
18. Cooperage	412	414 (21)
19. Lumber	404	474 (18)
20. Paper	403	675 (10)
21. Construction Materials	341	442 (19)
22. Clothing	265	388 (22)
23. Gas	—	738 (7)
Processing Group	718	717
Craft Group	437	477
Agricultural Group	584	663
Other Group	539	744
Wisconsin	609	656

[SOURCE: Manuscript Censuses for the State of Wisconsin, 1850 and 1860.]

west which was still in the initial stage of developing a lumber industry.[38]

In 1850, Sheboygan County ($530) excepted, the highest value added per worker in boot and shoe manufacturing was found in the southeastern counties of Racine ($590), Rock ($540), Kenosha ($515), and Walworth ($513). This again indicates that the earlier settled southeastern part of Wisconsin was the more technologically advanced, or at least was the more productive part of the state in respect to manufacturing. Ten years later Milwaukee had asserted leadership in the boot and shoe industry, with an average of $626, followed by Rock ($595), Jefferson ($506), Green ($493), and Sauk ($442) counties. The ascendancy of Milwaukee indicates that part of the city's manufacture was in ready-made footwear rather than custom-ordered boots and shoes. The high rank of the older counties once more points out that they were more receptive to mechanization and factory modes of operation.

Apparently the more populous southeastern part of Wisconsin was also the region where the traditional household and craft forms of manufacturing were breaking down. Yet the county statistics of manufacturing, by number of hands in each establishment, and by value added per worker, do not reveal any distinct locational pattern. (Table 9 and Table 10.) In 1850 the counties which had the largest average establishments, in terms of workers, were the sparsely settled northern counties which housed only the large lumber firms. Again, in 1860 the same pattern prevailed — the large sawmill raised the average size of the operations located in the lumbering regions. In 1850 the measure "value added per worker" in the different counties showed no consistent pattern. Lumbering, mining, and agricultural manufacturing counties were all present in the top rankings. The situation was similar a decade later, although the lumbering counties tended to be more prominent.

The breakdown of craft industries and the beginnings of larger-scale manufacturing and factory organization in Wisconsin

[38] The high average figures for Milwaukee County appear to be the result of the activities of a small number of large lumberyards which retailed lumber to the city and its hinterland and also traded with Chicago. This was in marked contrast to the processing activities of the logging mills in the northern parts of Wisconsin.

TABLE 9

TEN LEADING WISCONSIN COUNTIES, 1850,
ALL MANUFACTURING, BY VALUE ADDED PER WORKER AND
HANDS EMPLOYED PER ESTABLISHMENT

(Value Added Per Worker in Current $'s.)

Rank	County	Value Added per Worker	Rank	County	Number of Hands in Each Establishment
1.	Fond du Lac	1766.2	1.	Chippewa	40.0
2.	Columbia	1024.1	2.	St. Croix	31.5
3.	Calumet	883.6	3.	Brown	13.7
4.	Sheboygan	862.2	4.	Marathon	8.3
5.	Kenosha	832.8	5.	Manitowoc	7.8
6.	Lafayette	825.8	6.	Portage	7.7
7.	Walworth	776.4	7.	Milwaukee	6.8
8.	Rock	745.9	8.	Racine	6.0
9.	Winnebago	678.9	9.	Crawford	5.9
10.	Jefferson	675.5	10.	Winnebago	5.8

[SOURCE: Manuscript Census for the State of Wisconsin, 1850.]

can not be systematically attributed either to particular industries or to particular locations. Many of the lumber operations,
either in the northeast with access to Lake Michigan, or in the
northwest with access to the Mississippi River, were, from the
start, large commercial enterprises funded with outside capital.
They did not necessarily have a high value added per worker,
a category that might indicate the degree of mechanization or
skill. But lumbering operations were a type of primary processing which was beginning to call for considerable capitalization
and which required little skilled labor to manufacture bulky
products from standing timber.

Many of the towns and cities on the western shore of Lake
Michigan or in southeastern Wisconsin also had large establishments in various branches of manufacturing — flour, agricultural
implements, clothing, brewing, tanning, and iron products. But
the gross county figures do not reveal their incidence and im-

portance because they existed alongside more numerous craft operations. Locational factors in the southern half of the state were becoming more conducive to production on a large scale in some lines, but the possibilities of scale economies had not fully emerged and each community still supported craft shops and small mills producing goods for local demand.

Manufacturing in antebellum Wisconsin was neither homogeneous nor ubiquitous. Some parts of the state concentrated on those branches of manufacturing for which there was a plentiful supply of raw materials. Other parts of the state were more concerned to produce for the outside market and to use technological and managerial skills. At the same time some industries, notably processing, contributed a larger share to the Wisconsin aggregate than did others, for example craft and agricultural industries. While generally Wisconsin had, by 1860, developed well beyond the traditional household manufacturing

TABLE 10

TEN LEADING WISCONSIN COUNTIES, 1860,
ALL MANUFACTURING, BY VALUE ADDED PER WORKER AND
HANDS EMPLOYED PER ESTABLISHMENT

(Value Added Per Worker in Current $'s.)

Rank	County	Value Added per Worker	Rank	County	Number of Hands in Each Establishment
1.	Trempeleau	2422.2	1.	Dunn	44.7
2.	Kewaunee	1902.0	2.	Oconto	44.6
3.	Shawano	1167.5	3.	Chippewa	43.0
4.	Green	1090.6	4.	Eau Claire	18.3
5.	Outagamie	1083.4	5.	Kewaunee	18.2
6.	Rock	990.9	6.	Marathon	12.8
7.	Monroe	967.7	7.	Jackson	10.8
8.	Sauk	900.4	8.	Wood	10.8
9.	Waukesha	895.4	9.	Manitowoc	10.7
10.	Buffalo	883.7	10.	Portage	7.2

[SOURCE: Manuscript Census for the State of Wisconsin, 1860.]

of earlier pioneer communities, the nature of industrialization was still largely moulded by the presence or absence of natural resources and the distribution of population. The scale of manufacturing growth largely depended on the size of the market area, which in turn was connected to population agglomeration and transportation facilities.

Business entrepreneurs thus had a limited choice among the kinds of manufacturing in which they could rationally invest. Only those industries which utilized abundant natural resources and required minimal reserves of capital could hope to be immediately successful in local markets. To be sure, with the arrival of an all-weather transportation system, in the form of railroads, there was a wider range of possibilities for the development of manufactures. But locational factors relating to both demand and supply suggested that antebellum manufacturing would be closely tied to the availability of local raw materials. Access to natural resources, in conjunction with population, determined the discrete distribution of the main types of products, each with its distinctive features. The size of the various markets, which was related to urban centers and the adequacy of capital and transportation facilities, was more important in limiting the scale of the manufacturing plant.

However, more accurate judgments on the nature and scope of manufacturing on the frontier of settlement in early Wisconsin can only be made after a closer and more intensive inspection of industrial developments at a county level.[39] At this microlevel it is possible to ascertain what, if anything, the several parts of Wisconsin had in common when venturing into manufacturing; how the presence of raw materials and population influenced manufacturing potential; how transportation facilities and technological improvements affected industries in a new economy; and whether local demand was paramount, or whether there was any statewide or regional market.

Six Wisconsin counties — Jefferson, Grant, Winnebago, Eau Claire, Racine and Milwaukee — were selected from the avail-

[39] The county unit has the advantage of practicality with respect to reporting of data. Census data is usually given by county; the Dun and Bradstreet reports were bound by county; and newspapers, with the exception perhaps of those in Milwaukee, were often oriented towards their local administrative unit.

able fifty-five in 1860. With the exception of Milwaukee, each county concentrated to a degree on one or two particular branches of manufacturing, yet still carried on more limited manufactures in other lines.[40] (Table 11.) The six were not necessarily the most important counties in terms of value added by manufacture or in terms of any other particular measure. Nevertheless they illustrate the development of the major industries of Wisconsin in the antebellum years, and they also present a microcosm of continuous development, thus portraying the complexity of various patterns of growth. Furthermore these six counties were dispersed geographically throughout the state and, with the exception of Jefferson, had access to major arteries of water transportation. (Map 1.)

Jefferson County, located in the heavy wheat-growing region of southeastern Wisconsin, might be regarded as typical of many western prerailroad counties. The main resource was land; the main occupation was farming. Yet there also developed a remarkable range of small-scale manufacturing. The county had adequate water power, was well placed with respect to wheat areas, and had access to centers of population and markets — three important conditions which influenced the growth of flour milling in Wisconsin. Both the larger merchant mills and the gristmills serving a local population contributed to the aggregate county output. Lumber processing, using local timber resources, was of secondary importance, while the remaining operations were oriented towards the local consumer market. Jefferson County was essentially a lower-order market area functioning within the changing orbit of a larger regional network.[41]

[40] These six counties were *not* selected by random sample. They were chosen deliberately after a survey of the statistical data and historical literature revealed the general outlines of manufacturing developments in Wisconsin.

[41] The treatment of several county units within Wisconsin is reminiscent of the "central place" theory of size, spacing, and functions of urban settlements. While this general deductive theory has the most meaning as a guide to the location of tertiary activities in predominantly agricultural regions, and usually ignores considerations of manufacturing, urban agglomerations, and scale economies, it does point to a hierarchy of market centers organized to provide services for their surrounding tributary areas. These centers are ranked according to the range of services offered, but deviations from the market principle are explicable in terms of traffic or sociopolitical principles. The major theorist of central place is Walter Christaller, *Central Places in Southern Germany* (trans. C.W. Baskin; Englewood Cliffs, 1966). Since his original contribution, there has been a multitude

The manufacturing economy of Grant County in the southwestern corner of Wisconsin was likewise tied to primary processing, though here products could be transported with relative ease down the Mississippi River. Two stages of manufacturing developed in Grant County in the antebellum years. The region was settled earlier than most other parts of Wisconsin on account of the lead deposits. Initially the economy was extractive, and settlement took the form of numerous and sometimes short-lived lead-mining towns. By the late 1840's and early 1850's however, lead mining and smelting were becoming secondary in importance to agricultural pursuits, which in turn stimulated the development of flour milling. However, the dispersed nature of the population discouraged the growth of any major producers for retail markets.

Winnebago County in the Wolf River region of east-central Wisconsin was representative of a "transitional" type of lumber processing economy. Lumbering, in its primary stage of logs planed and sawed, and in its secondary stage of construction materials, barrelmaking, and woodenware, was of overwhelming importance in the manufactures of Winnebago County. Although itself lacking large forest reserves, the county's location enabled it to become the focus for nearly all the logging production of the Wolf River pineries. Wood was put to as many uses as possible, especially in Oshkosh, which served as the main local depot for the lumber industry. Yet Winnebago County was not concerned exclusively with processing lumber, for it was also able to draw on an agricultural hinterland and developed a notable flour-milling industry, especially in Neenah. The remainder of the county's manufacturing was dependent on local markets, and here the industrial economy was restrained by lack of good transportation, scarce capital, and few adapting entrepreneurs.

Eau Claire County in the Chippewa River Valley represented a more primitive lumber-processing economy. In contrast to Winnebago, Eau Claire was explored and settled at a later date.

---

of studies and articles in geography and in the related areas of sociology, marketing, ecology, planning, business, and economics. For a concise bibliography and review of the theory and its multitudinous applications, see Brian J.L. Berry and Allan Pred, *Central Place Studies: A Bibliography of Theory and Applications (Including a Supplement Through 1964)* (Philadelphia, 1965).

Here in northwestern Wisconsin large lumber firms were established in the vast Chippewa drainage area in advance of general settlement. Thus the primary activity of lumber planed and sawed was the only industrial activity in 1850 and virtually the only activity ten years later. The Eau Claire manufacturing economy was in fact a monolithic exploitation of timber resources which were readily exported by river. Population concentration was hardly a factor in influencing manufacturing.

Racine County, like Jefferson County, was located in the wheat belt of southeastern Wisconsin, but unlike Jefferson, was also adjacent to the wheat belt of northern Illinois. Its proximity to the water transportation of Lake Michigan aided its early entry into regional market hierarchies. In this county the manufacture of agricultural implements, suited to prairie farming, came to have a more significant status than flour milling in the aggregate manufacturing output. In addition to its direct dependence on agriculture, either as an output or an input factor, manufacturing in Racine County was also encouraged by the "induced outlays" of commercial agriculture. Small towns increased both in size and number to meet the requirements and extension of prairie farming. The distribution of farm products, the retailing of goods and services by such craftsmen as blacksmiths and carpenters, were subsidiary functions built around the farming community, much along the line envisaged in "central place" theory. Racine County was in fact a sophisticated version of the traditional frontier society, and contained examples of the coexistence of many types of manufacturing activity: the family system; the shop stage of the handicraft system; the merchant-manufacturer; and the mills — all catering to local pre-railroad types of demands while the machine shops and factories served the needs of state and even regional Western markets.

If Racine County showed the emergence of a dynamic agrarian frontier manufacturing, then Milwaukee County, the urban center of Wisconsin, illustrated the greater potential for manufacturing in the commercial entrepot of an agrarian state. Manufacturing in Milwaukee the county, which for all practical purposes was the same as Milwaukee the city, was significantly different from the rest of Wisconsin in the antebellum period. The area was responsible for about one quarter of the state's output in terms of both value added and employment. Not only was manu-

THE MANUFACTURING FRONTIER

TABLE 11

MANUFACTURING IN WISCONSIN, 1850 AND 1860

(Percentage Contributions of the Two Leading Industries in Each County,
by Value Added by Manufacture.)

	1850			1860		
County	First Leading Industry	Second Leading Industry	First & Second Together	First Leading Industry	Second Leading Industry	First & Second Together
Adams	—	—	—	54.45	37.97	92.42
Ashland	—	—	—	83.72	11.02	94.74
Bayfield	100.00	—	100.00	92.44	7.56	100.00
Brown	63.66	34.98	98.64	40.87	22.01	66.88
Buffalo	—	—	—	66.67	24.85	71.52
Calumet	78.82	21.18	100.00	40.39	23.14	63.53
Chippewa	100.00	—	100.00	99.09	0.53	99.62
Clark	—	—	—	91.07	8.93	100.00
Columbia	61.48	11.03	72.51	29.07	12.07	41.14
Crawford	50.83	14.43	65.26	78.69	19.16	97.85
Dane	24.24	16.36	40.60	27.21	15.88	43.09
Dodge	53.96	18.39	72.35	18.73	18.29	37.02
Door	—	—	—	64.77	29.84	94.61
Douglas	—	—	—	82.54	10.51	93.05
Dunn	—	—	—	97.73	2.27	100.00
Eau Claire	—	—	—	81.72	7.79	89.51
Fond du Lac	70.77	12.64	83.41	23.37	16.66	40.03
Grant	27.66	26.36	54.02	30.16	28.86	59.02
Green	30.44	25.62	56.06	53.59	14.27	68.22
Green Lake	—	—	—	33.29	15.95	49.24
Iowa	43.03	37.25	80.28	48.91	39.60	88.51
Jackson	—	—	—	100.00		100.00
Jefferson	39.37	20.57	59.94	26.58	16.17	42.75
Juneau	—	—	—	79.09	8.26	67.35
Kenosha	23.88	19.16	44.04	19.03	15.23	34.26
Kewaunee	—	—	—	99.66	0.34	100.00
La Crosse	—	—	—	41.19	14.67	55.86
Lafayette	59.10	26.83	85.93	93.48	1.47	94.95
Manitowoc	81.18	8.65	89.83	60.39	9.72	70.11
Marathon	100.00	—	100.00	95.67	1.83	97.50
Marquette	65.34	34.57	100.00	69.08	15.07	84.15
Milwaukee	11.41	8.88	20.29	16.67	9.89	26.56
Monroe	—	—	—	49.24	34.37	83.61
Oconto	—	—	—	93.04	2.41	95.45
Outagamie	—	—	—	35.09	21.88	56.97
Ozaukee	—	—	—	27.32	18.99	46.31
Pepin	—	—	—	70.11	12.54	82.65
Pierce	—	—	—	44.23	34.31	78.54
Portage	100.00	—	100.00	69.88	20.94	90.82
Racine	27.43	14.98	42.41	26.79	15.03	41.82
Richland	92.14	7.86	100.00	40.77	12.59	43.36
Rock	36.02	12.11	48.13	17.77	10.19	27.96
St. Croix	100.00	—	100.00	62.38	37.62	100.00

(Continued opposite)

MANUFACTURING IN WISCONSIN, 1850 AND 1860

(Percentage Contributions of the Two Leading Industries in Each County, by Value Added by Manufacture.)

(Continued)

County	1850			1860		
	First Leading Industry	Second Leading Industry	First & Second Together	First Leading Industry	Second Leading Industry	First & Second Together
Sauk	36.72	23.02	59.76	36.41	12.81	49.22
Shawano	—	—	—	100.00	—	100.00
Sheboygan	46.78	14.08	60.86	18.76	13.43	32.19
Trempeleau	—	—	—	48.62	45.87	94.49
Vernon	—	—	—	51.43	28.22	79.65
Walworth	37.89	17.04	54.93	34.44	22.94	57.38
Washington	45.45	25.43	70.88	41.09	19.12	60.21
Waukesha	31.63	23.10	54.73	35.63	11.36	46.99
Waupaca	—	—	—	35.17	19.87	55.04
Waushara	—	—	—	31.97	21.12	53.09
Winnebago	59.58	24.09	83.67	47.99	12.18	60.17
Wood	—	—	—	81.13	6.26	87.39
Wisconsin Aggregate By Value Added	25.10	16.39	41.49	24.07	17.52	41.59
Wisconsin Aggregate by County	57.56	17.93	71.06	54.75	16.47	70.44

[SOURCE: Manuscript Censuses for the State of Wisconsin, 1850 and 1860.]

facturing output highly concentrated in Milwaukee, but the character of this urban manufacturing was also peculiar for Wisconsin in the degree of its diversity. While the highest-ranked industry in Milwaukee contributed 11 per cent of the county aggregate by value added in 1850 and 17 per cent in 1860, the average contribution of the leading industry in Wisconsin counties at the two dates was respectively 58 and 55 per cent.

The major manufacturing activities of Milwaukee County might be classified as industries processing primary products from the city's agricultural hinterland. But there was already a growing proportion of manufacturing output focused on consumer industries of the housekeeping variety and on heavier producer goods. The former, using division of labor and sometimes also machinery, supplied not only the city population but also some of the rural hinterland. The latter had a widespread, if small, state market. The structure of manufacturing in the urban frontier gave Milwaukee yet another highly distinctive trait. Milwaukee had establishments of all sizes ranging from very large to minute, for it catered to a hierarchy of markets; and by the 1850's the city had become a comparatively higher-order city.

From an analysis of the character, growth, and distributional pattern of manufacturing in each of these six counties it is possible to make some more pertinent and precise observations about the development of manufacturing in an agricultural state of the Middle West in the mid-nineteenth century.

CHAPTER TWO

Jefferson County:
Traditional Manufacturing
in the Wisconsin Wheat Belt

THE ECONOMY OF WISCONSIN in the antebellum period has always been described as pre-eminently agricultural, and so it was. Wheat was king, and by 1860 Wisconsin was at the center of the empire. Situated in the prairie belt of the Old Northwest, Wisconsin contained some excellent agricultural lands, especially in the southern and southeastern counties. In these regions the land was largely composed of limestone soils which made the heavy silt prairies very fertile. There were no major undulations and very little bare rock; groves of timber needed for building and fencing were frequently found on land unsuitable for cultivation. Hence by 1860 the majority of the land in southern and southeastern Wisconsin was in farms which were primarily devoted to the cultivation of wheat.[1]

The achievements of the farmers in Wisconsin were slight in the early years of settlement, and only 15,151 acres of land were planted in wheat in 1839.[2] However, wheat production expanded rapidly during the 1840's and 1850's and by the outbreak of the Civil War Wisconsin was probably the most intensive wheat-growing state in the Northwest. In 1859 the wheat crop ap-

---

[1] For details of the agricultural protential and settlement pattern of this region, and of the state in general, see Joseph Schafer, *Four Wisconsin Counties, Prairie and Forest* (Madison, 1927), *passim*; Joseph Schafer, *A History of Agriculture in Wisconsin* (Madison, 1922), *passim*; Thompson, *passim*; Lampard, 2–56; John G. Clark, *The Grain Trade in the Old Northwest* (Urbana, 1966), 206–211, 251–263; Merk, 15–58.

[2] Thompson, 15.

37

proached 15.8 million bushels, three times the size of the 1849 crop, and in the following year, 1860, the crop was a record 27 million bushels.[3]

The geographical distribution of wheat in these years was concentrated in the southeastern counties. Most of the 4,286,131 bushels of wheat grown in 1849 came from the counties south of Green Bay and east of the Wisconsin River. The "wheat belt" had pushed into the third and fourth tiers of counties, as far north as Fond du Lac and Green Lake counties. But the focus of intense production was in the first tier, for Rock and Walworth counties together contributed 33 per cent of the state crop. A decade later the center of production had shifted a little northward — the four most northerly counties of Green Lake, Fond du Lac, Dodge, and Columbia producing 27.3 per cent of the state crop — but was still within the southern and southeastern part of Wisconsin. In 1859 the ten leading counties, all in the south, produced 60 per cent of the crop. Each of these counties grew over 500,000 bushels of wheat and five of them contributed over a million bushels.[4]

Yet the dependence on agriculture and on wheat in particular did not exclude the growth of manufacturing in the southern and southeastern counties. On the contrary, the two occupations were often significantly intertwined, for agriculture provided a basis for industrial development in a number of ways. The most important influence lay in the stimulus given to the primary processing industries, notably flour milling and, to a lesser extent, tanning, meatpacking, brewing, and wool carding. But agriculture also functioned as a market as well as a source of inputs. Prairie farming in the Old Northwest and in Wisconsin in particular moved rapidly into commercial production. There was thus a high demand for specialized farming equipment, for plows, reapers, and threshers suited to the environment; and this demand prompted the local manufacture of agricultural implements. An indirect incentive was also given to manufac-

---

[3] *Seventh Census, 1850,* 931; *Eighth Census, 1860, Agriculture,* Vol. 11, 167; Thompson, 39–70; J.G. Clark, 207–208.
[4] J.G. Clark, 207–208. It should, however, be noted that Clark places Racine and Jefferson counties in the top ten wheat producing counties in 1860, whereas he should have cited Green and Grant.

turing through the need to distribute farm products and to service farm demands.[5]

Jefferson County, located in the fertile belt of silt prairies, but lacking a major artery of transportation, had potential for developing local industries focused on agricultural production. Its wheat output rose from 6,647 bushels in 1839 to 182,545 bushels in 1849 and to 418,095 bushels in 1859, then placing Jefferson twelfth among the state's wheat-growing counties. The manufacturing activities of the county reflected the emphasis on wheat growing. In 1850 40 per cent of Jefferson's value added and 55 per cent of the value of the product was in flour milling. A decade later the value added had decreased to 26 per cent, but the value of the product remained the same. Other agricultural processing industries — tanning, brewing, wool carding, and meatpacking — contributed a small share to the aggregate value added, as did the manufacture of agricultural implements. Timber resources provided a further basis for local processing activities; lumber mills produced 21 per cent of the county's value added in 1850 and 16 per cent in 1860. (Table 12 and Table 13.)

In sum, Jefferson County was a lower market area functioning mainly in terms of small manufacturing plants processing natural resources for local consumption. There was no major connection with markets other than local markets prior to the advent of the railroad in 1855. Even when the railroad came, it merely brought merchandise manufactured in other places. Jefferson, in spite of its oft-quoted advantages as incentives to industrial location, was actually only suited to be a local manufacturing center, or at best, prior to the centralization of flour milling, a region which could process agricultural goods for sale outside the county.

The population distribution within the county emphasized a hierarchical network of local markets. Jefferson had received its earliest settlers in the mid-1830's after the close of the Black

[5] For a perceptive general statement of the impact of commercial agriculture on manufacturing in the Middle West, see Fishlow, 226–235. Evidence of the interrelationship of the two activities is also scattered throughout Danhof. Contemporaries also noted the close relationship, but viewed the growth of manufacturing as the means of preventing the drain of currency eastwards rather than as a means of taking the positive advantages of site location. See *Wisconsin Farmer*, 12 (1860), 99–100, 293–295; 16 (1864), 47–48; WSAS *Trans.*, 6 (1860), 77–79.

Hawk War and the acquisition of former Indian lands by the federal government.[6] Suffering minor setbacks following the Panic of 1837 and the stringent financial conditions of the late 1830's, settlement grew steadily from its total of 915 in 1840.[7] At midcentury Jefferson contained 15,319 residents, or 5.0 per cent of the state's population. An increase of 88 per cent in the 1850's gave the county an aggregate of 28,771 in 1860 or 3.7 per cent of the Wisconsin total. Much of this population was dispersed in small towns, each tending to have about 5 per cent of the county's inhabitants. Two minor urban centers, Jefferson and Fort Atkinson, each had about 10 per cent of the population, while the major center of Watertown contained about one fifth of the county's residents.

The structure of this urban network influenced the location of manufacturing activities in Jefferson County. Watertown was the leading center, having 45 per cent of the aggregate value added in 1850 and 53 per cent in 1860. One of the minor centers, Jefferson, managed to accumulate 10 per cent of the value added in both years, but Fort Atkinson fared less well. The remainder of the industrial activity was spread unevenly between small towns and villages whose relative contribution depended on the type of manufacturing involved. There was little close correlation between the distribution of population and the distribution of manufacturing, though both operated on a hierarchical system. This disparity was possibly a result of the proximity of the regional urban center of Milwaukee — a center which provided some service manufactures. The small towns might thus have had their own saw- and gristmills, but not always their own craft shops, since ready-made goods could be imported from Milwaukee.

The distribution of manufacturing in Jefferson County may in part be responsible for the contrast between the county and the state in any given branch of industry. On the whole, Jefferson made a relatively low contribution to the Wisconsin aggregate, namely 4.5 per cent of the value added in 1850 and 2.6 per cent in 1860. This was lower than the county's relative share of Wis-

---

[6] *The History of Jefferson County, Wisconsin* (Chicago, 1879), 331, 333–349.
[7] *Sixth Census, 1840, Compendium,* 94.

TABLE 12

MANUFACTURING IN JEFFERSON COUNTY, 1850

(Value Added in Current $'s.)

Industry	Value Added	Per Cent of Total	No. of Workers	Per Cent of Total
Processing Industries				
Lumber	35,150	20.57	52	20.55
Flour	67,283	39.37	60	23.72
Cooperage	3,524	2.06	13	5.14
Leather	1,300	0.76	5	1.98
Construction Materials	720	0.42	2	0.78
Wool	3,575	2.09	5	1.98
Aggregate	111,552	65.27	137	54.15
Household-Craft Consumer				
Boots and Shoes	5,561	3.25	17	6.75
Furniture	7,619	4.46	16	6.31
Blacksmiths	12,909	7.28	20	7.90
Confectionery	5,463	3.20	7	2.76
Tin, Copper, etc.	3,159	1.85	8	3.16
Aggregate	34,711	20.04	68	26.88
Agricultural Industries				
Agricultural Impls.	5,710	3.34	9	3.56
Wagons	9,335	5.46	24	9.48
Aggregate	15,045	8.80	33	13.04
Other Industries				
Iron	6,650	3.89	8	3.16
Miscellaneous	2,940	2.00	7	2.77
Aggregate	9,590	5.89	15	5.93
Jefferson County	170,898	100.00	253	100.00

[SOURCE: Manuscript Census for the State of Wisconsin, 1850. Jefferson County.]

consin's population for the same years, namely 5 per cent and 3.7 per cent. The only two industries of some statewide importance in which Jefferson provided a noteworthy share were blacksmithing and flour milling in 1850. But with the extension of milling to other parts of the state and the decline of blacksmithing, Jefferson was unable to maintain this proportion over the ensuing decade.

Furthermore the county's manufacturing plants were smaller than those in Wisconsin generally. In 1850 the average number of workers employed in Jefferson's establishments was 3.4, in contrast to 4.8 men in the state as a whole. A decade later the comparative figures were 3.6 and 5.4. Indeed there were only eleven establishments in the county which might be considered large, and only one of these — a flour mill — qualified under both measures, work force and value of product, which were used to determine size.[8]

Yet size need not be the sole determinant of the evolution of industrial progress. To ascertain the degree of industrialization it is also necessary to assess other measures such as value added per worker, division of labor, the absence or presence of different kinds of motive power, availability of capital, techniques of production, and entrepreneurial ability.

Although the Jefferson County establishments were small when compared to the average Wisconsin establishment, the value added per worker in the county was higher than that in the state; the comparative figures were $675 for the county and $609 for the state in 1850, and $708 for Jefferson and $656 for Wisconsin in 1860. This relatively high labor output in Jefferson, however, did not reflect a growing industrial maturity, for it stemmed from the use of skilled labor in many branches of manufacture rather than from widespread mechanization or division of labor.

There was little room for the development of even a rudimentary kind of division of labor. Most firms in Jefferson County were very small operations, employing one or two skilled artisans together with sufficient general labor to carry out the odd and extra jobs. The larger establishments in the handicraft

---

[8] The measures generally used to determine "large" manufacturing establishments in this study are fifteen or more hands per establishment and a minimum value of product of $20,000.

TABLE 13

MANUFACTURING IN JEFFERSON COUNTY, 1860

(Value Added in Current $'s.)

Industry	Value Added	Per Cent of Total	No. of Workers	Per Cent of Total
Processing Industries				
Lumber	47,983	16.17	77	18.38
Flour	78,878	26.58	45	10.74
Cooperage	11,004	3.71	19	4.53
Liquors	17,056	5.75	10	2.39
Leather	9,664	3.26	16	3.82
Construction Materials	10,370	3.50	19	4.53
Meat Packing	2,050	0.69	10	2.39
Wool	3,350	1.13	10	2.39
Minerals	1,750	0.59	2	0.48
Aggregate	182,105	61.38	208	49.65
Household-Craft Consumer				
Boots and Shoes	29,328	9.88	58	13.84
Clothing	9,564	3.22	23	5.49
Furniture	16,693	5.63	40	9.55
Blacksmiths	900	0.30	4	0.95
Tin, Copper, etc.	3,570	1.20	5	1.19
Aggregate	60,055	20.23	130	31.02
Agricultural Industries				
Agricultural Impls.	14,252	4.81	16	3.82
Wagons	11,435	3.85	30	7.16
Aggregate	25,687	8.66	46	10.98
Other Industries				
Iron	8,060	2.72	6	1.43
Gas	4,800	1.62	5	1.19
Miscellaneous	15,995	5.39	24	5.73
Aggregate	28,855	9.73	35	8.35
Jefferson County	296,702	100.00	419	100.00

[SOURCE: Manuscript Census for the State of Wisconsin, 1860. Jefferson County.]

manufacturing of footware and clothing were not factories; at
most they were manufactories where the workers merely applied
their skills under one roof rather than specializing in certain
aspects of production by making use of special machinery or
tools. On the whole there were few signs of progress in production techniques in Jefferson County's manufacturing establishments.

The use of different kinds of motive power in Jefferson likewise showed little indication of progress, but rather reflected the
accessibility of the natural resource of water. Most establishments
which needed motive power availed themselves of the abundant
water, mainly from the Rock River. Watertown was well located
on both sides of a sharp bend in the river, making it an ideal site
for dams.[9] The fall of some thirty feet in the heart of the city
could be used to great advantage, and by 1856 three dams had
been built to provide power for manufacturing establishments.
Jefferson the city, located at the junction of the Crawfish and
Rock rivers, had constructed a dam across the Rock River for
motive power in 1842. Fort Atkinson, like Watertown, was situated on both banks of the Rock River. Other towns not located
on the Rock were nevertheless able to use smaller streams, such
as the Bark, the Whitewater, and the Scupernong.[10]

Yet the Rock and lesser streams did not supply as steady a
source of motive power as might have been desirable. The natural
hazards of drought and floods interrupted the flow and threatened
the existence of manufacturing establishments. In the late summer of 1853, for example, the Rock River was very low for several
weeks and work at the mills was seriously retarded because of
lack of motive power. Yet in June of 1858 the steady increase
in the volume of the river resulted in floods which swept away
many dams and caused heavy property damage.[11] These hazards,

[9] Watertown, located on both sides of the Rock River, fell partly in Jefferson
County and partly in Dodge County. The figures for manufacturing and population
include only those parts of Watertown in Jefferson County; namely the Town
of Watertown, the 1st, 2nd, 3rd, 4th and 7th wards. From the standpoint of
manufacturing the wards in Dodge County did not differ significantly from those
on the Jefferson side of the county line.

[10] History of Jefferson County, 312, 476; L.C. Smith, 284-317; E.B. Quiner,
City of Watertown, Wisconsin, Its Manufacturing and Railroad Advantages and
Business Statistics (Watertown, 1856), 10-11; Territory of Wisconsin, Wisconsin
Laws, 1842 (Madison, 1842), 9-10.

[11] The Jeffersonian, Sept. 29, 1853; Weekly Democrat, June 10, 1858.

to be sure, were not annual, but they did militate against the ready investment of capital and steady manufacturing progress.

However, the cheapness and abundance of water was such an attraction that few steps were taken to develop alternative means of power. Steam was used in but three of the seventy-five manufacturing operations reported in the 1850 census, and in but ten of 118 establishments in the 1860 census. These few steam-driven operations were mainly sawmills, which implied the large requirements of these plants.[12] Yet even these enterprises did not comprise a majority of the sawmills in the county — accounting for only 13.3 per cent in 1850 and 40.1 per cent in 1860. Until shortly before the war, steam power was employed only on a very limited scale.

Abundant water worked against the introduction of steam power in Jefferson County. But the reliance on water may also have been heightened by the lack of local coal resources. Jefferson had no native coal, and transportation facilities for importing coal prior to the advent of the railroads were negligible. Jefferson was not a lakeshore county, and the upper Rock River was very difficult, if not impossible, for upstream navigation of coal barges. Water power was plentiful and cheap, and coal for use in steam power was expensive. Jefferson's manufacturing plants thus tended to be confined to water sites.

The natural resources of the county were the most important factors determining the character of Jefferson's manufacturing output. Other institutional factors carried much less, if any, weight. Financial assets which were locally available for industrial entrepreneurs were marginal. Although the county boasted three banks with assets of $667,557, or 4.4 per cent of Wisconsin's total bank assets in 1860, it appears that manufacturers had little access to these resources, which tended to be more a reflection of money brought into the county for use in land deals and railroad construction. Newspaper editorials around 1860 were still calling for manufacturers with capital to locate themselves in Jefferson, or for local businessmen and property owners to spend more money on developing manufactures.[13]

[12] Temin, 203–205, claims that sawmills were the largest single users of steam power in the United States in 1838.

[13] *Watertown Democrat*, July 7, 1859; *Fort Atkinson Standard*, March 29, 1860; *Weekly Jeffersonian*, Aug. 2, 1860.

Advertising and promotional efforts favoring manufacturing were vigorous. Local newspapers were only too willing to advertise the various towns, especially Watertown, as ideal locations for manufacturing ventures. If manufacturing did not advance by leaps and bounds, it was certainly not due to negligence in boosterism. Praise of the water power created by the Rock River was loudly sung, as it was for the fertility of the surrounding farmlands, the abundant resources and timber in the immediate hinterland, the access to the pineries, and the county's inland location — which was alleged to be far enough from Milwaukee to allow freedom from competition.[14] But advertising could not in itself create a favorable situation for manufacturing and Jefferson could not overcome the handicap of limited transport facilities.

Manufacturing Activities in Jefferson County

The industrial structure of antebellum Jefferson County reveals the local orientation of its manufacturing. In 1840, when the county was still in its infancy, lumber milling and the construction of houses were the only reported industries, having a value of product of $15,780 and $5,020 respectively. The initial needs of the settlers for housing, fencing, and barns was indicated in the limited manufacturing output.

A decade later, in 1850, when there had been time to develop more varied manufactures, primary processing branches provided the largest share of the county total, 65.3 per cent. Within this processing group flour milling contributed the largest share — almost 40 per cent of the value added — and lumber planed and sawed furnished 20.6 per cent. Jefferson County was concentrating on processing its local products. As in many counties of southern and central Wisconsin where lumber processing did not overwhelmingly predominate, about one fifth of the manufacturing structure fell to the lot of the household-craft consumer group. The remaining 15 per cent of the county manufacturing

[14] Quiner, 11–12; *Watertown Chronicle*, Apr. 17, 1850; Apr. 23, 1851; *Watertown Democrat*, Nov. 2, 1854; Apr. 17, June 5, 1856; July 7, 1859; *Fort Atkinson Standard*, March 29, 1860; *Weekly Jeffersonian*, Aug. 2, 1860.

was divided between the agricultural industries and the miscellaneous "other" group. (Table 12.)

Ten years later, in 1860, the county offered a similar overall industrial profile. The contribution of the processing group had decreased slightly to 61.4 per cent of the total, but within this broad category the balance had shifted. Flour milling still ranked highest, followed by lumber planed and sawed; but these two industries now only supplied 26.6 per cent and 16.2 per cent of the value added respectively. Other processing branches, especially liquors, contributed a larger share to the county's manufacturing activities. Household-craft consumer industries, as in 1850, were responsible for one fifth of the Jefferson aggregate. However, as with the processing industries in 1860, so here also the balance within the craft group had shifted. Blacksmiths had contributed one third of the value added by the craft group in 1850. But in 1860 boot and shoe making furnished virtually 50 per cent of the craft group total. Agricultural industries continued to provide about 9 per cent of the county aggregate, while the "other" group increased its contribution to 9.7 per cent. (Table 13.)

In 1850 Jefferson County thus tended to follow the Wisconsin norm by having over 50 per cent of its aggregate value added contributed by two industries. Then flour milling and lumber planed and sawed provided 59.9 per cent of the value added, as compared with the 71 per cent for the two leading industries in the average Wisconsin county. Jefferson did not match the common trend of highly specialized manufacturing, but was moving in that direction. In 1860, however, flour and lumber furnished only 42.8 per cent of Jefferson's value added, or well under the 70.4 per cent contribution for the two leading industries in the average Wisconsin county. This reversal could be interpreted as a sign of maturity, in that the county was diversifying its production. More likely, however, was the fact that primary processing industries utilizing local resources had a limited expansion threshold. Jefferson was in a transitional stage typical of many counties settled in the late 1830's and early 1840's which had no particular locational advantage for developing a regional manufacturing base.

Flour Milling

Three principal conditions influenced the distribution of flour milling in antebellum Wisconsin. To become a milling center it was necessary to have a good water power site, to be within the wheat-growing areas or to have good transportation connections with them, and to have access to both local agglomerations of population and wider markets.[15] The ideal location would be a lakeshore town, situated on a river, in the southeastern section of the state. Yet in the prerailroad days it was possible to become a minor flour center without the combination of all three factors. Location within the general wheat-growing area plus water power appear to have been sufficient to create a small center supplying flour to the inhabitants of an immediate hinterland. Mills could draw on wheat crops from a radius of thirty to forty miles and could distribute flour a similar distance. But most mills would have a limited output unless they could import wheat and export flour to more distant markets, and this required good transportation.

Jefferson County mills were typical of the small flour mills which took advantage of good water power and location in intensive wheat-growing areas. With only 6,647 bushels of wheat grown in the county in 1839, there was little incentive to build gristmills. Early settlers took their wheat or corn downriver to Beloit to get it ground or purchased their flour from Whitewater, Milwaukee, or other accessible points.[16] It was not until the early 1840's that entrepreneurs started to process the crop locally, and it was later in the decade before mills really became numerous.

The first gristmill in Jefferson County was built on the water power at Lake Mills in 1842. A second mill was built on the middle dam at Watertown in the same year and was subsequently expanded. In the middle and late 1840's other mills were built at Watertown, Jefferson, Palmyra, Milford, and Cold Springs, in response to the increasing output of wheat and the cost of taking it some sixty or seventy miles to be ground in

---

[15] Thompson, 103.
[16] *History of Jefferson County*, 338, 467.

Milwaukee, the nearest lakeshore point. By midcentury Jefferson had at least twelve flour and grist mills employing sixty hands and yielding a value added of $67,283. These establishments were dispersed throughout the county, though the major concentration of milling activity was located at Watertown. The four mills of this city accounted for 49 per cent of the value added and 68 per cent of the workers in the county's flour production.[17]

If some Watertown mills provided examples of the technology and methods of production used in the county flouring industry, then Jefferson millers were making efforts to keep abreast of modern developments. The five-story Emerald Mills owned by E. & J. C. Cramer of Milwaukee and B. F. Fay of Watertown were designed to incorporate the newest techniques in labor-saving machinery and were located so that operations were not affected by high water. Heavy investment in equipment and planning seems to have paid off, for in July of 1850 alone the mills purchased 47,000 bushels of wheat which were turned into 10,000 barrels of flour valued at $25,000. However, the Emerald Mills were probably exceptional, for at midcentury they were responsible for one quarter of the county's flour production by value added.[18] The other three Watertown mills, two of which were equipped with modern machinery in 1847 and 1848, were not so productive. Together, the three turned 78,500 bushels of wheat into 16,000 barrels of flour valued at $65,250.[19]

The three Watertown mills run by Cole & Bailey were not as sophisticated as the Emerald Mills, but they were more advanced than the remaining eight mills dispersed throughout the county. In 1850 these eight mills produced 37,502 barrels of flour, valued at $109,473; or approximately $2.92 per barrel in contrast to the $4.08 per barrel commanded by the Cole & Bailey mills.[20] Yet

[17] *Watertown Chronicle*, June 23, 1847; Aug. 18, 1847; July 3, 1850; *Rock River Pilot*, Nov. 3, 1847; *History of Jefferson County*, 424, 468, 481, 529, 540, 566; MCSW, Jefferson County, 1850.
[18] *Watertown Chronicle*, June 23, 1847; March 28, 1848; July 31, 1850; *Rock River Pilot*, Nov. 3, 1847; MCSW, Jefferson County, 1850.
[19] *Watertown Chronicle*, June 23, Oct. 6, Nov. 10, 1847; Aug. 2, 1848; March 28, 1849, adv.; July 31, 1850; MCSW, Jefferson County, 1850.
[20] The figures for the annual production of the Watertown flour mills given in the *Watertown Chronicle*, July 31, 1850, vary slightly from those reported in MCSW, Jefferson County, 1850. Presumably this resulted from using a different

the price of flour and meal itself might not be a clear indication of poor technology, for it could fluctuate with market conditions. Watertown's urban population and commercial outlets may have been prepared to pay more than the buyers found by the other Jefferson mills.

However, the three mills run by Cole & Bailey also had a higher output than the other mills, producing an average of 5,333 barrels to the other mills' average output of 4,688 barrels. The fact that one of these Watertown mills was run by steam had little, if any, influence in giving them a higher average. Three of the non-Watertown water-powered mills had a higher value added than the Steam Mill. The other mills probably had a slightly less sophisticated technology and physical capacity than those managed by Cole & Bailey. Certainly their production did not seem to have been limited by their immediate agricultural hinterland. The intake of all twelve mills in 1850 was about 274,010 bushels of wheat, probably not counting that ground for the custom trade.[21] This was 91,465 bushels more wheat than was raised within the county bounds. Some, if not all, of the flour mills — particularly those in Watertown — must have been drawing on the wheat production of other counties.

The Jefferson County flour mills of 1850 thus appear to have formed a hierarchy of productive capacity, but even the sophisticated Emerald Mills could not claim to make either the county or the city the best wheat market in the state. Certainly Jefferson County grew only 4.3 per cent of Wisconsin's wheat in 1849, and yet had 7.1 per cent of the state's value added in the manufacture of flour. But the mean value added by Jefferson mills was much lower than that added by Wisconsin mills, being $5,507 and $8,012 per establishment respectively. Jefferson County ranked only thirteenth in the state, suggesting that its mills were not as advanced technologically as those in other parts of Wisconsin. This lag in technology is substantiated by the fact that the Jefferson mills only had a value added per worker of $1,121 compared with the state figure of $2,348. In 1850, Jefferson

---

year; the census worked with the year June to June, while the paper probably took the year July to July.

[21] This estimate is based on an average of five bushels of wheat per barrel of flour.

flouring establishments, though doing an active local trade, were not really competitive with other mills in Wisconsin.

The production of Jefferson mills, when compared to the Wisconsin mills, improved during the 1850's. By 1860 the county had a value added of $78,878, or 3.7 per cent of the state's flouring industry. Although this was a decline in the relative value contributed to the Wisconsin total, it was not altogether unexpected in view of the rapid expansion of wheat-growing areas. The mean value added by Jefferson mills was still lower than the Wisconsin mills — being respectively $4,640 and $5,450 — but the differential had narrowed from 31 per cent in 1850 to 15 per cent in 1860. Furthermore the output per worker was more in line with the state figures. The Jefferson mills had an average value added per worker of $1,753, while the Wisconsin flour mills had an average of $1,967. Jefferson was approaching the general pattern in respect to output per establishment and output per worker.

But though Jefferson mills had lowered the differential production rate between themselves and the state mills, they did not increase their flouring capacity. The twelve establishments of 1850 had an average output of 4,567 barrels of flour each. The seventeen establishments of 1860 had an output of 4,432 barrels of flour each. Only one plant — the Blanchard Mills of Watertown — had a noteworthy production, namely 25,000 barrels. N. S. Green of Waterloo was second with 15,000 barrels[22] The Jefferson mills seemed to have shrunk and to be playing a larger local role. The increasing competition of flour mills in other parts of Wisconsin lessened the potentialities of milling in Jefferson. Even though the mills were still drawing on wheat supplies outside the county bounds, they did not have an extensive hinterland. Their intake of 426,700 bushels of wheat was only a little larger than the 418,095 bushels raised in the county.[23]

The leading flour mills in the county were well equipped for both merchant and custom trade. H. W. Blanchard's merchant mill at Watertown was capable of making fifty barrels of superfine flour daily. The Watertown mill of V. D. Green & Co.

---

[22] MCSW, Jefferson County, 1850 and 1860.

[23] This intake figure does not include custom grinding; but custom grinding was equally if not more likely to have taken place in 1850.

had undergone extensive improvements in 1859 to accommodate a larger amount of both custom and merchant work. Joseph
Powers of Hebron owned a large gristmill and a splendid water-
power site in the early 1860's, while N. C. Hurlburt of Jefferson
had his mill equipped with the latest machinery.[24] But these
larger mills were not doing a flourishing business in 1860. Compared to the output of flour in 1855, the 1860 total possibly represented a decline of some 30 per cent.[25] This decline was partly
a result of the panic and depression of the late 1850's, but was
also due to the greater amount of wheat shipped out of the region by railroad. Any gains that the mills made in the early
1850's had been largely negated by 1860.

Jefferson County did not possess locational advantages for becoming a major milling center in the antebellum period. Although there were good water-power sites and access to wheat-
growing areas, these were insufficient assets for survival on a
regional scale. During the 1840's and early 1850's the county did
not have a viable connection with outside markets. Flour had
to be transported by road to Milwaukee for dispatch to points
further distant, and the cost of road transportation was prohibitive. Hence flour mills catered mainly to local demands. With
the establishment of railroads in the mid-1850's Jefferson was
still unable to seize the opportunity to gain a larger market.
The railroads merely enlarged competition for raw materials.
Instead of becoming a railroad terminal, Watertown was no
more than a railroad crossing.[26] For the remainder of the antebellum period at least, the county struggled to maintain itself as
a local center.

The locational disadvantages of Jefferson County were compounded by a general shortage of capital for manufacturing and

---

[24] D. & B. vol. 26: 104D, 104G, 105; *Watertown Chronicle*, Sept. 8, 1852, adv.;
Aug. 23, 1854; *Watertown Democrat*, Jan. 11, 1855; July 29, 1858; Sept. 1, 1859;
The Jeffersonian, June 29, 1854, adv.; Quiner, 10; *History of Jefferson County*,
547.

[25] Quiner, 17, 22, gives statistics for Watertown trade in 1855. These comparisons are based on figures for Watertown only and are generalized to imply the
whole county. In 1850 Watertown produced 47.4 per cent of the flour production
measured by barrels. In 1860 the percentage had dropped to 39.2. MCSW,
Jefferson County, 1850 and 1860.

[26] Quiner, 22; Chester V. Easum, *The Americanization of Carl Schurz* (Chicago,
1929), 156.

a lack of entrepreneurial drive. In 1855 Carl Schurz noted that all the wealth made in Watertown was made on the spot.[27] While this may have been praiseworthy from the standpoint of the rags-to-riches ethic, unfortunately for the county it did not allow Watertown to compete successfully with other towns which were able to benefit from the cost advantage of plants using large amounts of capital. The lack of outside capital for manufacturing, even in the relatively small amounts which some parts of Wisconsin managed to attract, was itself an indicator of substandard locational assets.

In addition to the lack of imported capital there was also a dearth of managerial talent. In the late 1850's *The Watertown Democrat* not only chided the businessmen and property owners for slipping, but even represented the energy of the city in Rip Van Winkle terms and suggested that unless money was spent on roads and manufacturing, Watertown would become a third-or-fourth-rate country village.[28] The locational disadvantages were strengthened by or perhaps even fostered the lack of initiative in manufacturing Jefferson's most suitable product.

Lumber Planed and Sawed

Lumber processing in Jefferson County before 1860 reflected some of the same industrial trends seen in flour milling. Both industries decreased in the relative amount of value added contributed to the Jefferson total, though they both increased in absolute value added. (Table 12 and Table 13.) In both branches there was a large number of firms, as compared to the number in other counties, and these firms tended to be smaller than the mean Wisconsin establishment. Furthermore both flour milling and lumber processing were mainly dependent on local resources for their supplies of materials.

Sawmilling was in fact the pioneer industry of the county, not only on account of the building and fencing needs of the early settlers, but also as a consequence of the local stands of oak and basswood. The surface of the county was sprinkled with oak openings while the uplands were generally well wooded

[27] Easum, 111.
[28] *Watertown Democrat*, July 7, 1859.

with white, bur, black, and red oaks.[29] When the original settlers wanted lumber there was an abundant supply in the vicinity.
The first sawmill was built at Hebron in the winter of 1836–37.
It was not alone for long. In 1837 George J. Goodhue built a
double sawmill at Johnson's Rapids, the future site of Watertown, and placed a dam across the Rock River — the first such
dam to be built on that river in either Wisconsin or Illinois.
In the same year a sawmill was completed at Hebron and in
1838 another was built at Cold Spring.[30] By 1840 the Sixth Census
reported that the county had $11,000 invested in four sawmills
which employed nine hands and produced lumber valued at
$15,780.

The lumber industry in Jefferson County continued to grow
in number of mills and volume of output in the early 1840's. In
1841 James Rogan built another mill at Watertown and in 1842
a sawmill was erected on the Rock River dam at Jefferson. In
the same year Myron Smith & S.D. Tenny built a mill and dam
on the Bark River and Abram Brink was building on the Scupernong River at Palmyra. A dam and sawmill were also built at
Waterloo in 1843.[31]

Sawmills grew in rough proportion to the influx of settlers.
The number of people required to establish and support a mill
varied. When George Goodhue built his mill in 1837 the future
Watertown was a settlement of some seventy persons. Jefferson
had an even smaller population in 1842 and Waterloo may not
have had more than twenty inhabitants in 1843.[32] But lumber was
essential to any pioneer community and, in view of the initial
plentiful supply of timber, sawmills operated part-time or full-
time in virtually all small settlements. For example, when the
sawmill of Smith & Tenny at Sullivan burned shortly after its
completion in 1842, the demand for building materials was so
strong that Charles De Witt immediately began to build another
mill. Similarly in 1841–42 George Goodhue commenced rebuild-
ing his mill which had been partially damaged by fire.[33]

[29] History of Jefferson County, 317; A.R. Whitson, et al., Soil Survey of Jefferson
County, Wisconsin (Madison, 1916), passim.
[30] History of Jefferson County, 336, 338–339, 529, 547.
[31] Ibid., 339, 467, 521, 529, 562.
[32] Ibid., 406, 467–68, 562. These population figures are estimates.
[33] Watertown Chronicle, June 23, Nov. 24, 1847; History of Jefferson County, 520.

By midcentury the county could boast of fifteen sawmills which had an annual value of product of at least $500. Probably many more smaller mills were not reported in the census. Those mills counted by the census were all relatively small, having an average capital invested of $3,953 and an average value added of $2,343, which approximated the state mean at the time. The Jefferson mills were not as large as those of the more intensive lumbering counties in the pineries, for the mills of such counties as Winnebago and Marathon had a mean value added of $4,880 and $3,527 respectively. But they did surpass those of such less densely wooded southern counties as Dane or Walworth which had an average value added of $1,054 and $1,250. Given the size of its population, therefore, Jefferson was capable of producing sufficient wood for domestic needs, having a total of 7,650,000 feet of logs for sale in 1850.

During the 1850's the number of mills increased to twenty-two, but the size of the firms declined. By 1860 the average Jefferson sawmill had a capital invested that was 11 per cent smaller than that of 1850 and a value added which was 7 per cent smaller. The mills, which for the most part were processing local timber, were maintaining their basic function of catering to local building demands. In doing this, however, there may have been some need to buy pine lumber floated down the Rock River, since the local lumber output of board feet had fallen off by 2 per cent over the decade while the population had meanwhile increased by 88 per cent.[34]

Not surprisingly, there was no large-scale investment of capital in Jefferson sawmilling. The largest firm reported in the census of 1860 had a capital invested of $8,000, while the average sum invested was $3,532 and the average value added was $2,181. The mills were processing a locally available raw material for the local market. In the mid-1850's Foster & Jeffries of Watertown were content to furnish builders, mechanics, and farmers with sawed and planed lumber. H.B. Blanchard, one of Watertown's more

---

[34] There is little reference to lumber yards as opposed to sawmills. However, in 1860 two firms in Fort Atkinson were selling pine lumber and other planed lumber, and Enos Salsich of Watertown was using pine in his sash-and-door factory. *Fort Atkinson Standard*, March 1, Dec. 17, 1860, advs.; MCSW, Jefferson County, 1860.

prominent businessmen, installed a modern planing machine in the Old Yellow Mill in 1858 but seemed to be mainly concerned with using it to supply local builders. The Messrs. Green of Watertown were even proud of their capacity to do custom work.[35]

The parochial nature of lumber manufacture in Jefferson County was further demonstrated by the unusually high percentage of sawmills which were run in conjunction with flour mills. The two types of processing were not necessarily housed under the same roof, but they were operated by the same owner. In 1850 Cole, Bailey & Co. ran a joint enterprise, while J. Heath of Sullivan produced 1,000 barrels of flour in his establishment which, for census purposes, was classified as a lumber mill. A decade later the trend had become more marked. Seven of the twenty entrepreneurs active in lumber planing and sawing also engaged in flour milling. Owning two types of mills did not necessarily imply that one suffered at the expense of the other, but it did suggest that neither by themselves was sufficiently developed to make a large profit. Few, if any, economies of scale were gained by putting together two such diverse manufacturing operations. The only advantage lay in the fact that the same firm could supply two elemental needs of the local population.

Yet in spite of this narrow orientation in lumber milling, there had apparently been some efforts to make technological changes through the introduction of steam power. While only two out of fifteen mills had opted for steam rather than water in 1850, by 1860, nine out of twenty-two were using the more modern means of power. Steam power did not increase the capacity of the lumber mills for, if anything, those mills using steam power had an average output in board feet which was less than that of the water-powered mills. The use of steam did, however, cheapen the cost of production, for the nine mills accounted for well over half the value added by lumber mills in 1860.

Such was the local character of the Jefferson sawmills that they did not compare favorably with the Wisconsin average. The latter had increased in all aspects of value and production, owing to the rapid development of the northern pineries. By 1860 the average Wisconsin mill had a capital invested of $12,864, em-

---

[35] *Watertown Democrat,* Nov. 2, 1854; Oct. 5, 25, 1855, advs.; July 28, 1858; March 3, 1859, adv.; *Weekly Jeffersonian,* Nov. 12, 1854; Apr. 3, 1856.

ployed 10.4 hands, and had a value added of $5,261. Jefferson, by contrast, had a capital invested of $3,532, employed 3.5 workers per establishment, and had an average value added of $2,181. The new lumber operations on the northern rivers had greatly expanded the overall potential of lumber manufacturing, but Jefferson was faring better than many counties in southern Wisconsin where the oak openings had quickly been denuded and local sawmills were dying out, or were using imported wood. By 1860 counties such as Waukesha and Walworth had an average value added of $1,342 and $1,148 respectively, while Dodge reached a slightly higher value of $1,758.

On the whole, sawmilling activities in antebellum Jefferson County were dependent on the availability of natural resources and the local demand for building materials. The industry was shaped by its immediate environment. The preference for a larger scatter of small mills rather than a small number of large mills was a reflection of the domestic character of an industry which catered mainly to home needs; it underscored a lack of capital and initiative to develop lumber manufacture on a commercial scale.

Construction Materials and Cooperage

Flour milling and lumber processing accounted for the overwhelming proportion of primary processing in Jefferson County, but the secondary processing of wood in the form of barrels and sash, doors and blinds made a small contribution in 1850 and played a slightly larger role in 1860. (Table 12 and Table 13.) Both activities followed the pattern established by the sawmills: they were small in size, used local resources, and sold their products in a local market.

The manufacture of construction materials increased in both relative and absolute amount in the 1850's, reflecting the growth of a more sophisticated market. Whereas in 1850 and previously, purchasers had been content to buy roughly sawed and planed lumber from the mills, by 1860 builders, at least in the larger urban centers of Watertown and Jefferson, were calling for a more refined product. Brickmakers mainly supplied local customers from small shops, even though the railroad permitted the shipment of goods in the late 1850's.[36]

Coopers used local wood to supply the domestic needs, primarily of the flour mills, but also of the breweries and meatpacking establishments. The barrelmakers of the late 1840's and early 1850's ran very small establishments; the largest firm, M. Coon of Palmyra, had a capital of $600 and a value added of $1,632. The average firm involved a capital of only $363 and produced a value added of $881. Evidently these establishments had only a local significance and may even have been run on a custom basis.

A decade later, however, the seven establishments of 1860 had increased their value added, though their capital remained very small, the respective figures being $1,572 and $335. Part of the increase in productivity may have stemmed from the introduction of machinery. As early as 1855 local newspapers advertised stave machinery and some barrelmakers undoubtedly employed this faster method of production.[37] The use of machinery, however, did not necessarily lead to exports beyond the local hinterland. The establishment of the leading producer, O. B. Sanford of Watertown, was burnt down in January 1860 and no doubt had not fully recovered before the census was taken in June of that year. Yet even Sanford appeared to sell many of his staves to local millers.[38] Jefferson's coopers generally followed the marketing pattern of other processing industries.

Other Processing Industries

The remaining processing industries in antebellum Jefferson County contributed a lesser amount of the manufacturing profile. (Table 12 and Table 13.) The relative backwardness of these branches was due to the lack of raw materials and the competition from imported goods, especially those from Milwaukee. As has been indicated, the manufacturing structure of the county was essentially oriented to home needs. If the raw material was not

[36] *Watertown Chronicle,* June 25, 1851, adv.; Apr. 6, 1853, adv.; *Watertown Democrat,* Sept. 11, 1856; June 24, 1858, adv.; March 22, 1860; MCSW, Jefferson County, 1850 and 1860.

[37] *Weekly Jeffersonian,* Sept. 6, 1855, adv.; May 19, 1859, adv.; *Watertown Democrat,* March 17, Nov. 3, 1859.

[38] *Watertown Democrat,* Nov. 3, 1859; Jan. 12, June 7, 1860.

conveniently to hand, it was cheaper to import the finished product rather than the raw materials to be manufactured on a small scale. Any temporary fluctuations in production were explicable in these terms. The increase in brewing in the 1850's was a result of the growing number of Germans in the county and the fairly easy access to barley. The relatively moderate contribution of the woolen industry in 1850 was an attempt to introduce a new industry based on the willingness of local farmers to raise sheep.

HOUSEHOLD-CRAFT CONSUMER INDUSTRIES

The household-craft consumer industries furnished about one fifth of the value added of Jefferson County manufacturing in the antebellum period. Their contribution measured by labor input was higher, as was typical of most craft industries. The relative importance of the several manufacturing branches within this group fluctuated noticeably, possibly as a result of changing local market conditions, but also possibly as a result of the methods of census taking or *mis*taking. Blacksmiths were the most significant branch in 1850, but a decade later they were virtually nonexistent. In 1860 cobblers produced almost half the value added of the group, whereas in 1850 they had only been able to account for one sixth of the total. (Table 12 and Table 13.)

Boots and Shoes

Cobblers were probably five to ten years in coming to any given settlement after its initial founding. There is little indication that any of the villages or towns supported such craftsmen before the mid-1840's, though farmer-cobblers or carpenter-cobblers who could do repairs may have been pressed into service at an earlier date.[39] The shoemakers of the middle and late 1840's were somewhat more sophisticated than repair men; they practiced a custom trade either in their own small shops or as ancillaries in a retail shoe store.[40] The extent to which these

---

[39] *History of Jefferson County,* is relatively good for citing the names and dates of the "firsts" in each settlement. However, it makes little reference to shoemakers, though blacksmiths and cabinetmakers receive fair attention. It is possible that these craftsmen were slow in establishing themselves in view of their very small output in the late 1840's.

[40] *Watertown Chronicle,* June 23, Dec. 8, 1847, advs.; June 28, July 5, 1848, advs.; Aug. 7, 1850, adv.

craftsmen supplied the county footwear demands is unknown, but possibly more imported than locally-made shoes were sold, in view of the belated arrival of craftsmen and the proximity of Milwaukee.

By midcentury the census reported only four shoemakers with a value of product over $500. For the most part these ran two- or three-man shops, with a capital of $1–300 and a value added of some $500. One exception, Andrews & Young of Watertown, had a larger establishment, employing ten men and having a value added of $4,000. This shop, however, was merely a central location — a manufactory — where each craftsman made shoes and did repairs. The $500 capital invested in this establishment suggests that little attention was paid to machinery or tools, while the output of 4,000 pairs of boots and shoes indicates no great measure of division of labor or factory production. The shoe shops of the county were minute establishments which could not possibly have supplied sufficient wares for local inhabitants. Racine County, with a slightly smaller population than Jefferson County in 1850, had a value added of $30,660 — a figure which was five-and-half times as large as that of Jefferson.[41]

The number of shoe firms and their output rose in the 1850's. By 1860 eleven establishments, eight of which were located in Watertown, had a value added of $29,328 and employed fifty-eight men producing 20,722 pairs of boots and shoes. The shops consisted of small two- or three-man firms like those of the previous decade and some medium-sized establishments having a value added approaching $2,000. The small firms did custom work and repairs on a limited basis. The medium-sized shops carried a larger stock of ready-made ware of their own manufacture as well as catering to the individual taste.[42] H. Betram, who had the largest shoe shop, employing sixteen hands in 1860, was doing a profitable business in the late 1850's, but he was still only considered a practical bootmaker.[43] On the whole there

[41] Unfortunately it is not possible to make this comparison in pairs of boots and shoes, for the census marshals failed to report the number made in three small footwear firms in Jefferson. Racine firms made 23,150 pairs of boots and shoes, which was possibly five times as many as were made in Jefferson.

[42] The Jeffersonian, May 31, 1855, adv.; Watertown Democrat, Nov. 20, 1856, adv.; Jan. 19, 1860, adv.; Weekly Jeffersonian, Jan. 8, 1857, adv.; Jan. 26, 1860, adv.; Fort Atkinson Standard, Oct. 18, 1860, adv.; Wisconsin Chief, Oct. 31, 1860, adv.; D. & B. vol. 26: 47, 67.

[43] D. & B. vol. 26: 37.

was little improvement in the shoe business other than an increase in the size of some firms.

The growth in shoemaking stemmed mainly from servicing the demands of the rising population. Possibly the production of leather in the two tanneries also helped by supplying materials. It is noticeable, however, that Jefferson was one of the few counties where boot and shoe manufacturing was gaining rather than losing capacity. Usually shoemakers found their livelihood challenged by the competition of ready-made goods, especially when railroads eased the transportation problem. Jefferson craftsmen appeared, at least on the surface, to be better equipped to meet the threat of competition, though they were by no means able to cope with the county's full demands. With a population of 28,771 as potential clientele in 1860, Jefferson shoemakers manufactured only 20,722 pairs of shoes per annum. Racine shoemakers, by contrast, possibly made as many as 30,000 pairs of boots and shoes, for a population of 21,340, and even with this output, retailers were beginning to dominate the shoe trade.[44] The increase in boot and shoe manufacturing in Jefferson County seems unusual only because this branch had weak beginnings in the 1840's.

Blacksmiths

Blacksmiths were among the first craftsmen to ply their trade in the new settlements of Jefferson County in the late 1830's and early 1840's. As such they were the all-round village toolmaker, wagonmaker, and repairman. Their number is impossible to ascertain at any given time since they were not all recorded in the manufacturing censuses. However, all villages with a population of from 75 to 100 people probably had a handyman who qualified for the title blacksmith.

By midcentury ten blacksmiths were reported as having a value of product over $500. Presumably these did not represent a full sample; small towns probably had part-time or even full-time blacksmiths whose product was not large enough to make them

---

[44] The census marshals failed to report the number of boots and shoes made in five firms in Racine the city in 1860. Four of these five were the largest firms in the county. As the value added produced by these firms amounted to over 50 per cent of the industry's total, it is probable that the production of 14,319 shoes by the five firms reported was at least doubled.

manufacturers. The larger towns of Watertown, Jefferson, and Fort Atkinson not only supported such blacksmiths, but also others artisans, such as wagonmakers, who specialized in one or more of the blacksmith's functions.

Those blacksmiths recorded in the census in 1850 usually ran owner-operator shops aided by a wheelwright and a helper. The work consisted of horseshoeing, ironing wagons and plows, making plows, wagons, carriages, and tools, and doing repairs. There was no clear correlation between the size of the establishment and the type of articles produced. It might be expected that the shops with a larger value added, for example over $1,000, made plows and wagons, while the smaller shops shod horses, but this did not seem to be the case. The blacksmith, being a general service man, took orders and made or repaired goods according to customer demands.[45]

As was common in most parts of the state, blacksmithing in Jefferson County declined both absolutely and relatively in the 1850's. By 1860 only two blacksmiths were reported in the census schedules. Either the function of these artisans had been pre-empted by other craftsmen or they had been relegated to the position of repairman. There is no indication of upward mobility or increasing specialization in wagonmaking among the blacksmiths of Jefferson County, as there was in Grant County.[46] Hence they probably went out of business altogether, migrated, or remained repairmen.

Jefferson County was not unique in this trend towards eliminating blacksmiths as manufacturers. The number of blacksmiths in Wisconsin remained stable in the 1850's — 116 in 1850 and 115 in 1860. But considering that twenty-five new counties made manufacturing reports in the same period, then the average dropped from 3.9 to 2.1 blacksmiths per county. The Jefferson establishments did not decline in size over the decade, for they employed 2.0 workers both in 1850 and in 1860, but they did decline markedly in value added, having $1,245 per establishment in 1850 and $450 in 1860. This 62 per cent decline was sharper than in Wisconsin as a whole, where the value added only fell

[45] *Watertown Democrat*, Sept. 3, 1851, adv.; Nov. 29, 1855, adv.; *Jeffersonian*, June 9, 1853; *Weekly Jeffersonian*, Nov. 6, 1856, adv.; Aug. 18, 1859.
[46] MCSW, Grant and Jefferson counties, 1850 and 1860.

from $1,209 to $990, or by 18 per cent. The county, being in the southern and more highly settled portion of the state, may have experienced the demise of these craftsmen at an earlier date.

Furniture

The manufacture of furniture in Jefferson County increased both absolutely and relatively, compared to other craft industries. (Table 12 and Table 13.) This increase, though not as unusual as the relative increase in boot and shoe production, contrasted with the trend in many counties, where the sale of ready-made furniture appeared to be forcing local craftsmen out of business. As with shoemaking, however, the rise in furniture production in Jefferson is remarkable only because it grew from a small base. The increase probably reflects changing local conditions of access to lumber and to urban markets and methods of census reporting.

Chair and bedstead makers, turners and carpenters found their place in the villages and towns of Jefferson County early in the 1840's. Fort Atkinson's pioneer cabinetmaker, Joseph Goodrich, came about 1843. In Hebron, Joseph Powers was manufacturing bedsteads shortly after 1845. By 1845 Stephen March had a cabinet shop in Watertown, and two years later S.S. Keyes had built a shop in Lake Mills. These establishments operated on a parochial level, manufacturing diverse articles of furniture and doing all kinds of wood turning, often in exchange for lumber or farmers' produce.[47] But the cabinetmakers, or at least those in Watertown, did not enjoy a monopoly, for by 1847, retail merchants and merchant manufacturers were advertising ready-made goods at competitive prices.[48]

In 1850 the census reported seven furniture manufacturers employing sixteen men and turning out articles with a value added of $7,619. These craftsmen ran small shops aided only by one or two hands; the largest among them had a capital of $800 and made a value added of $1,887. The average had a capital invested of $629 and a value added of $1,088, which was 45 per cent and 52 per cent smaller respectively than the state mean. Jefferson had no furniture makers who ran manufactories, let alone factories.

[47] *History of Jefferson County*, 501, 547; John H. Ott, *Jefferson County, Wisconsin and Its People*, 2 vols. (Chicago, 1917), 150, 232; *Watertown Chronicle*, June 30, 1847, adv.; May 23, Oct. 3, 1849, advs.

[48] *Watertown Chronicle*, July 7, Oct. 13, Dec. 29, 1847, advs.; May 23, 1849, adv.

The furniture shops, nevertheless, grew in number and in output in the 1850's. The size of the average Jefferson firm increased 82 per cent when measured by capital invested and 40 per cent when measured by value added. However, they remained in the same relationship to the average Wisconsin firm, being 47 per cent below the mean firm in capital invested and 52 per cent in value added. The antebellum Jefferson establishments, when considered in a statewide context, were clearly small and catered only to domestic demand.

Within the county context, furniture making in Jefferson was composed of different-sized enterprises. There was not the marked dichotomy in size of firms that existed in Milwaukee, but it was easy to differentiate between one- and two-man shops and the larger establishments, which were attempting to provide a service for the consumers of the county rather than simply confining their market horizon to the town or village. The small shops such as those run by H.W. Hays of Palmyra or B.L. Buckingham of Sullivan often custom-made furniture for the local trade either for cash or in exchange for goods. In contrast the largest firm, Clark, Cole & Co. of Jefferson the city, who had expanded their business considerably in the 1850's despite the hard times, had installed steam power and in 1860 employed twelve men to make chairs and bedsteads, some of which were transported by wagon to Whitewater and Madison.[49] John Keck, who probably ran the second biggest establishment in the county in 1860, had likewise met with financial difficulties in the late 1850's, but he still maintained a steady business catering to clientele in the city and adjacent country.[50] Other large establishments were sophisticated versions of the one- or two-man shops and were often located in the larger towns.[51]

Furniture-making establishments in Jefferson County increased in size during the 1850's and expanded at a faster rate than overall manufactures in the county. The major increase, as in most branches of manufacture in most counties, took place in the first

[49] MCSW Jefferson County, 1860; *History of Jefferson County*, 478–479.

[50] *Watertown Democrat*, Nov. 2, 1854, adv.; Jan. 15, 1857, adv.; D. & B. vol. 26: 42.

[51] *Watertown Democrat*, Nov. 2, 1854, adv.; Jan. 25, 1855; July 17, 1856, adv.; Nov. 26, 1857, adv.; *Wisconsin Farmer*, 9 (1857), 165, adv.; MCSW, Jefferson County, 1860.

half of the decade for, the panic and depression impeded substantial growth in the late 1850's. Yet the rise in furniture production was neither spectacular nor of lasting significance, for the craftsmen met many difficulties in competing with the increasing sales of ready-made merchandise imported into the county.[52]

Other Household-Craft Consumer Industries

The other craft industries, clothing, confectionery, and tinware, contributed only a minute share of the county manufacture in the antebellum period, but they are worth noting. Sheet iron, copperware, and tinware produced a steady but small amount of value added; clothing manufacture appeared to start up in the 1850's; confectionery goods apparently ceased to be manufactured in the same decade. (Table 12 and Table 13.)

Tinsmiths, as in many Wisconsin locales, never established themselves as a major branch of business in Jefferson County. There was too much competition from the sale of ready-made stoves and kitchen utensils. Smiths were thus ancillaries to hardware merchants, either in their own shops or in the retail store, and they turned out limited amounts of custom-ordered stove furniture, stove pipes, roofing and other ware, or did repairs.[53]

Confectionery shops, bakeries, candy stores, or other food establishments were generally very small and most often were not recorded in the manuscript census.[54] One bakery reported in 1850 had quite an extensive trade, but must have shut down sometime thereafter, since no confectioner was regarded as a manufacturer by 1860.

The manufacture of clothing in Jefferson County is peculiar in that it seemed to be increasing in the 1850's. However, this apparent increase was merely a result of the failure of small tailors and milliners to be reported in 1850. These craftsmen did

---

[52] *The Jeffersonian,* June 9, 1853, adv.; Apr. 27, 1854, adv.; May 31, 1855; *Watertown Democrat,* Nov. 2, 1854, adv.; Nov. 26, 1857, adv.; D. & B. vol. 26: 39.

[53] *Watertown Chronicle,* June 27, 1847, adv.; Sept. 27, 1848, adv.; *Jeffersonian,* May 12, 1853, adv.; D. & B. vol. 26: 21, 17, 71.

[54] The reporting of confectionary shops in the manufacturing census was haphazard. Obviously there were bakeries and candy manufacturers in many Jefferson County towns in both 1850 and 1860, and probably several had a product valued at over $500 per annum. The Dun & Bradstreet reports indicate that there were at least two such establishments which might have been reported. D. & B. vol. 26: 38, 68.

exist and were, for the most part, custom tailoring on a limited basis.[55] In the 1850's tailors generally became less able to compete successfully with retailers and merchant manufacturers, who were growing in number.[56] Indeed the three firms reported in the census were all engaged in retailing as well as manufacturing.[57] Tailors in Jefferson County, as in most other Wisconsin counties, came to play a subsidiary role to retailers and had to be content with taking special orders from individual customers or with doing repairs.

AGRICULTURAL INDUSTRIES

Agricultural Implements

Although Jefferson was basically an agricultural county concentrating on wheat growing, local farmers did not stimulate the growth of either a large local agricultural implements industry or a wagon and carriage industry. Watertown did not become celebrated for the manufacture of farm machinery as did Racine. Indeed the agricultural implements branch of manufacturing was merely supplementary to the import trade, contributing only 8 or 9 per cent of the county's aggregate by value added. (Table 12 and Table 13.)

Manufacturers of farm equipment, whether specialized in function or being part-time blacksmiths, were few. Two such establishments were reported in the census of 1850 and three in that of 1860, while a few firms also came into and went out of existence within the census intervals. Of these enterprises possibly only Sewell Keyes' rake and hoe manufactory commanded an extensive business. The firms were usually medium sized, employing four or five workers, and making a value added of some $4,000.[58] The reason for this restricted business was the importation of imple-

[55] Rock River Pilot, May 18, Sept. 20, 1848, advs.; Watertown Chronicle, Aug. 30, Oct. 4, Oct. 25, Nov. 28, 1848, advs.; Aug. 22, 1849, adv.; June 5, 1850, adv.

[56] Watertown Chronicle, Sept. 7, 1853, adv.; March 7, 1855, adv.; Watertown Democrat, Oct. 26, 1854, adv.; March 1, 1855, adv.; Feb. 25, 1860, adv.; Weekly Jeffersonian, Oct. 9, 1856, adv.; July 30, 1857, adv.; Wisconsin Chief, March 23, 1859, adv.; Fort Atkinson Standard, Dec. 20, 1860, adv.; D. & B. vol. 26: 28, 39, 94.

[57] Watertown Democrat, Sept. 18, 1856, adv.; Nov. 11, 1858, adv.; D. & B. vol. 26: 40F, 53; MCSW, Jefferson County, 1860.

[58] Watertown Chronicle, Feb. 2, 1848, adv.; Watertown Democrat, Nov. 16, 1854; July 22, 1858; Wisconsin Farmer, 4 (1852) 214; D. & B. vol. 26: 45, 77; MCSW, Jefferson County, 1850 and 1860.

ments sold by agents. As early as 1847 L.D. Phelps of Dodge County was acting as the local agent for the sale of Pitts' Horse Powers, Threshing Machines and Separators of Rochester, New York. Even George Dickinson, who was making fanning mills in Waterloo in 1850, was a partner of R.E. Ela of Rochester, Racine County, who ran the larger main plant.[59] During the 1850's especially after the opening of the railroads, pressure from salesmen representing outside manufacturers in Wisconsin and elsewhere became even stronger. Jefferson farm implements makers, lacking competitive stamina, were thus reduced to playing a secondary role in servicing and repairing the equipment of the local farmer.

Wagons and Carriages

Wagon and carriage making, though less subject to outside competition than agricultural implements, was basically a minor branch of manufacturing in antebellum Jefferson County. The men producing wagons and carriages were specialized blacksmiths. While concentrating on wagonmaking and doing little repairing, they still retained the aura of blacksmiths' shops, being small two- or three-man shops employing an average capital of $840. In 1860, even the largest of these firms only employed four men in the manufacture of twenty-six wagons and other work.[60]

"OTHER" INDUSTRIES

The "other" industries in Jefferson County likewise contributed only a small share to the manufacturing output. The Vulcan Iron works of Watertown, established in 1846, made limited amounts of castings, farm equipment, mill irons, and other articles for local consumption throughout the 1850's.[61] The Watertown Gas Works, established in 1856, were an unusual phenomenon and might even be regarded as a sign of progress since only two other cities in Wisconsin, namely Milwaukee and Racine, had gas supplies. Finally the miscellaneous industries consisted of an odd assortment of petty manufactures ranging from potash to the making of melodeons and safes.

[59] *Watertown Chronicle,* Nov. 17, 1857, adv.; MCSW, Jefferson County, 1850; R.E. Ela to George Dickinson, *passim,* Ela Correspondence, State Historical Society of Wisconsin.
[60] MCSW, Jefferson County, 1850 and 1860.
[61] *Watertown Chronicle,* June 23, 1847, adv.; Dec. 24, 1851, adv.; *Watertown Democrat,* Nov. 9, 1854; May 8, 1856; June 14, 1860; D. & B. vol. 26: 43.

Conclusions

Manufacturing activities in antebellum Jefferson County reflected an agricultural economy in a state of transition. The main emphasis was understandably placed on the processing of locally available raw materials — namely wheat and, to a lesser extent, lumber — for local consumption. The remainder of the industrial enterprises catered to practical and household needs, when and if they proved to be economical. Some attention was thus given to household-craft consumer industries insofar as they could withstand the competition of retailed ready-made goods, and a small amount of agricultural machinery was manufactured if the pressure from outside firms was not too severe.

The structure and output of manufacturing in Jefferson was essentially small-scale and limited. The majority of firms, with the exception of some flour mills and one clothing and one footwear manufactory, catered to a local hinterland. This type of development was probably typical of many pioneer economies, which, prior to the construction of the railroad, lacked good connections with other areas. Having failed to firmly establish any large-scale industry prior to the arrival of the railroad, Jefferson County entrepreneurs were neither in a financial position in the late 1850's nor in a locational situation to easily withstand competition from goods made in Milwaukee or made in other parts of the country and imported through Milwaukee. On the whole, the Jefferson County pattern of manufacturing was that of a lower-order market area functioning within the orbit of a larger regional network.

CHAPTER THREE

Grant County: Manufacturing in the Mining Region

LUMBER AND RICH SOIL were not Wisconsin's only natural assets, for the state was also well endowed with mineral deposits. Abundant lead deposits, together with small quantities of zinc and copper, underlay the southwestern corner of the state. Bog iron ores were dispersed throughout the marshes of Wisconsin, especially in the southeastern counties. More extensive deposits of iron were worked in the Black River Falls region and in Sauk, Crawford, and Dodge counties, though the rich Superior deposits remained virtually untouched in the antebellum years. Wisconsin also possessed a wide variety of natural building materials such as limestone, granite, gravel, marble, and clay for brickmaking.[1]

Lead was the most important mineral resource in antebellum Wisconsin. It was located in the lead region of the Upper Mississippi Valley which extended some seventy miles north and south on both sides of the river and some sixty miles east and west, encompassing parts of Iowa, Illinois, and Wisconsin. The

---

[1] U.S. *Senate Reports,* "Report of a Geological Exploration of part of Iowa, Wisconsin and Illinois," 28 Cong. 1 Sess., 1844, Report 407; U.S. *Senate Executive Documents,* 30 Cong. 1 Sess., 1848, Doc. 57; State of Wisconsin Assembly, 5 Legis., 1852, 7 Legis., 1854, 10 Legis., 1858, *Reports* of the Committee on Mining and Smelting; State of Wisconsin, Assembly, 7 Legis., 1855, 8 Legis., 1856, *Annual Report* of the Geological Survey of the State of Wisconsin; Chamberlin, *passim;* J.B. Whitney, *Geological Survey of the Upper Mississippi Lead Region,* Reprinted from the Wisconsin Geological Survey Report Vol. 1, 1862; Ulysses S. Grant, *Preliminary Report of the Lead and Zinc Deposits of South Western Wisconsin* (Madison, 1906). Most of the secondary sources — for example, Schafer, *The Lead Region,* passim; Merk, 111–122; Lake, *passim;* and the relevant county histories — all draw heavily on these reports.

Indians and then the French had intermittently worked the ore in the early years of the nineteenth century, to be followed by more extensive American ventures in the late 1820's. But prior to the Black Hawk War of 1832 American miners were periodically threatened by hostile Indians and it was not until the middle and late 1830's that lead output increased significantly, rising from a total of 4,281,876 pounds in 1832 to 25,044,950 pounds in 1839.[2]

The mining boom was of relatively short duration. Surface prospecting by individuals with a pick and shovel soon gave way to larger and more costly operations. Moreover the growing private ownership of lead-bearing land, the change in the tariff of 1846, and the attractions of the Mexican War and the California gold mines all further discouraged interest in lead mining. Output fell from a peak of 54,494,850 pounds in 1845 to a total of 24,453,100 pounds in 1860.[3]

Grant Country, situated in the heart of the Upper Mississippi Valley lead region, was settled at an earlier date than other parts of Wisconsin, and often by Southerners traveling up the river. Estimates of population in the lead area as a whole in the 1820's have varied, but by the end of the decade there was probably a minimum of 4,000 residents.[4] Following the end of Indian dis-

---

[2] For further information on early mining activities, see Daniel Parkinson, "Pioneer Life in Wisconsin," *Wisconsin Historical Collections*, 2 (1856), 326–364 [hereinafter cited as *Wis. His. Colls.*]; Moses Meeker, "The Lead Region," *Wis. His. Colls.*, 6 (1872), 271–296; M. Palmer Strange, "Western Wisconsin in 1836," *Wis. His. Colls.*, 6 (1872), 297–307; R.G. Thwaites, "Notes on Early Lead Mining in the Fever River Region," *Wis. His. Colls.*, 13 (1895), 271-292; Theodore Rudolph, "Pioneering in the Wisconsin Lead Region," *Wis. His. Colls.*, 15 (1900), 338–389; John N. Davidson, "Some Distinctive Characteristics of the History of Our Lead Region," *Wisconsin Historical Proceedings* (1898), 183–195 [hereinafter cited as *Wis. His. Proc.*]; John H. Evans, "Some Reminiscences of Early Grant County," *Wis. His. Proc.* (1909), 232–245; John W. Taylor, "Reservation and Leasing of the Salines, Lead and Copper Mines of the Public Domain" (unpublished Ph.D. dissertation, University of Chicago, 1930), *passim*; Schafer, *The Lead Region*, 21–46; Margaret S. Carter, *New Diggins On The Fever, 1824–60* (n.p., 1959), 8–59; James E. Wright, *The Galena Lead District, Federal Policy and Practice, 1824–1847* (Madison, 1966), *passim*.

[3] For contemporary explanations of the declining output of the lead mines, see State of Wisconsin, Assembly, 5 Legis., 1852, *Report* of the Committee on Mining and Smelting; Wisconsin Assembly, 7 Legis., 1854, *Annual Report* of the Geological Survey. Schubring, 11–14, also notes the reasons stated by several geologists who explored the region.

[4] Mary J. Read, "A Population Study of the Driftless Hill Land During the Pioneer Period, 1832–1860" (unpublished Ph.D. dissertation, University of Wisconsin, 1941), 315.

turbances, numerous small mining villages sprang up throughout Grant County in the 1830's. By 1840 the census officially recorded a population of 3,926 in the county. Population continued to increase in the antebellum years, reaching 16,169 by 1850 and 31,207 by 1860; but it retained its widely dispersed character. The initial pattern of small settlements clustered around lead mines was maintained, even though some mining towns became defunct. New small towns were centered on agricultural potential or access to water or rail transportation routes.[5]

This distribution of population had a marked effect on the development of manufacturing activities in Grant County. Though the complete breakdown of figures is not available for 1840, possibly every mining center had its own blacksmith, cobbler, tailor, and miller, even though their value of product did not exceed $500 per annum. Certainly by 1845 the towns with a population of 200 or more were supporting several artisans or miner-artisans, while the larger centers of Platteville and Potosi contained several men who might be classified as manufacturers.[6]

By 1850 manufacturing activity appeared to becoming more centralized, in that Platteville accounted for some 40 per cent of the total value added. Possibly Platteville, which had some 13.4 per cent of the county's population, was trying to assume the function of a higher-order center. If this were the case, however, the town did not succeed, for in 1860 it only contributed 13.6 per cent of the county aggregate value added and contained less than 10 per cent of the population. The bulk of the manufacturing was by then dispersed throughout the many towns, and showed a close relationship to localized natural resources.

Manufacturing in antebellum Grant County emphasized activities relating to mineral deposits, but the manufacturing structure was not entirely focused on the presence of lead. Minerals only provided 26.4 per cent of the Grant County value added in 1850 and 30.2 per cent in 1860. Flour milling vied with minerals as the leading branch of manufactures, contributing 27.6 per cent of the county value added in 1850 and 28.9 per cent in 1860. (Ta-

---

[5] *Ibid., passim.*
[6] *Grant County Herald,* Aug. 30, 1845; *Independent American,* May 9, 1845, both quoting Julius B. McCabe, "Gazeteer of the State of Wisconsin," 1845. This "Gazeteer" was never published.

ble 14 and Table 15.) Grant County in fact had a dual-based manufacturing economy. Not only did the county possess some of the richest lead veins, but it also had good agricultural soil which provided wheat crops for the local flour-milling industry. The original incentive to farming had been the high cost of foodstuffs, but agriculture soon became a profitable end in itself.[7]

The presence of two leading industries in 1850 and 1860 put Grant at odds with the general Wisconsin county pattern of having an overwhelming proportion of value added in one branch of manufacture. Whereas the average Wisconsin county had 57.6 per cent and 54.8 per cent of its value added in one industry in 1850 and 1860 respectively, Grant County had only 27.7 per cent and 30.2 per cent respectively. The contrast was nearly as sharp when it was noted that Grant's *two* leading industries combined only contributed 54 and 59 per cent of the county aggregate by value added in contrast to the Wisconsin mean county figures of 71 and 70.4 per cent in 1850 and 1860.

Rich and diverse natural resources in Grant County meant that entrepreneurs were better able to diversify their processing activities than were their counterparts in many northern Wisconsin counties. Lumber planed and sawed, using either local oak or upriver pine, furnished an important third branch after minerals and flour milling. There was also a scattering of activity in other processing branches, giving the group as a whole a total of 68.5 per cent of the Grant manufacturing by value added in 1850 and 75.7 per cent in 1860. (Table 14 and Table 15.)

The household-craft consumer industries in Grant County, as in Wisconsin in general, declined in their share of total manufacturing output. This group contributed one sixth of the county aggregate in 1850 and one eighth in 1860. The downward trend pointed to two facets of industrial development on the western frontier. In the first place certain craftsmen, such as blacksmiths, were taking on more specialized functions and were becoming classified as wagonmakers. In the second place other artisans, for example cobblers and tailors, were giving up their trades because

[7] *Grant County Herald*, Aug. 19, 1843; *Wisconsin Herald*, May 15, 1847; *Independent American*, Apr. 28, 1854; State of Wisconsin, Assembly, 5 Legis., 1852, *Report* of the Committee on Mining and Smelting, 279; State of Wisconsin Assembly, 7 Legis., 1854, *Annual Report* of the Geological Survey, 57–58; Schafer, *The Lead Region*, 2–20, 131–147; Read, *passim*; Taylor, 122–125.

TABLE 14

Manufacturing in Grant County, 1850

(Value Added in Current $'s.)

Industry	Value Added	Per Cent of Total	No. of Workers	Per Cent of Total
Processing Industries				
Lumber	11,697	8.47	28	13.40
Flour	38,200	27.67	24	11.47
Cooperage	2,462	1.78	4	1.91
Leather	3,410	2.47	8	3.83
Construction Materials	1,780	1.29	8	3.83
Wool	650	0.47	1	0.48
Minerals	36,399	26.36	41	19.62
Aggregate	94,598	68.51	114	54.54
Household-Craft Consumer				
Boots and Shoes	3,017	2.18	9	4.30
Clothing	660	0.48	2	0.96
Furniture	4,215	3.05	12	5.74
Blacksmiths	11,093	8.04	28	13.40
Tin, Copper etc.	3,650	2.64	6	2.87
Aggregate	22,635	16.39	57	27.27
Agricultural Industries				
Agricultural Impls.	8,701	6.30	15	7.18
Wagons	8,575	6.21	16	7.66
Aggregate	17,276	12.51	31	14.84
Other Industries				
Iron	1,575	1.14	3	1.44
Miscellaneous	2,000	1.45	4	1.91
Aggregate	3,575	2.59	7	3.35
Grant County	138,084	100.00	209	100.00

[Source: Manuscript Census for the State of Wisconsin, 1850. Grant County.]

of competition from retailed ready-made goods. Craft industries were dying out. In fact the only household-craft consumer branch in Grant County to grow in relative as well as absolute amount in the 1850's was the manufacture of furniture. The increase in this particular line was probably attributable to the accessibility of lumber, both locally and from the pineries.

During the 1850's less attention was also paid to the agricultural group of industries in Grant County. Despite the increased output of farm products, the manufacture of farm implements declined both relatively and absolutely. Local entrepreneurs were unable to compete successfully with equipment brought into the area by agents of large firms. Possibly the increase in the output of wagons and carriages may also have supplied some of the less specialized needs of rural living. The "other" group of industries provided but a small share of the county's value added by manufacturing. (Table 14 and Table 15.)

The only branch of manufacturing in which Grant contributed a substantial amount to the state total was mineral production. In 1850 the county provided 23.5 per cent of the Wisconsin aggregate; this amount fell to 19.2 per cent in 1860. This high percentage stemmed from the fact that Grant County had a larger commitment to manufacturing than did either of the other Wisconsin lead-mining counties of Iowa and Lafayette. Thus, although minerals only provided some 25–30 per cent of Grant's aggregate, their absolute value could still bear favorable comparison to the absolute value of minerals produced elsewhere in the state.

In other manufacturing activities Grant County failed to make a significant contribution to the Wisconsin aggregate. The second-highest figure was 7.9 per cent of the Wisconsin blacksmiths in 1850, followed by 5.8 per cent of the state's cabinetmakers in 1860. Both of these figures were larger than Grant's share of the Wisconsin total population, namely 5.3 per cent in 1850 and 4.0 per cent in 1860. However, the overall contribution of Grant County manufacturing was less than the county's proportion of Wisconsin's population — being 3.6 per cent in 1850 and 2.7 per cent in 1860 — indicating that the industries were not fully supplying local consumer needs.

The parochial character of Grant County manufacturing also emerges from a comparison with the average size of the state's manufacturing establishments. In 1850 Grant only had industrial

TABLE 15

MANUFACTURING IN GRANT COUNTY, 1860

(Value Added in Current $'s.)

Industry	Value Added	Per Cent of Total	No. of Workers	Per Cent of Total
Processing Industries				
Lumber	34,212	11.24	49	13.50
Flour	87,895	28.87	43	11.85
Cooperage	735	0.24	2	0.55
Liquors	8,470	2.78	10	2.75
Leather	4,355	1.43	12	3.31
Construction Materials	1,600	0.53	9	2.48
Meat Packing	330	0.11	2	0.55
Wool	1,139	0.37	15	4.13
Minerals	91,590	30.16	102	28.10
Aggregate	230,326	75.73	244	67.22
Household-Craft Consumer				
Boots and Shoes	3,666	1.20	10	2.75
Clothing	735	0.24	3	0.83
Furniture	23,948	7.86	33	9.09
Blacksmiths	6,352	2.09	14	3.86
Tin, Copper etc.	1,153	0.38	11	3.03
Aggregate	35,854	11.77	71	19.56
Agricultural Industries				
Agricultural Impls.	7,855	2.58	9	2.48
Wagons	19,584	6.43	32	8.82
Aggregate	27,439	9.01	41	11.30
Other Industries				
Iron	405	0.13	2	0.55
Miscellaneous	10,226	3.36	5	1.37
Aggregate	10,631	3.49	7	1.92
Grant County	304,250	100.00	363	100.00

[SOURCE: Manuscript Census for the State of Wisconsin, 1860. Grant County.]

plants larger than the general state average in one category, minerals. In fact the largest single establishment reported in the censuses was a lead mine — not strictly a manufacturing plant — which employed sixteen miners in 1860. While the average number of workers per establishment did increase from 2.6 in 1850 to almost 3.0 in 1860, it did not match the increase in the size of the average Wisconsin firm over the same period — from 4.8 to 5.4. These figures suggest that the county had no large operations like the northern lumber mills or the Milwaukee clothing manufactories. Most manufacturing was done in a traditional way, in small shops employing two or three workers.

Although the distinction between traditional and modern methods of production need not be determined solely by the size of the establishment, there was little else in Grant County to show that a particular operation was using new techniques and equipment. There appeared to be little division of labor. Each worker might specialize in a certain task in some of the larger firms, but they were merely applying a skill which could be equally well applied at home or in a small shop. At most, the larger establishments in Grant County could only be called manufactories.[8]

Furthermore the industrial establishments were all using the cheapest source of power available: water, horse, or hand power. This did not necessarily indicate backwardness or a reluctance to employ new or more advanced means of motive power such as steam; it did, however, mean that mills and shops had to be located on a river and were subject to seasonal hazards. This in turn implied a somewhat restricted market and output.

Manufacturing activities in antebellum Grant County were not in a strong position for future growth. The lead veins were becoming exhausted. The market for flour was becoming highly competitive, and Grant County had no special cost advantage over other Wisconsin flour-producing areas. In other industries, especially the craft branches, entrepreneurs were competing against the encroachments of the retail trade and were satisfied if they could hold on to the neighborhood trade. Grant County manufacturing, with the notable exception of lead processing, was

---

[8] This designation is rather anomalous when applied to a lead-smelting furnace or a lead mine, but it implies the transitional stage in the growth of and definition of industry.

locally oriented, and even this limited market was threatened by competition from imported goods.

PROCESSING INDUSTRIES

Minerals

Although lead mining and lead smelting would not be considered manufacturing occupations in the twentieth century, both activities were included within the scope of mid-nineteenth-century "products of industry" schedules, and both were of major significance in analyzing the industrial evolution of southwestern Wisconsin. In Grant County, lead mining probably began in the early 1820's, but the first miners were itinerants who merely traveled around scratching the surface for ore. It was not until 1824 that the first permanent settlement was made, at Hardscrabble, to be followed by many new mining camps in the next two years. Yet few positive steps were taken towards permanent village and agricultural development until the end of the Indian threat in 1832.[9] In the 1830's more miners came to the region to work the ore either legally, under the federal leasing system, or illegally by purchasing supposedly non-mineral lands. By 1840 the census reported 794 men occupied in mining in Grant County, while four years later there were reputedly some 600 miners in the county.[10]

In this early period most mining operations were extremely crude. Digging on the pock-marked surface might be random or might be guided by surface signs such as linear depressions or the growth of certain types of vegetation, possibly indicating the presence of ore veins.[11] Methods of digging varied with the depth of the ore. Surface or near-surface deposits meant an attack on the side of the hill with a spade and shovel, windlass and tub. Deeper deposits were mined by digging a shaft and then tunneling along the vein, or by pumping water out of the diggings with

---

[9] *History of Grant County, Wisconsin* (Chicago, 1881), 478–479, 482; "Early Reminiscences of J.H. Rountree," Rountree Papers, State Historical Society of Wisconsin.

[10] *Sixth Census, 1840, Compendium,* 95; *History of Grant County,* 489.

[11] Miners soon found by practical experience that the lead ore usually occurred in groups of veins, running parallel to each other and most often running from east to west. U.S. *Senate Reports,* 28 Cong. 1 Sess., 1844, Report No. 407; Schafer, *The Lead Region,* 95.

a horse-powered pump. But even then little capital was invested, and mining was essentially a short-term project.[12]

Promotional efforts to encourage large-scale investment in mining were not made until the late 1840's and early 1850's, when it had become obvious that the lead output was diminishing. But still capital was lacking. Locally, the smelters or speculators with money, prior to 1846 and the end of the leasing system, were not prepared to sink money into government lands. Shortly thereafter gold prospecting in the Far West offered a more tantalizing prospect than did the marginal profits to be gained from deep mining in an area which had already been dug over and which required heavy expenditure for machinery. Furthermore the boosterism of the Wisconsin government failed to attract substantial outside investment. By the 1850's the mining potential of the lead district was on the wane.

Indeed, of the sixteen mining establishments reported in Grant county in the census of 1860, only one employed more than ten men. Perhaps manpower does not necessarily indicate potential, but it should be noted that only seven of the sixteen reported operations were obviously companies rather than partnerships, and that the average capital involved was $606, the largest single investment being $5,000, and the smallest $25. None of these investment figures suggest the presence of sophisticated plant and machinery. Those companies like the American Mining Company (1853) or the Rountree Company (1854) which proposed to carry out deep mining operations either never got off the ground or had a very short life span.[13] With an average value added of $736 per minor in 1860 — which for the smaller operations dropped to about $400 — the profit was going out of mining. Those establishments reported in the census may have been only a fraction of the mines in Grant County, but they could probably be regarded as a fair sample.

Smelting operations revealed another facet of the lead industry. Smelters were essentially men with considerable financial assets. Prior to 1846 they not only had to post a bond of $10,000 with the government superintendent before acquiring a license, but

---

[12] History of Grant County, 479–481; Wright, 28–29; Schafer, The Lead Region, 95–97.

[13] Independent American, Aug. 11, 17, 1854; History of Grant County, 743.

they were often the first local settlers to buy mineral lands when they came on the market. Despite this capital availability, smelting did not appear to return good profits. The twenty-one licensed smelters of 1827–28 had a combined value added of $80,475 which rendered a mean return of only $3,832.[14] To be sure, this profit was not necessarily equally distributed among the group members, but even so smelting could hardly be called a highly remunerative operation. Profits may well have decreased in the 1830's, for John Rountree's furnace on the Platte was up for sale in April, 1838, because none of the owners were willing to attend to the business.[15]

Much of the explanation for low or uncertain profits in lead smelting in the early years of settlement may well have been inefficient means of production; smelting was done in primitive log and ash furnaces heated by wood and fire and bellows. But also of importance was the fact that smelting was carried out under federal government supervision, and the smelter had to agree to pay the government a certain percentage of his product.[16] Furthermore the markets and transport routes for the finished product fluctuated with Eastern demands, the tariff rates and the season of the year, thus making smelting even more financially hazardous.[17]

The situation did not seem to improve with the demise of the public mines in 1846. In the mid-1840's the quantity of lead actually fell by half in comparison to earlier seasons. Then, in 1846, many lead furnaces closed because of the diminishing quantity of ore, though the effects of the tariff of 1846 were also being felt.[18] By 1850 the seven Grant County smelters recorded

[14] Wright, 24–25, 65–66.

[15] J.H. Rountree to Hempstead & Beebe, Dec. 19, 1835; J.H. Rountree to Hooper, Rock & Scales, Apr. 18, 1838; Vol. 11, Letter Book, 46–47, 81, Rountree Papers.

[16] Under the terms of John Rountree's license for smelting, Apr. 18, 1833, he was to pay the government six pounds of every hundred pounds of lead he smelted. See Rountree Papers, "Licence for Smelting," 1833, 1834, and "Licence Bonds," 1832–1834; Wright, 17; Carter, 32.

[17] Vol. II, Letter Book, Rountree Papers, contains correspondence, 1828–1847, which indicates that most of the lead was sent downriver through Galena or St. Louis agents. These letters also show a keen awareness of the price of lead, the desirability of storing lead for higher prices, and the dangers involved in shipping lead down the Mississippi when the river was either in a very low stage or in near-flood.

[18] J. H. Rountree to Emmerson, Harris & Potter, Sept. 14, 1846; J.H. Rountree

in the census had an aggregate value added of only $36,399, or an average of $5,200. The smelters had small operations; the largest employed ten men.

A decade later the situation had deteriorated. Ten smelters could only produce 2,542 tons of lead in contrast to the 3,121 tons of 1850.[19] Lead smelting operations had decreased in size, falling from an average of 5.9 men per establishment in 1850 to 3.9 by 1860, and their average value added had also declined by some 18 per cent. The long-standing smelters appeared to have made little or no effort to come to grips with a diminishing ore production. Instead of amalgamating in order to cut production costs, the number of smelters had increased. Furthermore newcomers were doing a better business than the old hands, for the three smelting operations which existed both in 1850 and 1860 declined 32 per cent in terms of value added compared with the overall decline of 18 per cent.

The lead industry in Grant County, as the oldest economic activity in Wisconsin apart from the fur trade, had a life span of over thirty years in the antebellum period. During this time lead mining and smelting were subject to booms and, after 1847, to slumps. Lead still continued to be mined and smelted, but in diminishing quantities. The lead industry had followed the usual see-saw pattern for mineral development, in the course of which Grant's industrial economy changed both internally and in comparison to the state as a whole. Internally the industry influenced the location and spread of other servicing manufactures in the county and then was replaced in importance by these branches. Externally the industry placed Grant County among Wisconsin's leading manufacturing counties in 1840, but it did not maintain a high value added and failed to preserve the county's position within the state.

---

to P.T. Southworth, Sept. 4, 1846, Vol. 11, Letter Book, Rountree Papers. The tariff of 1846 lowered the protection on lead from 3¢ per pound "specific" to 20 per cent "ad valorem" and allowed Spanish lead, which was being produced in large quantities, to enter the American market on a competitive basis. However, the price of lead at Galena increased fairly steadily from $2.24 per thousand pounds in 1842 to $4.125 in 1852, which suggests that diminished ore output may have been responsible for the smaller quantity of lead smelted.

[19] MCSW, Grant County, 1850 and 1860; computations, using the 2,000-pound short ton and seventy pounds per pig of lead, and inserting average figures where none are recorded.

Flour Milling

Flour milling, though later in developing than the lead industry, was of equal, if not greater, importance in the manufacturing economy of Grant County in the 1850's. The initial stimulus to milling was provided by the presence of mining camps and villages scattered throughout the county. The high cost of food early encouraged miners to become miner-farmers and grow food crops on the side. Of more importance, by the mid-1830's farmers were moving into the Grant River district, which was endowed with excellent soil, timber, good water supplies, and easy access to the markets of the lead region. By 1840, 604 men out of a total population of 3,926 were engaged in agricultural pursuits and the ratio of men to women in the general population was 100:58, suggesting both an increasing number of families and settlement of a more permanent nature.

The existence of early gristmills is difficult to document, but the first such mill is reputed to have been built on the Platte River about 1829, while the second was built on Pigeon Creek near Lancaster in 1835. These mills were primitive, using what was locally known as "lost rock," from the Iowa side of the Mississippi River, as mill burrs for grinding wheat and corn.[20] It was thus not surprising that these and other pioneer establishments only supplied part of the demands of the mining camps which still imported large quantities of flour up the Mississippi. By 1840 two of Grant's reported five flour- and gristmills had become more efficient for they had an aggregate production of 500 barrels of flour. The other three gristmills, with a production of $500 or more, probably catered to the custom trade.

The mills grew in number and capacity during the 1840's, but they still served an essentially local market. In 1840 the mill belonging to Rountree, Virgin & Grey could grind 150 bushels of wheat per twenty-four-hour day, producing flour for sale or on a custom basis. McKee's mill on the Little Platte had reputedly ceased to do custom work in 1841, but McKee would still grind farmers' crops by special contract, exchanging meal for corn at the ratio of 5:6. The Bass flour mill, built at Platteville in the fall of 1847 at an estimated cost of $4,500,

[20] History of Grant County, 483.

would grind corn and wheat for "the Eighth toll."[21] Solomon
Lightcap's mill near Hazel Green, completed in March 1848, at
a cost of $11,000, was probably only grinding wheat and corn
for neighborhood customers.[22]

By 1850 the census reported twelve grist- and flour mills with
an average value of product of $11,143 and an average value of
$3,183. These Grant figures compared unfavorably with the
overall Wisconsin values of $28,192 and $8,012, and to even
greater disadvantage with the outputs of the older wheat-producing counties in the southeastern part of the state. Kenosha mills
had a mean value of product of $63,458 and a mean value added
of $14,891; the comparative figures for Rock County were
$60,594 and $17,531. The Grant mills, widely dispersed throughout the county, were catering mainly to local demand. All powered
by water, they were basically small operations producing an
aggregate of 27,670 barrels of flour and other grains. Some
flour may have been exported upriver to the lumber mills, but
the home market remained the primary consideration.[23]

During the 1850's there was both an extension and a modifica-
tion of the Grant pattern of flour milling. The number of mills
increased from twelve in 1850 to twenty in 1860; value added by
manufacture rose by 130 per cent and the output of flour increased by 123 per cent to some 61,708 barrels.[24] Yet for the
most part the mills remained small, the mean value of product in
1860 being $16,115 and the mean value added being $4,395.
They were still in the rearguard of the wheat-producing counties,
for the average Wisconsin flour mill had a value of product of
$29,653 and a value added of $5,450.

Although the Grant County mills were small, used water power,
and were widely dispersed, it would appear that they were not
completely backward. The prominent millers, at least, were
attempting to keep abreast of technological changes. In 1852

[21] *Northern Badger*, Jan. 8, 1841, adv.; *The Wisconsin Whig*, Apr. 27, 1842, adv.;
Independent American, Dec. 2, 1848, adv.; *History of Grant County*, 719–721, 809.

[22] Account Book, 2 Vols., 1856–1862, Solomon Lightcap Papers, State Historical
Society of Wisconsin; *History of Grant County*, 755.

[23] MCSW, Grant County, 1850; *Independent American*, Dec. 2, 1848; Sept. 17,
1852.

[24] This is the minimum amount of flour produced, because several mills failed
to state their product. MCSW, Grant County, 1860.

the new Ellenboro mills contained all the necessary machinery for making good flour. In the same year N. H. Virgin's Platteville Mill was repaired and equipped with all the machinery required for making "Extra Superfine" flour. Virgin continued to improve his plant, and when he opened the Genessee mills in 1857 he acquired modern equipment for properly cleaning wheat and making high-quality flour. His example was not lost. In 1859 D. R. Sylvester refitted his mill with new machinery and in 1861 G. H. Rector and J. Caspare put the Ellenboro mills in better running order.[25]

Such technological improvements might explain why the millers seemed to be placing a greater emphasis on producing grain for sale rather than for the custom trade.[26] Though they were still prepared to oblige the farmer by custom grinding if and when he desired, they seem to have expanded their market horizons. Virgin & Teesdale were anxious for flour dealers, as well as local customers, to try their products. John Rountree was even more ambitious, for he exported flour up and downriver to St. Paul and St. Louis and also to Chicago in the late 1850's.[27] It is impossible to ascertain the amount of flour exported from the county, but probably leading millers did actively engage in the Mississippi River trade. Although they could not compete with their counterparts in southern and southeastern Wisconsin for the Milwaukee and Chicago markets, they were probably able to furnish some supplies for the logging camps in the pineries, even after the railroads reached the Mississippi in 1857–58 and made flour more easily available from Milwaukee and other inland centers in Wisconsin.

Flour and gristmilling in antebellum Grant County progressed, from the frontier stage of grinding wheat either for the custom trade or for consumption in the lead-mining centers, to a more

[25] *Independent American*, March 12, adv,. Sept. 17, 1852; March 6, adv., June 12, 1857; *Grant County Herald*, Oct. 22, 1859, adv.; June 6, 1861, adv.

[26] This statement is based on scattered information available in newspaper advertisements. When the miller did all types of flouring he usually indicated by the order in which he listed the varieties — namely, merchant, custom, or share grinding — that he preferred a certain type of arrangement. See *Grant County Herald*, Oct. 22, 1859, adv.

[27] D. & B. vol. 20: 14, 32, 54; *Grant County Witness*, June 21, 1860, adv.; *Grant County Herald*, Oct. 22, 1859, adv.; *Independent American*, March 6, 1857, adv.; H.F. McCluskey to J.H. Rountree, Aug. 3, Sept. 3, Sept. 20, 1859, Rountree Papers.

sophisticated level of making flour for sale both locally and in the export trade. There was no distinct shift from one stage to the other, for as late as 1860 most mills were still grinding wheat on a custom basis. But milling activity had expanded along with the increased grain output of the county, and, with increased capacity, some millers, at least, showed an awareness of the need to modernize their plants and sell to more distant markets. The mills might not be of a size or in a location to compete success-fully with the mills of southern and southeastern Wisconsin, but they could still find a viable market upriver or downriver, and were not yet forced out of business by the economies of scale practiced in the larger mills. Prior to the centralization of in-dustry and the heavy use of railroads, flour milling, even though the situation was tight in hard times, could still be regarded as a growing industry in Grant County.

Lumber Planed and Sawed

Lumber planed and sawed was another processing industry which grew steadily in the antebellum period, both in relative and absolute amounts. (Table 14 and Table 15.) Local supplies of lumber came from scattered groves which contained abundant stands of marketable timber, while a much larger area was covered with stunted oak. Even when such resources were depleted by the needs of the smelting furnaces and housing construction, Grant County, with its long frontage on the Mississippi River, could import timber from the northern pineries.

Sawmills supplying the timber needs of the mining camps and villages were established more frequently and at an earlier date than gristmills. The first recorded sawmill was built on the Platte River in 1829, though doubtless there were earlier mills, if only of a temporary nature. As settlement became more wide-spread in the 1830's there was a slow but steady growth of the industry. Evidence is slight, but in 1833 McKee erected a mill on the Little Platte, and he was kept busy supplying lumber to various parts of the territory. In 1835 John Rountree began building a sawmill which was completed the following year. Coates' mill must have been in existence and working order by 1837, if not earlier, for it was rented out in 1838. These estab-lishments were limited in scope. Jared Warner was probably one of the more successful pioneer sawmillers, but even his second mill, built in 1844, had a capacity of only 2–3,000 feet per day. Business either with the miners or the villages was limited.[28]

The thirteen sawmills reported in the census of 1850 still operated on a restricted basis. They generally had a small capital and a small value of product, the average figures being $1,505 and $1,676 respectively — figures which were below the state averages of $3,708 and $4,244. All mills were located on water sites and usually processed oak lumber, which suggests a nearby supply cut from the oak groves, possibly even on a custom basis.[29] Moreover the owners of about one third of these establishments also ran gristmills in conjunction with their sawmills, indicating, as in Jefferson County, that both types of mill were doing neighborhood work. Jared Warner, still the leading sawmill operator, was the only exception. Producing some 34 per cent of the county's value added in lumber, he was catering to a wider market threshold.[30]

During the 1850's the number of sawmills in Grant County seemed to remain stable around thirteen, but the size of the mills increased. By the end of the decade the average capital invested was $4,165, an increase of 177 per cent, while the average value of product was $5,215, an increase of 211 per cent. Notwithstanding the size increment of the mills, however, the output of rough lumber only grew some 34 per cent. This relatively slow growth resulted from two developments. On the one hand some mills were planing as well as sawing lumber and were also making lath, shingles, railings, pickets and slabs, suggesting a more sophisticated stage of lumber processing. On the other hand, several mills were suffering from the competition of lumber yards established on the Mississippi River and selling lumber from the pineries to Grant County carpenters and joiners.[31]

[28] History of Grant County, 480, 483, 720, 869; "Articles of Agreement between J.R. Vineyard, Benjamin Coates and Thomas Coates of Grant County and Francis Gulleman and James Burk of the same county and Territory, Nov. 19, 1838," George W. Lakin Papers, State Historical Society of Wisconsin; D. & B. vol. 20: 25; Grant County Herald, Sept. 9, 1843, adv.

[29] MCSW, Grant County, 1850; Wisconsin Herald, Jan. 6, 1848, adv.

[30] D. & B. vol. 20: 25; MCSW, Grant County, 1850.

[31] Independent American, Apr. 30, 1852, adv.; Aug. 3, 1855, adv.; Grant County Herald, Sept. 21, 1853; May 28, 1859, adv.; Oct. 27, 1860, adv.; Feb. 14, July 24, 1861, advs.; Grant County Witness, Apr. 29, 1861, adv.; MCSW, Grant County, 1860.

Thus, although the antebellum lumber industry in Grant County was growing steadily both in relative and absolute amounts, there were indications, at least by the late 1850's, that local establishments were suffering from the competition of downriver firms. Previously settlers had been satisfied with local oak and linden, crudely sawed. But with the increasing downriver trade in pine, originating on the Wisconsin, Black, and Chippewa rivers, the Grant County mills found their markets saturated and their survival threatened. Their larger size indicated the diseconomies of the small local mill, while the increased attention to secondary processing suggests an alternative way of remaining in business.

Other Processing Industries

The other processing industries in antebellum Grant County contributed only a small share of the country's aggregate value added, being responsible for 6.0 per cent in 1850 and 5.5 per cent in 1860. Secondary wood processing in the form of construction materials and cooperage yielded some $4,242 in 1850, but this sum declined to $2,335 by 1860. Such figures suggest that carpenters, joiners, and builders generally operated on a limited scale or a part-time basis and were probably not making sufficient money to be regarded as manufacturers.[32] The leather industry was essentially a local activity which held little prospect of advancement. The only firm which survived long enough to be reported in both censuses of 1850 and 1860 was owned by Philip D. Hendershot of Platteville. Even his saddlery and harness business seemed to be run on a custom basis and only netted some $4,000 profit.[33] The brewing industry likewise consisted of small firms catering to local demand, while the wool processing branch was a highly unstable venture. Woolen mills or their machinery changed hands with notable rapidity — there were at least sixteen partnerships or companies in the county between 1844 and 1861.[34]

[32] Advertisements in local newspapers suggest the existence of such craftsmen. *Platteville Examiner*, Feb. 25, 1858, adv.; *Grant County Witness*, Apr. 11, 1861, adv.
[33] D. & B. vol. 20: 10; *Platteville Examiner*, Apr. 15, 1858; *Grant County Witness*, Oct. 13, 1859.
[34] MCSW, Grant County, 1850 and 1860; *Independent American*, June 19, 1846, adv.; June 25, 1848, adv.; May 14, 1852, adv.; May 13, June 17, 1853, advs.; May

HOUSEHOLD-CRAFT CONSUMER INDUSTRIES

While most processing industries were increasing in value, both relatively and absolutely, the household-craft consumer goods manufactures were on the decline relatively and grew only 58 per cent in absolute value during the 1850's. (Table 14 and Table 15.) General, dry goods, and hardware stores had been established at an early date to satisfy the needs of the miners, and these retailing firms maintained a steady and even increasing control of the consumer market. The sales of goods imported from Galena, St. Louis, and New York provided strong competition for local craftsmen and manufacturers.

Furniture

Cabinetware manufacture was a popular occupation in pioneer Grant County during the 1830's and early 1840's. But the furniture makers then were not specialists; they tended to be carpenters or joiners who would do most kinds of work, whether constructing houses or making articles for their interiors. By the mid-1840's cabinetmakers were becoming distinguishable from general craftsmen and part-time handymen.[35] These cabinetmakers worked on a custom basis in small shops and generally made furniture from local wood, which they often bought in exchange for furniture. In some instances wood and iron turning and the manufacture of coffins and pumps were subsidiary activities.[36] The cabinetmakers, however, remained full-time artisans; they did not become merchant-craftsmen and sell furniture imported from St. Louis or New York. The retailing of ready-made imported furniture was done by the general merchandise store.

By 1850 seven furniture establishments were reported in the county. All of these firms operated on a limited scale, the largest having a capital invested of $1,000 and a value of product of $1,200, while the mean values were $507 and $801 respectively.

11, 25, 1855, advs.; June 5, 1857 adv.; *Grant County Herald,* June 15, 1844, adv.; Aug. 22, 1845, adv.; May 23, 28, Dec. 31, 1859, advs.; May 9, July 3, 1861, advs.; *Grant County Witness,* Apr. 12, 1860, adv.; June 6, 1861, adv.

[35] *Independent American,* May 9, July 4, 1845; *Grant County Herald,* Aug. 30, 1845, citing McCabe's "Gazeteer."

[36] *Independent American,* Jan. 11, July 4, Dec. 5, 1845, advs.; Aug. 7, Dec. 11, 1846, advs.; *Wisconsin Herald,* Nov. 15, 1845, adv.; Oct. 9, 1847, adv.; *Grant County Herald,* Mar. 15, 1845, adv.; *Wisconsin American,* Jan. 29, 1849, adv.

These figures were well under the Wisconsin average of $1,135 for capital invested and $3,144 for value of product. Although comparing favorably with furniture shops in the other lead-mining counties of Iowa and Lafayette, the Grant County shops were not as large or as specialized as those found in the counties of southeastern Wisconsin. Local furniture makers apparently had a much more restricted market threshold than their counterparts in other sections of the state.

During the 1850's the Grant County furniture firms increased in number and output, so that by 1860 they were providing 7.9 per cent of the county value added. Furniture making improved its standing within the county, and it also lowered the differential between the county firms and those of the state. In 1860 Grant cabinetmakers had an average capital invested of $1,129 and an average value of product of $2,299 — differentials of 111 and 91 per cent as compared to those of 124 and 293 per cent a decade earlier. Grant County in 1860 was much nearer the state average, and in fact had begun to outstrip some of the southeastern counties.

The improvement in the standing of furniture making in Grant County did not bring about any major change in the character of this industry. Firms were more widely scattered throughout the county, being located in seven towns; but they were still concentrating on manufacturing rather than involving themselves in the retail trade as merchant-craftsmen. The shops were indeed bigger and the warerooms stocked with a greater variety of articles for ready sale, but these goods were made on the premises. For example, W. & J. Grindell and E. Vanderbie, two large Platteville firms, had not changed their style; they both enlarged their shops in the mid-1850's and the Grindells added steam power, but they still continued to use local lumber to make their assortment of cabinetware. The Grindells were also undertakers, and Vanderbie was doing general wood turning, but neither firm yet engaged in retailing.[37]

The growth of the furniture industry in Grant County must have been based on the increase in the local population and an

---

[37] *Independent American,* June 25, Oct. 29, 1852, advs.; March 25, July 22, 1853, advs.; Nov. 24, 1854; *Platteville Examiner,* Feb. 11, 1858, adv.; Sept. 22, 1859, adv.; *Grant County Witness,* Aug. 18, Sept. 22, 1859, advs.; June 20, 1861, adv.

ability to compete with retailed articles. This growth is remark-able in view of the fact that retailed goods were squeezing cabinet-makers out of business in many parts of Wisconsin. There the combination of merchant craftsmen extended the merchandising side of the business, but since the merchant-craftsman was notably absent in Grant, the cabinetmakers were able to survive longer. Yet the ability of these artisans to withstand competition was not in itself sufficient to explain the increase. The availability of tim-ber supplies, either locally or from the pineries, must have helped by providing a ready source of raw material.

Boots and Shoes and Clothing

Boot and shoe manufacturing and clothing were the other two branches of the household-craft consumer group which grew in absolute terms. But their achievement in the 1850's was quite modest, the increases being 21.5 per cent and 11.4 per cent re-spectively. (Table 14 and Table 15.) Cobblers and tailors, like carpenters and joiners, were probably working in most settlements in Grant County by the early and mid-1840's. Possibly these artisans were later in getting established than their counterparts in many areas of Wisconsin because the early population clusters of Grant County, being focused on lead mining, tended to be short lived. Furthermore location on the Mississippi River, a main artery of trade and transportation, meant that it was relatively easy to import ready-made articles.[38] By the mid-1840's Julius McCabe's "Gazeteer" reported the existence of four shoemakers and ten tailors, but these could hardly cater to the needs of some 10,000 people. Either some artisans were not included in the "Gazeteer," or the retail trade in these lines had assumed a very great importance.

Those cobblers and tailors who were in business in the 1840's were small-scale entrepreneurs. Like most other Wisconsin crafts-men, they did cutting and repairs as well as maintaining ready stock and working on a custom basis.[39] As with the cabinetmakers,

[38] Accounts of early settlements in Grant County do not mention cobblers or tailors, though references are made to blacksmiths. More emphasis is given to the establishment of stores. From this lack of evidence and the nature of the economy, it seems that in the early days of settlement, consumer demands may well have been met by retail stores rather than by local craftsmen.

[39] *Northern Badger*, Aug. 21, 1840, advs.; *Grant County Herald*, Dec. 23, 1843,

these artisans do not seem to have taken on any retailing functions. They concentrated on manufacturing and let the general or specialized merchants handle the sale of imported ready-made articles.

By 1850 there were three boot and shoe firms and one clothing firm with annual products valued over $500. These branches of the craft industry had not necessarily declined in number in the late 1840's; probably they had failed to grow large enough to be included in the census. In such circumstances it was not surprising that these industries fell below the state average. Grant County establishments had a mean value added of $1,006 in boots and shoes and $660 in clothing, while Wisconsin firms had a mean value added of $2,288 in boots and shoes and $2,206 in clothing. Grant shoe and clothing shops were evidently only catering to a small portion of the county's market.

During the 1850's there were indications that shoemakers, tailors, and milliners may have increased in number. By 1859 there were some nine tailors, two milliners, two merchant tailors, and nine shoe shops scattered through the county.[40] But this increase was not reflected in the 1860 census, which recorded only six shoe firms and two clothing establishments. As the census did not count those artisans with a minute value of product, it is likely that most cobblers and tailors fell into this category. But even taking the eight establishments which were reported, they had made little advance over the firms of 1850. (Table 14 and Table 15.) Not only had they failed to substantially increase in value added, but they also compared unfavorably with Wisconsin shoe and clothing manufacturers. The Wisconsin value added for boots and shoes was two and a half times larger than that of Grant's, while the state's value added for clothing was twelve times larger.[41] These comparisons underline the relatively limited size of the county's establishments.

---

adv.; March 30, adv.; Oct. 19, adv., Dec. 14, 1844; *Wisconsin Herald,* Dec. 11, 1845, adv.; *Independent American,* Dec. 11, 1846, adv.; Mar. 25, May 6, Oct. 21, 1848, advs.

[40] *Platteville Examiner,* Apr. 22, 1858, adv.; *Platteville Witness,* June 9, 16, 1859; *Grant County Witness,* Aug. 18, adv., Oct. 6, Nov. 10, 1859; May 3, June 21, Nov. 29, 1860, advs.; Apr. 11, 1861, adv.; *Grant County Herald,* June 16, 1860.

[41] The mean value added for boots and shoes in Grant County in 1860 was $611; for Wisconsin it was $1,635. The comparative figures for clothing in 1860 were $368 and $4,114.

The smallness and infrequency of cobblers' and tailors' shops may have been attributable in part to the widely scattered population. There was no urban concentration large enough to stimulate the growth of local consumer manufactures on any scale. However, the backwardness of these industries was probably more attributable to the prominence of merchandising and the habit of buying ready-made articles, which had been established early in the development of the lead region.[42] Merchants' stores were stocked with articles of clothing and footware, and by 1860 some merchants were beginning to specialize in retailed clothing and were even taking on the function of merchant tailors.[43] The cobbler and the tailor of Grant County do not seem to have risen to the challenge of imported ready-made merchandise.

Blacksmiths and Tinsmiths

By 1860 blacksmiths and tinsmiths in Grant County were on the decline, both relatively and in absolute terms of value added. These branches of the household-craft consumer industries, although numerous enough in the early settlements, were dying out by the time of the Civil War. They were, however, declining for different reasons. Tinsmiths were suffering from the competition of hardware stores. Blacksmiths were taking on specialized functions and were becoming classified as wheelwrights, machinists, and foundrymen.

Tinsmiths, unlike other artisans in Grant County, were from the first closely associated with merchants. They generally looked after the jobbing trade, and their function was therefore subordinate to and less remunerative than the retailing side of the hardware business.[44] It is uncertain when tinsmiths first settled in the area. Hardware and dry-goods stores were found in most villages by the late 1830's, but craftsmen may not have been

---

[42] It seems rather anomalous that tailors and cobblers should suffer from the competition of the retail trade, whereas cabinetmakers did not seem to be greatly affected by this trade. Presumably it was easier to import ready-made clothing and footware than it was to import ready-made furniture.

[43] Grant County Herald, June 16, 1860, adv.; Grant County Witness, Nov. 29, 1860.

[44] Independent American, Jan. 25, 1845; Wisconsin Herald, Nov. 1, 1845; June 27, 1846; Grant County Herald, Sept. 6, 1845.

taken on, either as partners or as jobbers, until the mid-1840's, when the market threshold had expanded.[45]

Tinsmiths continued to work as merchant-craftsmen or as jobbers throughout the 1840's, but they did not appear to expand numerically. In fact in 1850 only two establishments had an annual product over $500. Neither firm operated on a larger scale. Together they had a capital invested of $1,500, a value of product of $3,650, and a value added of $1,825 — figures similar to those of the Wisconsin tinsmiths, namely $1,893, $3,677, and $1,634 respectively. It would seem that when Grant County artisans took on retailing functions they became more like craftsmen in other parts of the state.

Tinsmiths grew in number during the early and mid-1850's, for by 1857 there were at least nine of these entrepreneurs. Nevertheless, they did not appear to increase in size; rather the reverse, for they all had a small capital and a modest trade.[46] This situation did not stem from lack of initiative, but rather from the nature of the industry, which was limited and had become cramped by competition. The tinware business became even more constricted in the immediate prewar years; the eighth federal census only reported five craftsmen, and these had fallen below their average Wisconsin contemporaries in terms of output. Having a capital invested of $890, a value of product of $852, and a value added of $231, the Grant County firms now had differentials of 104, 222, and 474 per cent respectively below their statewide counterparts. The Wisconsin tinsmith had maintained a fairly stable trade during the 1850's, but the Grant tinsmith made fewer products. The county entrepreneurs had chosen to fall back on the merchandising side of the trade rather than on the manufacturing side.

The firm of Lane & Eastman, which later became H.C. Lane & Co., illustrates this development. They commenced business in 1854 intending to manufacture and keep on hand a full line of goods as well as to take custom orders. By 1859, however, their stoves apeared to be mainly imported. M.M. Zeigler of Lancaster

---

[45] *Independent American,* May 9, 1845; *Grant County Herald,* Aug. 30, 1845, citing McCabe's "Gazeteer"; *Wisconsin Herald,* May 8, 1847; *History of Grant County,* 764.

[46] D. & B. vol. 20: 16, 22, 30, 32, 33, 48.

also made it very clear that, while he manufactured all kinds of tin, sheet iron, and copperware, he retailed cooking, parlor, and box stoves, kettles, pipes, shovels, and other hardware.[47] By the outbreak of the Civil War the local manufacture of tinware was becoming very much a minor auxiliary to retailing.

Blacksmiths seem to have set up their forges in the villages and towns of Grant County soon after initial settlement. Robert Chapman built his forge in Platteville in 1835 when the town was re-established after the Indian troubles. By 1836 he had been joined by another smith. Though statistical information is missing before the mid-1840's, the number of blacksmiths doubtless increased. Indeed by 1845 Platteville had six smithies and Edwardsville, with a population of some 200, had two. The work done in these shops was of a general nature, ranging from ironing wagons, sleighs, and sleds to shoeing horses and making miners' tools; payment was taken in kind or cash.[48] By mid-century those blacksmiths with a larger output numbered thirteen, but there was probably an equal if not greater number whose product did not exceed $500 annually. However, even the smiths who were recorded in the census ran small shops, having only an average value added of $853, a value which was 25–30 per cent smaller than the typical Wisconsin blacksmith.

During the 1850's the number of blacksmiths appeared to decrease; only four establishments were recorded in the 1860 census. These shops were on the whole slightly larger than the average Wisconsin smithy. But the census reporting may have distorted reality. On the one hand, blacksmiths who continued to do all kinds of jobwork probably did not attain a $500 annual value of product, and thus tended to be relegated to the function of village handyman.[49] On the other hand, leading blacksmiths gravitated upward and began specializing in one function — for example, making wagons or agricultural machinery.[50] They were

[47] *Independent American*, Dec. 29, 1854, adv.; *Grant County Witness*, Sept. 9, 1859, adv.; *Grant County Herald*, March 28, 1861, adv.; D. & B. vol. 20: 22.

[48] *History of Grant County*, 687, 688; *Independent American*, May 9, 1845; Jan. 1, 1847, adv.; May 27, 1848, adv.; *Grant County Herald*, Aug. 30, 1845, citing McCabe's "Gazeteer"; *Wisconsin Herald*, Apr. 3, 1847, adv.; Aug. 26, 1848, adv.

[49] Some blacksmiths who advertised in the local newspapers were not recorded in the census. They seemed to be concentrating on horse-shoeing or general services. *Platteville Examiner*, May 18, 1858, adv.; *Grant County Witness*, March 15, 22, 1860, advs.; *Grant County Herald*, Feb. 21, June 13, 1861, advs.

[50] The distinction between wagonmaking and blacksmithing is very fine. Several

thus reclassified in the 1860 census. But whatever the reasons, blacksmiths seem to have been decreasing in importance in ante-bellum Grant County.

Generally the household-craft consumer branches in Grant County were not holding their own in the growth of manufacturing. This weakness stemmed from three causes. In addition to suffering from the competition of retailed mass-produced goods and from the limited nature of the local market threshold, many Grant craftsmen failed to adopt the strategic retailing function and become merchant-manufacturers. They therefore lacked any transitional help in becoming manufacturers. If they wanted to increase their business, they had to do so without the prop of the retail trade to help them through economic crises and structural change. This was a very difficult task.

AGRICULTURAL INDUSTRIES

The agricultural industries of Grant County, like the craft industries, were neither maintaining their growth rate in comparison to manufacturing as a whole nor to the processing industries in particular. Wagons and carriages increased in value both absolutely and relatively, but the making of agricultural implements decreased in both amounts. (Table 14 and Table 15.) This decline might seem paradoxical in view of the increased attention paid to farming, but Grant farmers preferred to buy their machinery from outside manufacturers, particularly in the late 1850's when the railroad facilitated the import of heavy goods.

Agricultural Implements

The pioneer agricultural implements manufacturers of the 1840's concentrated almost exclusively on the production of fanning mills.[51] By the 1850's some entrepreneurs were also making threshing machines and plows, but they appeared to have little staying power. Only Joel Potter, who had started making plows

---

entrepreneurs carried out both functions, but they generally had a higher value of output in either wagons or carriages or in smith work, and they were thus classified as one or the other type of craftsman.

[51] *Grant County Herald,* March 2, 1844, adv.; Dec. 20, 1845, adv.; *Independent American,* May 16, 1845, adv.; June 17, 1848, adv.

around 1845, continued to do a good business throughout the antebellum years, even to the extent of selling his plows in Iowa and Minnesota.[52]

By the 1850's local manufacturers were suffering from the competition of imported machines. As early as 1853 H.R. Beebe was claiming that his fanning mills were superior to those hawked by traveling peddlers. He cannot, however, have been fully confident in his products, for by 1856 he had become the agent for Enery's Chicago Agricultural Works. In the same year A.G. Marselin of Schullsburg was acting as local agent for Manny & Co. of Rockport, Illinois, and a year earlier, in 1855, Norman & Cowan had stopped making threshing machines because they could not compete with cheaper imported Eastern machines.[53] By 1860 outside competition was much stronger. Agents for such large midwestern firms as Cyrus McCormick of Chicago and J.I. Case of Racine seemed to be doing a flourishing business.[54]

The Grant County output of farm equipment reflected this inability to cope with strong rivalry. In 1860 the average capital invested per firm was $2,266, while the average value added was $2,618. Such small establishments were unable to produce goods cheaply enough to compete with firms in Racine, Chicago, or even Rochester, New York, which could afford to absorb transport costs owing to the economies of scale practiced in manufacturing. The Grant craftsmen had to be content with doing local specialized jobs and repair work. Agricultural implements was yet another branch of manufacturing in Grant County in which the retailed article undercut the local manufacturer.

Wagons and Carriages

Wagon and carriage manufacturing seemed to be a more flourishing business than agricultural implements in antebellum Grant County. (Table 14 and Table 15.) Although many wagonmakers often commenced as blacksmiths, and even continued to work at the smithy part-time, they found a viable local trade in wagons,

[52] D. & B. vol. 20:35; *Independent American,* May 19, 1859, adv.; *Grant County Witness,* Aug. 18, 1859, adv.; March 7, 1861, adv.; MCSW, Grant County, 1850 and 1860.
[53] *Independent American,* July 15, 1853, adv.; May 11, 18, 1855; March 21, adv., May 9, 1856.
[54] *Grant County Witness,* Jan. 26, 1860; Apr. 4, 1861, adv.; *Grant County Herald,* June 6, 1861, adv.

carriages, buggies, sleighs, and repairs.[55] Business might be limited, but by 1860 the census did report the existence of twelve firms.

THE "OTHER" INDUSTRIES

The other group of industries contributed little to the aggregate county value added. It consisted of various small firms catering to the servicing needs of their communities. For example, the Platteville iron foundry did a restricted business in castings, machinery, pumps, and repairs.[56] But any large piece of machinery or castings was imported from one of the major firms outside the state or perhaps from Milwaukee. The Platteville Oil Mill was also striving to make a paying venture out of turning locally-grown flax into linseed oil.[57]

Conclusions

Antebellum Grant County manufacturing appeared to pass through two stages. In the first period, up to the late 1840's, minerals were the main focus of attraction, both as a processing activity and as a general impetus to settlement and thus to service industries. However, with the decline in lead output in the late 1840's and early 1850's, manufacturers increasingly turned to other processing industries, such as flour milling and lumber planed and sawed. The dispersed settlement pattern of small mining villages, and the early emphasis on retailing groceries, dry goods, and hardware to miners, discouraged the growth of any major consumer craft manufactures. Artisans such as tailors, cobblers, cabinetmakers, and blacksmiths either tended to keep very small shops serving the custom trade and repair needs of the population, or were forced out of business by strong competition from retail shops.

[55] D. & B. vol. 20: 44; *Wisconsin Whig,* Apr. 27, 1842, adv.; *Independent American,* Jan. 23, May 15, 1846, advs.; *Wisconsin Herald,* Nov. 21, 1850, adv.; *Platteville Examiner,* Apr. 22, 1858, adv.; *Grant County Witness,* Sept. 1, 1859, adv.; Oct. 18, 1860; *Grant County Herald,* March 10, adv., Nov. 24, 1860; Jan. 12, 1861.

[56] MCSW, Grant County 1850 and 1860; *Wisconsin Herald,* Sept. 26, 1850, adv.; *Independent American,* May 18, 1855, adv.

[57] D. & B. vol. 20: 24, 148; *Independent American,* Jan. 13, Apr. 21, adv., 1854; Feb. 2, Nov. 30, 1855; July 25, 1856; *Platteville Examiner,* May 27, 1858.

Manufacturing in the Upper Mississippi lead region, as revealed by Grant County, was, as in most Wisconsin counties, centered on the primary processing of local natural resources. Although not as narrowly confined as industrial patterns in the northwestern lumbering regions, Grant County still illustrated the advantage of primary processing, whether for export or for the local market. The area was poised in an intermediary position between breaking out of the traditional mould of manufacturing for neighborhood needs and entering into a regional or even national market, where outside large firms using division of labor, machine technology, and more reliable transport were able to penetrate and sell in local markets.

CHAPTER FOUR

Winnebago County: A Transitional Manufacturing Economy in the Wisconsin Lumber Belt

ANTEBELLUM WISCONSIN WAS RICH in timber resources. Possibly 30 million of the state's 35 million acres originally held some useful trees, though most of valuable forest lay in the north. In the prairie regions to the south, hardwoods, especially oak, were early cut down to make way for farm cultivation and were generally used for building farmhouses, barns, and fences. In northern Wisconsin, which formed part of the Great Lakes lumber belt, the forest consisted of valuable hardwoods of oak, basswood and elm, white pine, and other conifers. This forest was drained by several rivers which not only gave access to the major water arteries of Lake Michigan, Lake Superior, and the Mississippi River, but also divided Wisconsin into six lumbering regions: the Wolf River and Green Bay districts in northeastern Wisconsin; the Wisconsin River region in central Wisconsin; and the Black, Chippewa, and St. Croix districts in northwestern Wisconsin. Of these six, the Wisconsin, Wolf, and Green Bay pineries were the most well developed. The other three were just beginning to feel the inroads of exploitation.[1]

[1] For general background information on the forest resources of Wisconsin, see Hotchkiss, 291–316; 380–517; Roth, 10–12; Fries, *passim*; Kleven, *passim*; U.S. Senate, *Executive Documents*, 30 Cong. 1 Sess., (1847–48), "A Geological Reconnaissance of the Chippewa Land District of Wisconsin," Document No. 57, 71 ff. For the use of the oak in southern Wisconsin, see Joseph Shafer, *Four Wisconsin Counties, passim*, and *The Winnebago-Horicon Basin: A Type Study in Western History* (Madison, 1937) *passim*.

Winnebago County, located to the west of Lake Winnebago in east-central Wisconsin, was well placed to develop an industrial economy focused on lumber.[2] Though lacking extensive resources within its own bounds, the county received most of the logging product of the Wolf River pineries. Lumber processing in its primary stage of lumber planed and sawed, and in its secondary stage of construction materials, barrels, and woodenware, formed the kernel of manufacturing activities. Indeed the concentration of manufacturing establishments in the three urban centers of Oshkosh, Neenah, and Menasha, which produced 54.3 per cent of the county's value added in 1850 and 89.1 per cent in 1860, indicated that the lumber industry was creating cities rather than seeking them as a location. Flour milling based on the agricultural hinterland was of secondary importance in the county manufacturing profile, while some craft shops oriented to local consumption added a broader industrial range.

As might be expected, Winnebago County's only major contribution to Wisconsin's aggregate manufacturing was in the planing and sawing of lumber. In 1850 the county produced 12.5 per cent of the state's total value added in lumber. The county industry expanded in absolute terms during the 1850's, but declined relatively so that by 1860 Winnebago contributed only 5.9 per cent of Wisconsin's manufactured lumber. By this date Winnebago was competing not only with the lumbering regions of the Wisconsin River and Green Bay, but also with newer regions in the northwest.

Other industries in the county composed only a fractional amount of the state's manufacturing output. In 1850 flour milling supplied 3.3 per cent of the Wisconsin flour output; in 1860 construction materials contributed 4.9 per cent and agricultural

---

[2] The county boundaries of Winnebago were changed twice before 1860. The county was first set off from Brown County in 1840, with a land area of 454 square miles. In 1849 the boundaries were enlarged by the addition of territory acquired by the United States in the 1848 treaty with Menominee Indians, resulting in a land area of 2,956 square miles. This additional area was later given to other counties, so that by 1856 Winnebago County was reduced to its original size of 454 square miles. *Origin and Legislative History of County Boundaries in Wisconsin* (Madison, 1942), 198–202; Series of Maps and County area figures for the State of Wisconsin, State Historical Society of Wisconsin; Richard J. Harney, *History of Winnebago County, Wisconsin, and Early History of the Northwest* (Oshkosh, 1880), 122.

implements contributed 3.9 per cent of their respective industries.[3] These branches kept pace with Winnebago's 3.3 per cent contribution to the Wisconsin aggregate population in 1850 and 3.1 per cent contribution in 1860.

In spite of the poor showing of Winnebago industries in comparison to the rest of Wisconsin, the county still had manufacturing establishments which were larger than the state mean. In 1850 the average operation in Winnebago employed 5.8 men in comparison to the 4.8 men employed in the average Wisconsin firm. A decade later the comparative figures were 6.8 and 5.4. This high average number of workers per establishment was a result of two distinct trends. On the one hand, the large proportion of lumber firms, nearly half the number of establishments in 1850, and just over a quarter of the establishments in 1860, raised the county average, since the lumber industry attracted greater investments and thus tended to maintain bigger operations. On the other hand, the poor showing of the household-craft consumer industries, namely 16.6 per cent of the county's workers in 1850 and 7.8 per cent in 1860, implied the absence of small self-employed craftsmen with one or two apprentices, a group which tended to lower the mean size of firms, as it did in Milwaukee County.

The size of the manufacturing establishments in Winnebago County, however, did not necessarily imply any degree of sophistication in methods of production. Size was but one indicator among other critical variables, such as labor output, division of labor, motive power, management techniques, and capital invested. Although firms grew larger in the 1850's, the level of worker productivity decreased. In 1850 the value added per worker was $679; in 1860 it was only $545. This drop stemmed from an inexplicably high value added per worker in the flouring industry in 1850 and a decline in the productivity of craft workers in the 1850's. The low county average in comparison to the state average in 1860 — $545 in contrast to $656 — was due to the county's poor standing in the craft industries and to the moderate

---

[3] This ranking ignores the miscellaneous industries, which are discounted because they comprised many diverse branches of manufacturing and were thus not strictly comparable to a single industry. In 1860 Winnebago County had 6.1 per cent of Wisconsin's miscellaneous manufacturing.

emphasis on secondary lumber-processing industries which generally employed unskilled labor.

The low value added per worker also indicated at most a minimal division of labor. Some division of labor may have been practiced in some of the larger sawmills, the flour mills, the agricultural machinery plants, and some cooperages, since these firms employed practical machinists and artisans to perform specific tasks. But the only establishment which clearly indicated that laborers had their own particular duties to perform, and even used day and night shifts, was the large Menasha Wooden Ware Factory. Division of labor was an indeterminate variable in Winnebago County, but probably even the larger firms failed to qualify as "factories" in this sense.

The form of motive power used in Winnebago manufacturing plants depended on location rather than technology. The extensive water resources of "The Rapids" at Neenah-Menasha could furnish enough power to supply any number of manufacturing establishments that might be built in that area.[4] Other towns in the county were not so well endowed. Oshkosh lacked a plentiful supply of water power and had to resort to steam power in the late 1840's. By 1860 all the city sawmills used steam power, as did the two flouring mills and the agricultural implements plant. The smaller towns in the county employed a combination of water and steam power. In Omro steam power was used in the sawmills and the flouring mill in 1860, whereas in Rushford both means of power were found in the sawmills and water power drove the machinery of the flouring mill.[5]

---

[4] The theoretical water power of the twin settlements of Neenah-Menasha was estimated to be 2411 horsepower available for use. See W.P. Trowbridge (compiler), "General Remarks Upon The Water Power of the Northwestern States," in "Reports on the Water Power of the United States: Statistics of Power and Machinery Employed in Manufactures," *Tenth Census, 1880, Vol. 27*, 15–27; L. Smith, *The Water Powers of Wisconsin, passim*. For contemporary estimates, see WSAS *Trans.*, 6 (1860), 355; *Menasha Advocate*, May 15, July 19, 1855; June 21, 1856; *Menasha Conservator*, May 14, 1856; Jan. 15, Apr. 16, June 11, Dec. 8, 1859; *Oshkosh Democrat*, Aug. 29, 1851; *Weekly Manufacturer*, June 6, 1861; *Wisconsin Farmer*, 11 (1859), 218.

[5] MCSW, Winnebago County, 1850 and 1860; *The Conservator*, Apr. 30, 1857, *Oshkosh Democrat*, Sept. 27, 1851; *Omro Republican*, March 4, 1858, adv.; WSAS *Trans.*, 6 (1860), 355; Mitchell & Osborn (Pub.) *Geographical and Statistical History of the County of Winnebago*, (Oshkosh, 1856) 92.

It is not possible to discern any differential rate of growth or any advance in technology resulting from the use of various forms of motive power. Taking the measures of a minimum of fifteen workers and a value of product of at least $20,000, three lumber firms in 1850 might rank as "large." Two of these used steam; the third used water power. In 1860 seven firms employed more than fifteen workers while sixteen firms had a value of product over $20,000. Only five of these establishments qualified under both measures: four lumber firms and the Menasha Wooden Ware Company. Of these, all the lumber firms were powered by steam, but the Wooden Ware Company used water power. Of the eleven flouring mills with a value of product over $20,000, nine employed water and two steam power. At the other end of the spectrum, all the household-craft consumer industries were dependent on hand power and rudimentary tools with little application of machinery. Motive power did not have any significant correlation with types of industrial production. Steam power was not regarded as an advance in technology, but merely as an alternative to poor or nonexistent water power.

Capital was essential to the development of large-scale manufacturing enterprises, but capital in Winnebago County was in short supply. By 1860 the three local bands, two in Oshkosh and one in Neenah, reported holding $279,111 worth of assets or approximately 1.8 per cent of the Wisconsin total. Winnebago County thus had poorer banking resources per capita than many other parts of the state. Yet even these meager assets were probably as much a reflection of the money already brought into the county, for investment in lumber and agriculture, as of the availability of local money for financing new manufacturing enterprises.

Those entrepreneurs who operated large firms usually brought their own capital to Winnebago, or had access to the capital of friends or relatives in the East. E.D. Smith of the Menasha Wooden Ware Company relied on his rich father-in-law to help him out of financial straits, while A.B. Knapp of the Oshkosh Gang Mill had a wealthy father. J. & H. Kimberly, in the flour-milling business in the 1850's, had started off in general stores with money brought from Troy, New York. Jonathan Mills, who built a flouring mill in Neenah, was able to borrow finances from Wing and

Mitchell of Chicago.[6] Not all of the leading entrepreneurs had access to capital, but those who did were more assured of surviving the periodic economic crises, the poor credit facilities of the frontier, the seasonal hazards of water power, and the omnipresent threat of fire, especially in Oshkosh.[7]

Manufacturing Activities in Winnebago County

The early manufacturing activities in Winnebago County were focused on two industries. In 1850, lumbering alone provided 60 per cent of the county total by value added, while lumbering and flour milling together furnished 84 per cent of the aggregate. (Table 16.) The county thus revealed the monolithic or duolithic manufacturing structure typical of most northern Wisconsin counties. Ten years later these two primary processing industries had declined in relative terms, supplying only 60 per cent of the county's value added. (Table 17.) During the 1850's Winnebago developed a more diversified manufacturing economy, especially in contrast to other northern counties which had 80–90 per cent of their manufacturing in lumber planed and sawed.

Yet within this diversification, the processing industries, and especially those based on lumber, far outstripped any other group of manufactures in Winnebago County. In 1860 the processing group was responsible for 73 per cent of the county's manufacturing by value added. Furthermore, if the Menasha Wooden Ware Company was counted in this group rather than with the miscellaneous industries, the 1860 total for the processing industries would then increase to 83 per cent. One other branch of manufacturing which showed some potential during the 1850's was that of agricultural machinery. (Table 17.) In some respects the making of farm implements was indistinct from the production of carriages, wagons, and iron goods, since all these activities catered to the needs of the local farmer and occasionally the lumber-

---

[6] D. & B. vol. 59: 335, 353, 357, 358U, 411, 418, 420.

[7] Fire struck Oshkosh several times during the 1850's. The great fire of May 10, 1859, burnt down almost all the business district. Earlier in 1856 a planing mill, sawmill, foundry, and other buildings were destroyed by fire. There was another fire in July, 1859, and yet another in the summer of 1860. Harney, 145; *History of the City of Oshkosh* (Oshkosh, 1867), 60; *Oshkosh Courier,* June 24, July 8, 1859; Aug. 3, 1860.

man. In this respect all were specialized blacksmiths serving their community, and their increase seemed to indicate peculiar local demands.

The household-craft group catering to the consumer needs of the county population was on the decline. This group only furnished 12 per cent of the county's value added in 1850 and 6 per cent a decade later, when improved transport facilitated the importation of goods for retailing. The consumer industries not only declined relatively during the decade, but their absolute value remained stable in spite of the doubling of population. This situation suggests that craftsmen could make little profit in supplying the local market. Winnebago's urban population was not large enough to encourage the local manufacture of mass-produced household goods; nor was the county sufficiently isolated to allow craftsmen free rein in the local market. Thus by 1860 it was becoming cheaper to import household articles from areas where unskilled labor and machinery were more widely utilized.

THE PROCESSING INDUSTRIES

Primary and Secondary Lumber Processing

Lumber processing provided the core of manufacturing in Winnebago County throughout the antebellum period. Although not heavily timbered, the county in general, and Oshkosh in particular, became one of the major lumber centers of the Old Northwest. The Wolf River, with its many tributaries, was one of the best lumbering streams in Wisconsin and provided easy means of water transportation for floating timber from the forests to the sawmills, which were springing up in increasing numbers in the Oshkosh area by the late 1840's.[8]

By midcentury sixteen sawmills in the county, often working on a custom basis, either for cash or goods in kind, produced 15,846,200 feet of lumber valued at $130,138. Much of this

[8] Harney, 109–110, 138, 196, 217, 264; Kleven, 277–278; Fries, 18–19; *Oshkosh City Directory for the Year 1857* (Oshkosh, 1857), 5–6 [hereinafter cited as *OCD*]; Richard N. Current, *Pine Logs and Politics: A Life of Philetus Sawyer, 1816–1900* (Madison, 1950), 20–21; G. A. Cunningham, *History of Neenah* (Neenah, 1878), 21, 82; *History of the City of Oshkosh*, 31; Publius V. Lawson, *History, Winnebago County, Wisconsin: Its Cities Towns, Resources, People* (2 vols., Chicago, 1908), 1: 520–521, 659–660; Reuben G. Thwaites, "Winnebago County," *Wisconsin Local History*, pamphlets, Vol. 5, No. 7, n.p.

TABLE 16

MANUFACTURING IN WINNEBAGO COUNTY, 1850

(Value Added in Current $'s.)

Industry	Value Added	Per Cent of Total	No. of Workers	Per Cent of Total
Processing Industries				
Lumber	78,078	59.58	130	67.35
Flour	31,566	24.09	5	2.59
Leather	900	0.69	2	1.04
Construction Materials	3,455	2.64	10	5.18
Wool	180	0.14	1	0.52
Aggregate	114,179	87.14	148	76.68
Household-Craft Consumer				
Boots and Shoes	6,345	4.84	13	6.74
Clothing	3,900	2.98	7	3.63
Furniture	3,200	2.44	8	4.14
Tin, Copper etc.	2,653	2.02	4	2.07
Aggregate	16,098	12.28	32	16.58
Other Industries				
Iron	750	0.58	13	6.74
Aggregate	750	0.58	13	6.74
Winnebago County	131,027	100.00	193	100.00

[SOURCE: Manuscript Census for the State of Wisconsin, 1850. Winnebago County.]

lumber was marketed rough and in bulk, and little processing was done other than to cut the pine into various sizes of logs.[9] For the most part the lumber was used locally in Winnebago County for the construction of houses, though sales may also have been made to the carpenters and builders of neighboring Fond du Lac, Marquette, and Dodge counties.[10]

[9] MCSW, Winnebago County, 1850; *Oshkosh True Democrat*, Feb. 4, May 4, June 1, adv., 1849; *Winnebago Telegraph*, Sept. 14, 1850; *Oshkosh Democrat*, Nov. 1, 1850.

[10] *Oshkosh Democrat*, Jan. 11, June 7, adv., Oct. 25, adv., Nov. 28, 1850; Jan. 10, adv., Jan. 31, Feb. 7, adv., Apr. 18, adv., Apr. 25, May 9, adv., June 6, adv., 1851.

In the first half of the 1850's the Wolf River lumber industry expanded rapidly and prospects were good. The fifteen or twenty mills of the main river and its tributaries were annually producing some 50,000,000 feet of pine logs which, in 1855, were estimated to be worth about $350,000. In addition, a large amount of manufactured pine lumber would probably gross some $250,000.[11] The towns in Winnebago County participated in this boom. In 1855 Oshkosh — "The Sawdust City" — reported six mills in the city limits and three others within a mile radius of the city. A year later there were sixteen mills in operation including a gang saw mill with sixty saws. Menasha in 1855 had at least three important lumbering enterprises. In Neenah, in 1856, there were four saw and planing mills as well as construction materials shops; Omro had four steam sawmills in operation in 1856.[12]

The lumber industry looked flourishing in the summer of 1857, but surface appearances were deceptive. If productivity was to continue, increasing lumber manufacturers needed better transport facilities. To be sure, they could use the water routes either by way of the Fox River and the Great Lakes to Chicago, or by Lake Horicon and the Rock River to southern Wisconsin and northern Illinois, or perhaps even to the Mississippi Valley via the Fox-Wisconsin waterway; but these routes were seasonal, hazardous, and difficult to navigate. After 1854 some lumber could be sent by rail from Fond du Lac, but entrepreneurs needed railroads running out of Oshkosh and other smaller lumber centers to expand their market threshold.

In addition to transportation difficulties, financial problems were also threatening the Winnebago lumber industry. Many businessmen had used all their capital or had gone deeply into debt to build sawmills and piers. And though the price of lumber was high in the early and mid-1850's, maintenance costs were also very high.[13] When the Panic of '57, followed by a severe depression, brought business to a standstill, few manufacturers had financial reserves and many failed to survive the period of low

[11] *Watertown Chronicle*, Feb. 25, 1852; *Oshkosh Courier*, June 27, 1855.

[12] *History of the City of Oshkosh*, 47; *Geographical and Statistical History of the County of Winnebago*, 82, 88, 92, 99; *Oshkosh Courier*, Aug. 8, 1855; Feb. 6, 1856; *Menasha Advocate*, May 17, 1855; *Menasha Conservator*, May 14, 1856; *The Conservator*, Apr. 30, 1857; Harney, 145.

[13] Isaac Stephenson, *Recollections of A Long Life, 1829–1915* (Chicago, 1915), 118.

TABLE 17

MANUFACTURING IN WINNEBAGO COUNTY, 1860

(Value Added in Current $'s.)

Industry	Value Added	Per Cent of Total	No. of Workers	Per Cent of Total
Processing Industries				
Lumber	151,500	47.99	222	38.34
Flour	35,114	11.12	52	8.98
Cooperage	6,055	1.92	35	6.04
Liquors	6,933	2.20	10	1.73
Leather	6,113	1.94	12	2.07
Construction Materials	22,410	7.10	47	8.12
Wool	2,500	0.79	7	1.21
Tobacco	300	0.10	2	0.35
Aggregate	230,925	73.16	387	66.84
Household-Craft Consumer				
Boots and Shoes	5,044	1.60	18	3.11
Furniture	5,540	1.75	13	2.25
Blacksmiths	950	0.30	3	0.52
Tin, Copper etc.	5,942	1.88	11	1.90
Aggregate	17,476	5.53	45	7.78
Agricultural Industries				
Agricultural Impls.	18,502	5.86	33	5.70
Wagons	1,281	0.41	4	0.69
Aggregate	19,783	6.27	37	6.39
Other Industries				
Iron	6,360	2.01	8	1.38
Paper	2,685	0.85	12	2.07
Miscellaneous	38,442	12.18	90	15.54
Aggregate	47,487	15.04	110	18.99
Winnebago County	315,671	100.00	579	100.00

[SOURCE: Manuscript Census for the State of Wisconsin, 1860. Winnebago County.]

prices.[14] In Oshkosh this situation was aggravated by a disastrous fire, which in May, 1859, caused $350,000 worth of damage in the business section of the city and temporarily paralyzed business. Another fire in July, 1859, burned the planing mill of Morgan, Watts & Jones, while a third in the summer of 1860 destroyed the buildings and damaged the machinery and stock of the steam sawmill of French, Wheeler & Co.[15] By 1860 the twenty-four lumber mills in the county were only producing some fifty-two million feet of lumber with a value of $279,500 — a volume equal to the 1855 production, but substantially lower in value.

The Winnebago lumber manufacturers who survived the economic crises of the late 1850's, and especially the Oshkosh entrepreneurs who produced 73 per cent of the county's lumber in 1860, usually had substantial means themselves or had access to other sources of money. For example, A.B. Knapp of the Oshkosh Gang Saw Mill, largest lumber concern in the county, ran a heavily encumbered business in the years 1859–61 and probably had to rely on his wealthy father for capital or credit. G.M. Paine, another leading lumberman, was in straitened circumstances in the late 1850's and tried to borrow money from the East to tide him over the bad times.[16] As with many frontier enterprises, it seemed that in primary lumber processing in Winnebago County, reserves of capital were needed in order to become a manufacturer serving a regional as well as a local market. The instability of market prices, inadequate transport arrangements, and the "natural" hazards of the weather and of fire meant that success was rare without financial backing.

Yet even when capital and credit were available, success was still the exception rather than the rule. Business skill, such as that shown by Philetus Sawyer, was essential to weather frontier conditions. He started off his Wisconsin lumbering career by operating a sawmill under contract. By 1853 he had gained enough experience to enter a partnership with Messrs. Brand & Olcott of

[14] *History of the City of Oshkosh*, 41; Sister Mary L. Phelan, "The Origins and Development of the Lumbering and Woodworking Industries in the Vicinity of Oshkosh, Wisconsin, 1830–1880: A Study In The Use And Exploitation of the Wolf River Pinery" (unpublished M.A. thesis, Catholic University of America, 1954), 41; Stephenson, 144; D. & B. vol. 59: 340, 358L, 381.
[15] Harney, 145; *Oshkosh Courier*, June 24, July 8, 1859; Aug. 3, 1860.
[16] D. & B. vol. 59: 358L, 395.

Fond du Lac, and was thus able to draw on their financial resources as well as on his own business acumen. But equally, if not more importantly, he laid strong foundations for his future by using money borrowed in the East to speculate in land in the Wolf River area. By 1862 he had accumulated sufficient assets to be able to buy out his partner at an advance of $70,000 above the original capital in the business.[17] Managerial initiative and ability, as well as capital, were needed in the growth of any large-scale lumber firm in northeastern Wisconsin.

Skill and capital were not, however, as critical in the development of secondary lumber processing in Winnebago County, because these branches of manufacturing were usually either local enterprises or were adjuncts of primary lumber processing firms or of farming activities. Businesses specifically manufacturing sash, blinds, doors, shingles, pickets, and lath were relatively slow to develop, and generally consisted of joiners or carpenters working on a custom basis for cash or country produce.[18] By the mid-1850's some advances had been made in the number of firms and in their use of modern machinery and steam power, but much work was still done for the custom trade.[19] Indeed it would seem that the industry weathered the depression of the late 1850's by conducting much trade on credit and by swapping accounts. Certainly Lawson & Co. of Menasha obtained their supply of lumber and paid their workers in kind, though some money must have passed hands, as the firm paid $300–400 annual rent for their premises.[20]

The construction materials industry in Winnebago County, though growing, did not become a major industry in the antebellum years. This was in part due to the production of lath in the sawmills themselves. Then also many products were custom-made by joiners and carpenters whose shops may well have been omitted

[17] Current, 22, 23, 28; *Commemorative Biographical Record of the Fox River Valley* (Chicago, 1895), 983–984; Hotchkiss, 396; Lawson, 2: 1124–1128; *United States Biographical Dictionary and Portrait Gallery of Eminent and Self-Made Men* (Wisconsin volume, Chicago, 1877), 491–492. [Hereinafter cited as *USBD*.]

[18] *Oshkosh Democrat*, May 31, 1850, adv.; *Oshkosh True Democrat*, Feb. 9, 1849, adv.

[19] *Oshkosh Courier*, Aug. 15, 1855, adv.; *Neenah Bulletin*, May 21, 1856, adv.; *The Conservator*, March 12, 1857, adv.; March 18, 1858.

[20] "Memoranda on the Life of P. V. Lawson," Box 5, 14–20, Lawson Papers, State Historical Society of Wisconsin; D. & B. vol. 59: 358a2; Lawson, 2: 704–705.

from the products of industry schedules. But of even more importance was the role of the farmers of northeastern Wisconsin in secondary lumber processing. Many farmers, especially Germans and Belgians, made shingles during the winter months when farming was impossible, and thus competed with carpenters and joiners for a share of the local urban market. Such dovetailing of small-scale lumber processing and agriculture was not evident in the statistical data on manufacturing. However, it cannot be disregarded. Prior to the Civil War, hand-shaved shingles may well have sold more readily than the products of Oshkosh's steam-powered shingle mills.[21]

Another form of lumber processing important in the industrial economy of antebellum Winnebago County was the manufacture of such wooden ware as barrels, spokes and hubs, churns, pails, and tubs. In the 1850's the cooperage branch was probably stimulated by the presence of a large flour-milling industry at Neenah.[22] Wagon parts were made at Menasha, and by 1861 these products may even have been exported through Green Bay for sale in Wisconsin and other states.[23] But the most important branch of the wood-using industries was the fabrication of pails and tubs. In 1860 the Menasha Pail Company, largest enterprise in the county, employed seventy-five men in the production of 20,000 pails, 1,500 tubs, 500 feet of broom handles, lumber, and sundry other articles valued at $58,250.

This pail-and-tub factory was started on a small scale in 1849, but the first two owners lacked the capital needed to increase the business. Elisha D. Smith, who bought the firm for $1,200 in 1852, was also financially encumbered; but he retained control thanks to the backing of his father-in-law, a wealthy Rhode Island banker. Given this sounder financial basis, Smith used his skills to expand output not only to towns in Wisconsin, but, using road and rail transport, to markets in Missouri, Michigan, Illinois, and the East. By 1856 the factory was carrying on an extensive

---

[21] *Oshkosh Democrat,* June 8, 1855; May 17, 1857; MCSW, Winnebago County, 1860; Merk, 76–78.

[22] *The Conservator,* May 14, 1856; *Weekly Manufacturer,* June 6, 1861; MCSW, Winnebago County, 1860.

[23] "Articles of Copartnership," Vol. 5, 40, Lawson Papers; *Menasha Advocate,* June 21, 1855; *Weekly Manufacturer,* June 6, 1861; Alice E. Smith, *Millstone and Saw: The Origins of Neenah-Menasha* (Madison, 1966), 67.

business and though the depressed business conditions of 1858
caused some distress, trade quickly recovered. By late 1859 Smith
was planning to branch out into the production of half bushels,
washboards, churns, and other woodenware. Already the largest
establishment of its kind in the West, it was estimated that, with
the new additions, the Menasha factory would have few rivals
in the country.[24]

Capital was critical in the success of this establishment. Smith's
entrepreneurial ability was also required in expanding the market
threshold and in improving production techniques; but if his
father-in-law had not nominally purchased the firm in 1854, Smith
would have been forced to go into bankruptcy. Once again, as
with so many Winnebago lumber-processing enterprises, a combination of wealth first and then business acumen was essential
to industrial progress. Business skill itself was insufficient. Money
or credit was needed to tide the entrepreneur over the slack periods and the unstable financial conditions of the frontier.

Flour Milling

Flour and gristmilling was the second-ranking processing industry in antebellum Winnebago County. In 1850 this branch, with
a value added of $31,566, was responsible for 24.1 per cent of the
county's manufacturing output; a decade later the corresponding
figures were $35,114 and 11.1 per cent. Yet these totals somewhat
understate the importance of the flour industry in the county's
manufacturing economy. Using the measure value of product, a
different picture emerges. Flour and gristmills produced goods
worth $108,216 in 1850, or 31.7 per cent of the county total, while
in 1860 they had a produce worth $454,443, or 47 per cent of
the Winnebago aggregate. The value of flour itself was high; it
was the value added by manufacture that was relatively low.

Early settlers in Winnebago County had to import their flour
either from Green Bay using the Indian trails, or from Manchester
on the eastern shore of Lake Winnebago.[25] It was not until 1848

[24] H. A. Miner, *Memorial of Elisha Dickinson Smith, 1827–1899* (Madison, 1903),
6–7; Lawson, 2: 669, 687–691; C. T. Kimball, "Reminiscences of the Beginnings of
the City," Box 8, Lawson Papers; D. & B. vol. 59: 353, 411, 418, 420; *Menasha
Advocate*, Aug. 24, 1854; May 17, 1855; *The Conservator*, Apr. 9, Dec. 22, 1859.
[25] Harney, 138; *Oshkosh Courier*, May 16, 1855.

that the pioneer mills provided a much-needed service for the local communities. Once started, however, the industry expanded rapidly in the 1850's, for the mills could produce flour for export as well as for home consumption. The wheat crops of Winnebago and Fond du Lac counties, with 10.7 per cent of the Wisconsin total in 1860, furnished plentiful supplies of raw materials. The enormous potential of the water power at Neenah-Menasha was an additional incentive to milling. Furthermore, the site location of the twin towns on a water route enabled mills to export surplus flour by means of the Lower Fox to Green Bay. Proximity to raw materials, available motive power, and access to markets were the three main conditions conducive to the establishment of pioneer flour milling. All that was needed were entrepreneurs who had the capital and ability to develop these resources.

Such men were not slow in coming forward and making Neenah-Menasha, but especially Neenah, the center of a flourishing industry.[26] The Kimberly brothers led the way. Using money brought with them from the East, they started off as merchants, but by 1851 they had also turned to flour milling. Though they began milling on a custom basis and had a struggle to make ends meet in the early 1850's, by the middle of the decade they were on a sound financial footing. Flouring capacity increased to such an extent that the merchandising store could be closed in 1856 and by 1859 the brothers were the richest millers in Neenah.[27]

Edward Smith, a Neenah merchant since 1850, Hugh Sherry, and Hiram Wheeler built another flour mill in Neenah in 1852–53. Wheeler was in charge of the construction; Sherry, who had some experience as a miller, looked after the running operations.

---

[26] In 1850 the census reported two flour mills in the county. The Neenah Mill of L. P. Jones produced 17,280 barrels of flour, while the Algoma mill of D. W. Forman & Co. produced 1600 barrels of flour. By 1860 the census reported 13 mills in the county. The six mills located in Neenah contributed 63.5 per cent of the county's value added in flour and 56.9 per cent of the value of the product. The eight mills of the twin settlements of Neenah-Menasha together furnished 67.2 per cent of the value added and 64 per cent of the value of the product. MCSW, Winnebago County, 1850 and 1860.

[27] D. & B. vol. 59: 335; Harney, 202; Cunningham, 185–186; Lawson, 1: 408, 411; *The Conservator*, May 14, 1856; July 22, 1858; Charles N. Glaab and Lawrence H. Larsen, "Neenah Menasha in the 1870's: The Development of Flour Milling and Papermaking," *Wisconsin Magazine of History*, 52 (1968), 27. [Hereinafter cited as *Wis. Mag. Hist.*]

However, this partnership was short-lived, and Smith soon took over the mill himself, paying special attention to custom grinding. In 1857 he was joined by John Proctor, and these two entrepreneurs did a large business in high-quality flour for the rest of the decade.[28] Smith's former partners were not as successful. Sherry associated with Thomas Richards in milling operations in September, 1854, but neither man was a shrewd financier, and the firm was dissolved in the same year. Sherry resuscitated his business in January, 1855, with two new partners, Davis and Roberts, but he again "overextended" and sold out a month later to these partners. He then became involved in building the Fox River Mills in 1856, which he later sold to E. & J.R. Ford. The mill of Davis & Roberts only returned small profits and was bought by W.J. Clements in 1857. Lack of capital and poor management negated the business efforts of these entrepreneurs.[29]

Other twin-city millers were more successful in the 1850's. In 1854 A.F. Cronkite and S.G. Burdick opened a merchant flour mill at Neenah and did a steady trade until 1862, when the failure of Cronkite & Co., bankers and hardware merchants, affected the stability of the firm. John R. Davis bought the old government mill at Neenah in 1854 and operated it successfully throughout the antebellum years. Mills and Peet ran the Atlantic Mills at Neenah from 1857 onwards, borrowing money from Wing & Mitchell of Chicago to skirt financial difficulties.[30] In Menasha, three flour mills were in operation by 1855. Four years later H.A. Burts built the Coral Mills, making them the tenth mill at the foot of Lake Winnebago, with more undergoing construction.[31]

The enterprises of Neenah-Menasha millers in the 1850's illustrate both the problems and the potential of flour milling in

[28] D. & B. vol. 59: 358a; *The Conservator*, June 5, 1856; Dec. 17, 1857; *Neenah Bulletin*, May 21, 1856; Cunningham, 186; Harney, 202; Glaab and Larsen, 27; Lawson, 1: 411–412.

[29] D. & B. vol. 59: 335; *The Conservator*, Jan. 1, 22, 1857; *Neenah Bulletin*, May 21, 1856; Harney, 203; Lawson, 1: 412.

[30] D. & B. vol. 59: 358a, 358u; Harney, 202–203; Lawson, 1: 412; Cunningham, 84–85, 198; *Menasha Advocate*, June 26, 1854; *The Conservator*, May 14, 1856, adv.; Dec. 29, 1859, advs.; *Neenah Bulletin*, May 21, 1856, adv.; *The Weekly Manufacturer*, June 6, 1861, advs.; July 3, 1862, advs.; A. E. Smith, *Millstone and Saw*, 63–65.

[31] John A. Bryan to his son Marshall, Island Home, Oct. 1860; March, 1861, Bryan Correspondence, State Historical Society of Wisconsin; *Menasha Advocate*, June 12, 1854; *The Conservator*, Jan. 1, Nov. 21, 28, Dec. 8, 29, 1859, advs.; Lawson, 2: 699–702; A. E. Smith, *Millstone and Saw*, 65.

Winnebago County in the antebellum years. The potential was definitely promising in view of the local wheat resources and the water-power capacity of the twin settlements. Indeed, in the last four months of 1859, the mills shipped some 25,930 barrels of flour, as well as producing an unspecified amount of custom work —a total which was less than 50 per cent of the mills' annual business.[32] But the problems were as difficult as the results were rewarding. Many enterprises were started on a small basis, either with capital built up locally in merchandising or raised or borrowed in the East by the entrepreneur himself. A sure source of money was essential to construct the mill, to obtain the machinery, to buy the wheat, and then to sustain the entrepreneur until profits could be realized from the sale of flour, either locally or in more distant markets. Frequent changes in ownership indicate the search for the combination of both skillful miller and financial backer. If the two assets could be combined, then the firm, as for example with the Kimberly Brothers, was nearly certain of success. Those flouring enterprises in pioneering regions which aspired to become more than local gristmills, once again, had to add the availability of finance and entrepreneurial talent to the natural resources of the environment.

Other Processing Industries

Other processing industries provided but an insignificant proportion of the county's manufacturing output, namely 0.8 per cent in 1850 and 4.8 per cent in 1860. (Table 16 and Table 17.) These branches of manufacturing grew in the 1850's in response to local demand. For example the breweries served the German population. They were thus small, having an average value added of $1,733 in 1860 compared to the average figure of $6,013 for Milwaukee firms, and were located in the urban centers of Oshkosh, Neenah, and Menasha. The leathergoods establishments were also small, having an average value added of $1,528 compared to the average figure of $5,384 for Racine. They merely processed local skins and hides and often made shoes as well as leathergoods. Woolen manufacturing suffered from the same

[32] *The Conservator*, Dec. 29, 1859.

limitations: modest resources and markets.[33] There was little opportunity to develop these types of processing branches other than on a marginal basis.

HOUSEHOLD-CRAFT CONSUMER INDUSTRIES

The household-craft consumer industries in Winnebago County were geared to the practical requirements of an underdeveloped area, and like the "other processing industries" were restricted in output. In 1850 this group furnished 12.3 per cent of the county's value added; a total which had declined to 5.5 per cent a decade later. (Table 16 and Table 17.) Rendering an average per capita value of $1.58 in 1850 and $0.74 in 1860, these industries were certainly not supplying all the local consumer demands. To be sure, some household goods were made in small shops or in the homes, but more often they were bought at retail stores which imported merchandise from Milwaukee, Chicago, or the East. Local craftsmen were unable to withstand the increasing competition of ready-made articles in the 1850's.

Boots and Shoes

Within the household-craft consumer group boots and shoes made the largest contribution to Winnebago manufacturing, having 4.8 per cent of the county aggregate in 1850 and 1.6 per cent in 1860. Most of the shoe shops were small, having an average capital invested of $1,280 in 1850 and $841 in 1860, and they were only absorbing a limited portion of the neighborhood trade. The decline in the size of the establishments in the 1850's reflected the increased mercantile activity in mass-produced footwear.

Pioneer footwear was made in either mercantile or craft shops. For example, in Oshkosh in 1849, Petersilea & Gerschwender ran a retail boot-and-shoe store selling Boston-manfactured work especially selected by an agent. However, the partners also made footwear to order. By contrast, Edward Edwards concentrated on the craft manufacture of high-quality shoes. Both kinds of shop

---

[33] D. & B. vol. 59: 358, 410; MCSW, Winnebago County, 1850 and 1860; *Oshkosh True Democrat*, June 22, 1849; *Oshkosh Democrat*, Sept. 14, 1850, adv.; Sept. 19, 1851, adv.; June 8, 1855, adv.; *The Conservator*, May 14, 1856; July 16, 1857, adv.; July 15, 1858; Lawson, 1: 396; Harney, 197.

were small, employing only the partners themselves and one or two journeymen or apprentices.[34]

In the early 1850's several new enterprises, generally following the pattern already established by the older shops, opened for business. In 1851 the merchant-manufacturers Petersilea & Gersch-wender dissolved their partnership to establish separate shops, but both continued to sell ready-made footwear and to manufacture for the custom trade. In the same year A.R. Montgomery set up a shoe manufactory in conjunction with his General Store in Omro. The artisans, as distinct from the merchant-craftsmen, concentrated on making boots and shoes on a custom basis. Their appeal rested on the use of skilled labor to guarantee quality, a good fit, and style, rather than on the price of the finished product.[35]

Some of these establishments were short-lived; others managed to acquire more stability by taking in new partners. Those which survived were joined by numerous other small firms in the second half of the 1850's. In all, at least eighteen boot-and-shoe operations came into being in Winnebago County in this quinquennium.[36] About half of these concentrated on the manufacture of customware; another 25 per cent combined both retailing and manufacturing, while the remaining 25 per cent appeared only to be interested in retailing.[37] The craftsmen seemed merely to eke out a living from their limited sales and their repair work. The merchant craftsmen and retailers were better off, probably because they had more capital invested in the business and could afford to sell at cheaper prices. For example, Oshkosh businessmen like the Fraker Brothers, the Stickney Brothers, or C.A. Johnson all had Eastern contacts either supplying ready-made

[34] Oshkosh True Democrat, Feb. 9, Nov. 16, Dec. 21, 1849, advs.; Harney, 138.

[35] Oshkosh Democrat, Jan. 24, Feb. 21, Aug. 15, Oct. 24, Dec. 26, 1851, advs.; Apr. 23, Nov. 19, 1852, advs.; June 17, 1853, adv.; Oshkosh Weekly Courier, June 29, adv.; May 17, 1854, adv.

[36] D. & B. vol. 59: 352, 358B, 358D, 358H, 358K, 358N, 358a6, 391, 406; Oshkosh Democrat, July 21, 1854; Oshkosh Weekly Courier, May 17, 1854, Oshkosh Courier, Apr. 4, May 20, 1855, advs.; Apr. 30, May 16, adv.; July 23, 1856; May 13, 1857, adv.; May 11, 1860; Menasha Advocate, May 31, 1855, adv.; The Conservator, June 5, 1856, Oct. 21, 1858; Neenah Bulletin, May 21, 1856; Weekly Manufacturer, June 6, 1861; The Northwestern, Sept. 14, 1860.

[37] Estimates worked out from statements made by the Dun & Bradstreet agents and from the advertisements in the newspapers.

footware or financial backing, and they were thus able to under-sell the more local firms.[38]

Despite the evidence of new activity in shoe manufacturing in Winnebago County during the 1850's, these enterprises were not reported in the 1860 census, which showed only six estab-lishments, producing 3,390 pairs of boots and shoes. Three pos-sible reasons, either separately or conjointly, account for this situation. In the first place many craftsmen may not have at-tained a $500 value of product, and thus may have been ignored in the census tally of manufacturers. But of more importance, in this instance, the shoe business seemed to have overextended its capacity in the late 1850's.[39] Supply outran demand. Then the general depressed business conditions of the late 1850's and the undercutting price policy of some retailers hastened the closure of some small shops. By 1860 the competition of medium-priced ready-made footwear was proving to be too strong for local shoemakers.

Clothing

Similar trends can be seen in the antebellum clothing industry in Winnebago County. Craftsmen were outnumbered by mer-chant-manufacturers and by retailers who had larger enterprises and more staying power. Numerous small shops sprang into existence in the 1850's, but their life span was short, owing to the uncertain economic conditions on the frontier in that decade and to the rivalry of retailed ready-ware. Though the industry contributed more to the manufacturing economy than the census figures suggested, the relative proportion was still meager and even diminishing.[40]

Early clothing establishments appear to have been doing busi-ness in Winnebago County by the late 1840's. For the most part

[38] D. & B. vol. 59: 352, 358B, 358K, 391, 414, 415; *Menasha Advocate*, May 3, 1856; *The Conservator*, June 3, 1856, adv.; *Oshkosh Courier*, May 11, 1860; Jan. 4, 1861; *The Northwestern*, June 1, Dec. 21, 1860.

[39] D. & B. vol. 59: 391; *The Northwestern*, Sept. 16, 1860.

[40] The Census of 1850 reported only two tailors with a joint value added of $3,900; the Census of 1860 reported no clothing establishments. This was clearly not the case, as other contemporary evidence indicates that there were at least four clothing manufacturers and four millinery shops in 1860 and that some of these had a value of product of $500 or more.

these firms were merchant-manufacturers who had a well-selected stock of ready-made clothing and also employed cutters and tailors to do custom work.[41] Craftsmen working for themselves seemed to be few and far between.

The clothing industry expanded in the 1850's, though to what extent is uncertain. There were at least four tailors at work in the county during the decade, and new millinery and dressmaking establishments also conducted a limited business.[42] But the merchant-tailors were cornering the bulk of the clothing business, at least in men's wear. Samuel Eckstein and Peter McCourt, who were worth some $6–7,000 each in 1859, were the leading clothiers. They bought merchandise in Eastern markets, had ready-made clothing of their own manufacture, and employed experienced tailors for the custom trade. The other six or more merchant tailors who opened shops in the second half of the 1850's also offered a variety of manufactured goods, but their trade was not so large.[43]

Not all merchant-tailors were successful. William Smith of Menasha only survived about three years, from 1853 to 1857, while J.P. Robey of Oshkosh lasted from 1854 to 1856.[44] But on the whole they were more stable than the tailors, probably because of their merchandising activities and their larger sources of capital. Cheaper ready-made clothing seemed to have a wider sales appeal than tailored goods; and retail sales were taking precedence over local manufactures, which were on the decline in antebellum Winnebago County.

Furniture

The making of furniture, though possibly a secondary lumber processing industry by reason of its raw material, displays more

[41] *Oshkosh True Democrat,* July 27, Nov. 30, 1849, advs.; *Oshkosh Democrat,* May 31, adv., June 7, adv., July 5, 1850; *Winnebago Telegraph,* Sept. 14, 1850, adv.; Harney, 139.

[42] D. & B. vol. 59: 358B, 358K; *Menasha Advocate,* June 12, 1854; May 3, 1856, adv.; *Neenah Bulletin,* June 4, 1856; *The Conservator,* May 14, 1856; May 7, 1857, adv.; July 8, adv., July 15, 1858; *The Omro Republican,* March 4, 1858, adv.; *The Northwestern,* May 18, 1860; Lawson, 1: 397.

[43] D. & B. vol. 59: 340, 358N, 358O, 399; *Oshkosh Courier,* July 12, 1854; July 30, 1856, adv.; March 26, 1857, adv.; *Oshkosh Democrat,* Feb. 7, 1851; June 17, July 13, adv., 1853; June 8, 1855; *Menasha Advocate,* Feb. 1, 1855, adv.; June 14, 1856, adv.; March 26, 1857, adv.; *The Northwestern,* Nov. 16, 1860.

[44] D. & B. vol. 59: 342, 354; *Menasha Advocate,* June 12, 1854.

marked characteristics of the domestic branches of manufacturing in organization and market potential. This industry, like the clothing and shoe branches in Winnebago County, was split between the craftsmen and the merchant-manufacturers who retailed imported goods as well as looked to the jobbing trade. Moreover, despite the accessibility of raw materials, the furniture industry also declined relatively, contributing 2.4 per cent of the county aggregate in 1850 and 1.8 per cent in 1860. Craftsmen in this branch could survive only in a very limited way.

Pioneer cabinetware shops were established soon after initial settlement in each of the three main urban centers of Oshkosh, Neenah, and Menasha. Some entrepreneurs concentrated on making furniture, mainly beds and chairs, either in a shop or in a "manufactory," if their labor input and use of machinery could justify that title. Often these cabinetmakers, who were usually carpenters or joiners by trade, also did wood turning. Occasionally they made coffins and acted as undertakers. Other cabinetmakers also retailed imported furniture. These entrepreneurs emphasized the merchandising side of the business.[45] Doubtless there were also carpenters and joiners in the smaller centers of Omro, Rushford, and Winneconne, and in other villages.

The furniture business in Winnebago County expanded in the 1850's, but at a rather laggardly pace. There was an extensive turnover among craftsmen, whether they were called cabinetmakers, carpenters, or joiners.[46] Even allowing for a 100 per cent underestimation of cabinetmakers in the 1860 census, the industry was still weakly developed and the outputs small. People must have either made their own furniture, brought it with them, or bought ready-made goods from a retail store.[47]

The extent of retail furniture sales in Winnebago County is difficult if not impossible to estimate. A.D. Seaman of Milwaukee early established a branch firm at Oshkosh, though it was taken over by E.R. Colton in 1851. Presumably, however, Colton was still supplied with furniture from Milwaukee. Other firms such

[45] *Oshkosh True Democrat*, Feb. 9, March 9, 1849, advs.; Jan. 25, 1850, adv.; *Oshkosh Democrat*, June 14, 1850, adv.; Harney, 139, 199, 217, Lawson, 1: 397, 658; Cunningham, 83.

[46] D. & B. vol. 59: 403, 407; *Oshkosh Democrat*, June 17, 1853, adv.; *Menasha Advocate*, June 12, 1854; Feb. 1, 1855; Feb. 15, 1856; *The Conservator*, Apr. 28, 1858, adv.; Jan. 15, July 23, adv., 1859.

[47] D. & B. vol. 59: 358R, 375, 389, 396, 407.

as Keyes & Blin of Menasha and Weil & Greenwald of Oshkosh retailed ready-made furniture, though they also sold homemade products.[48] Overall it would seem that furniture manufacturing was not an important enterprise in pioneer Winnebago. Cabinet-makers, either as craftsmen, merchant-craftsmen, or even as carpenters, existed on a local, limited and "high-class" trade, while the sale of cheaper retailed goods also had a rather slender market.

Blacksmiths and Tinsmiths

Blacksmiths and tinsmiths contributed very little to the manufacturing output of Winnebago County, providing only 2 per cent of the total value added in 1850 and 2.2 per cent a decade later. Blacksmiths usually had small shops and concentrated on repairs and minor job work like horse shoeing or carriage trimming.[49] As such they did not seem to qualify for listing in the census. Those smiths who were recorded were often entered as wagon-makers or as farm tool-and-machinery manufacturers. Obviously there were more blacksmiths in the county than were indicated by the census, for a business survey in Neenah-Menasha in 1858 listed nine such men, and the Oshkosh City Directory of 1857 listed twenty-nine blacksmiths, which, at a conservative estimate, would indicate nine or ten firms.[50] But it is difficult to ascertain the precise number of these men and the scope of their activities. Possibly they were regarded as servicing rather than manufacturing entrepreneurs.

Tinsmiths were reported with greater frequency in the census than were blacksmiths, presumably because their end products — stoves and kitchen utensils — were more tangible articles than the products contributed by blacksmiths. Yet those tinsmiths who did have an annual value of product over $500 were likely to be merchant-manufacturers and dealers in hardware, iron, and nails. As such they had a larger business than the artisan, and

---

[48] Oshkosh Weekly Courier, Aug. 3, 1853, adv.; Oshkosh Courier, Nov. 8, 1854, adv.; May 21, Sept. 3, 1856, advs.; June 24, Aug. 26, 1859, advs.; Menasha Advocate, Feb. 1, 1855, adv.; March 22, 1856, adv.; Oshkosh Democrat, June 8, 1855, adv.; Neenah Bulletin, May 21, 1856, adv.; The Conservator, Apr. 22, 1858, adv.; Nov. 21, 1859, adv.; Weekly Manufacturer, June 6, Sept. 12, 1861, advs.

[49] Oshkosh Courier, Nov. 12, 1856, adv.; Menasha Advocate, June 7, 1855, adv.; The Conservator, July 31, 1856, adv.; Sept. 24, 1857, adv.

[50] OCD, 97–124; The Conservator, March 18, 1858; Jan. 15, 1859.

often their retailing functions were more remunerative than their manufacturing activities.[51] There may well have been other tinsmiths whose main function was job work, and who were therefore bypassed by the census.

In sum, the household-craft consumer goods made in Winnebago County formed a small percentage of the total manufactures. Although increasing slightly in absolute value in the 1850's, they declined relatively. Some household products such as shoes, clothes, and furniture could have been made at home or by small-scale or part-time craftsmen, but it is equally likely that such goods were bought in increasing amounts from retailers who obtained their ready-made articles either from Milwaukee, Chicago, or from Eastern cities. Craft industries were dying out.[52]

AGRICULTURAL INDUSTRIES AND IRON PRODUCTS

The agricultural implements and wagon and carriage industries, together with iron foundries and machine shops, made their appearance in Winnebago County in the early 1850's, a few years after initial settlement of the region. By 1860 they had grown to the point that they contributed 8.3 per cent of the county's value added. Utilizing local wood and imported iron, these branches of manufacturing catered to the particular demands of the local farmers and lumbermen.

A pioneer agricultural implements firm made fanning mills as early as 1850, but this was not a profitable venture and was soon closed down. By the mid-1850's other entrepreneurs had ventured into the manufacture of fanning mills, grain cradles, grain separators and plows, but few were successful.[53] Only three firms had any staying power. The Smedley & Rogers Farmers'

[51] D. & B. vol. 59: 338; *Oshkosh True Democrat*, Feb. 9, 1849; *Oshkosh Democrat*, Nov. 22, 1850, adv.; June 21, 1851; June 8, 1855; *Menasha Advocate*, July 26, 1855, adv.; *Neenah Bulletin*, May 21, 1856; *Oshkosh Courier*, Feb. 18, 1857, adv.; *The Omro Republican*, March 4, 1858, adv.; *The Conservator*, July 1, 1858, adv.; *The Northwestern*, May 18, 1860, adv.

[52] It is difficult to make precise quantitative statements about craft industries in Winnebago County because the census marshal was obviously negligent in recording the existence of firms. These estimates are based on evidence provided by other contemporary sources.

[53] D. & B. vol. 59: 358V; *Oshkosh Democrat*, Sept. 13, 1850, adv.; Jan. 17, 1851, adv.; Jan. 28, 1853, adv.; July 21, 1854, adv.; June 8, 1855, adv.; *Oshkosh Weekly Courier*, May 3, 1854; *Neenah Bulletin*, June 4, 1856, adv.; *The Conservator*, July 17, 1856, adv.

Machine Manufactory in Oshkosh, which later became Powers, Rogers & Co.'s Foundry and Machine Shop and Threshing Machine Manufactory, was doing a good business in the mid-1850's, but it was sold to an Illinois firm in 1857. Smedley & Case increased their output of horse-powers, threshing machines, and other farming equipment in the second half of the decade and by 1860 were producing $18,000 worth of goods. R. Wyman, who concentrated on the manufacture of plows, was also successful in weathering the economic storms of the 1850's.[54]

There is no obvious reason for the success of some agricultural implements manufacturers and the failure of others. Presumably there was a limited market for these articles, as the large firms in southeastern Wisconsin and northern Illinois sold their farm machinery in northern Wisconsin.[55] The ability to stay in business may well have rested on managerial skills in catering specifically to local farmers and their peculiar soil and weather problems. Then, as usual, financial reserves were needed to tide the firm over slack periods or economic crises. The rapid turnover of firms suggests that an amalgam of both reasons operated.

Wagon- and carriage-making firms were generally smaller than agricultural implements establishments, but their existence seems to have been equally if not more precarious. Some proprietors such as J.C. Tingley and J.N. Gill may have stayed in business for about three years, but it is uncertain in what condition.[56] Again their ability to survive was probably dependent upon the state of the local market and the capital available to the entrepreneurs.

Iron foundries and machine shops in Winnebago County also shared the characteristic of instability. The foundry and machine shop built in Algoma in 1849 had a short life, even with changed

[54] D. & B. vol. 59: 356, 397; MCSW, Winnebago County, 1860; *Oshkosh Weekly Courier*, June 29, 1853; *Oshkosh Democrat*, June 17, 1853; July 21, 1854; June 8, 1855, adv.; *Menasha Advocate*, June 14, 1855, adv.; *Oshkosh Courier*, March 14, 1855, adv.; Apr. 16, adv.; May 14, 1856; *Oshkosh Weekly Democrat*, July 13, 1859; *The Northwestern*, May 18, 1860; *Geographical and Statistical History of the County of Winnebago*, Adv. Sec. 6.

[55] MCSW, Racine and Walworth counties, 1860; Ela Papers; J. I. Case Papers, J. I. Case Co., Racine.

[56] *Oshkosh Democrat*, June 14, 1850; June 8, 1855, adv.; Nov. 12, 1857; *Winnebago Telegraph*, Sept. 14, 1850; *Oshkosh Courier*, Oct. 7, 1856; *The Northwestern*, Nov. 9, 1860, adv.; OCD, 98, 105, 121; Harney, 203.

ownership. The Menasha foundry of Fargo & Thomas was unable to stay in business; the Oshkosh brass and iron foundry was destroyed in the fire of July, 1856.[57] By the late 1850's the only iron foundry was that built in Neenah by Moore, Wells & Co. in 1857. This firm did a good business in castings, mill irons, machinery, stoves, and other utensils. A keen sense of entrepreneurship and a local market for small castings and domestic utensils seemed to be the key to their success, since they had no capital other than what they had invested in the business.[58]

A local market existed for foundry goods and machinery, particularly in the lumber and flour-milling industries. But Winnebago firms seemed unable to compete in quality and price with products made by Milwaukee and Eastern firms. Lumbermen and millers preferred to import their equipment from established firms in more distant locations than to give their business to local founders. The Winnebago iron industry was thus reduced to taking occasional orders for mill gearing and repairing, probably from smaller firms, and to making wagons, carriages, farming utensils, and miscellaneous goods as required.

Conclusion

Manufacturing activities in antebellum Winnebago County reflected an underdeveloped economy dependent on forestry and farming. The main industries were lumber processing, either in its primary or secondary stage, and flour milling — industries which required capital investment in plant and machinery, but which utilized available natural resources. Other branches of manufacturing catered to practical and local needs, when and if they existed, and only if they were competitive with imported goods. At this time there were limits to the development of manufacturing in Winnebago County. The nature and rate of industrial growth was, for the most part, contingent upon a combination of accessible local resources, the willingness of capitalists to stake money in new enterprises, and the skill of the manufacturer to sell his goods either to a lightly scattered population or to a

[57] *Oshkosh True Democrat*, Feb. 9, 1849; *Oshkosh Democrat*, June 21, 1850; Feb. 14, 1851; June 8, 1855; MCSW, Winnebago County, 1850; *History of the City of Oshkosh*, 48; Harney, 200, 217.
[58] D. & B. vol. 59: 407; *The Conservator*, Dec. 24, 31, 1857; *Weekly Manufacturer*, Sept. 12, 1861; MCSW, Winnebago County, 1860.

regional market, using available transportation facilities. While raw materials were present in abundance, the combination of business acumen and financial backing was rare, especially in the household-craft consumer branches, which suffered growing competition from retail merchants.

The character of manufacturing in pioneer Winnebago County was transitional. Only one establishment, the Menasha Pail Factory, could be truly called a factory. Some of the lumber operations were large, but they employed unskilled or semiskilled labor working on a seasonal basis and often with crude machinery. Many of the flour mills yielded a high value of product, but their poor showing in the value-added category suggested room for improvement both in technology and management. Craft shops were on the wane. They had only a small capital, did a limited business, and had a marginal existence. Artisans were unable to cope with the sales of ready-made imported goods, which were evidently cheap enough to withstand the cost of transportation, often by poor roads.

The manufacturing interest was in a stage of indecision about which direction to take. By 1860 the days of the craftsman as an important manufacturer were over. Certain branches of the craft group were either dying out or were being replaced by more sophisticated industries. Yet some craftsmen could still earn a living. Ready-made clothing and footware had not completely taken over the market in the antebellum period. The obviously profitable industries of a well-endowed agricultural and lumbering area, namely those processing natural resources, had definitely made some headway, but before 1860 in Winnebago County there were insufficient initiative, capital, and transportation facilities to encourage investment and growth on any regional scale and with any marked degree of success.

CHAPTER FIVE

Eau Claire County: A Monolithic Manufacturing Economy in the Wisconsin Lumber Belt

OF THE SIX LUMBERING REGIONS in Wisconsin, the Chippewa River Valley was probably the richest. Contemporary lumbermen estimated that in 1840 about one sixth of all the pine lumber west of the Appalachians — approximately twenty billion board feet — stood in this area, which also included three or four billion feet of hemlock.[1] Some exploration and initial exploitation of these resources had taken place in the late 1840's and early 1850's. But it was not until the late 1850's that the vanguard of the lumber tycoons began building large-scale enterprises which were later to make the Chippewa Valley the most important lumbering area and Eau Claire one of the major lumber-processing counties in Wisconsin.

The earliest sawmill in the Chippewa Valley had been built by Lockwood and Street in 1828 when the land still officially belonged to the Indians. They soon added a second mill in the 1830's, but sold both to Hiram S. Allen, an important antebellum lumberman. Following the Indian Cession Treaty of 1837, other mills were constructed by pioneers in the hope of a quick and easy profit from the sale of lumber downstream. In the 1840's still more mills were erected in the Eau Claire region, and some of the earlier mills changed ownership.[2]

---

[1] Fries, 20–21; Merk, 64; Hotchkiss, 474; J. Gregory, 83.
[2] For more details on these pioneering lumbermen, see Thomas E. Randall, *History of the Chippewa Valley* (Eau Claire, 1875), *passim;* Kleven, 76–81; Hotchkiss, 475–477; *Chippewa County, Past and Present* (Chicago, 1913), 1: 97–100; Duane D. Fischer, "The Disposal of Federal Lands in the Eau Claire Land District of Wisconsin, 1848–1925" (unpublished M.S. thesis, University of Wisconsin, 1961), 14–22.

By the 1840's the lumber industry in the Valley was beginning to take some shape. Transients were being sorted out from more permanent entrepreneurs. Pioneers who lacked sufficient capital to absorb the costs of lumbering and who were unskilled in the management of the business soon sold their mill property to lumbermen like Carson, Eaton, and Allen who saw the long-term future of the region and were determined to succeed. These entrepreneurs realized that there were no sizable pineries south of the Wisconsin River, and that the whole of the southern Middle West was therefore a potential market. They were prepared to make heavy outlays on plant and labor. They were also able to bear the additional cost of importing the food, drygoods, and general merchandise needed to support lumber camps; for, prior to the late 1840's, no settlers came to the Valley for agricultural or retailing purposes only.[3]

The lumbermen were correct in their estimation of the manufacturing worth of the Chippewa Valley. By 1843 the lumber output of the area was some 5,500,000 feet, and it continued to rise in the next decade. In 1847 the five mills and seven saws on the Chippewa and its tributaries processed 5,350,000 feet of lumber, 3,110,000 pieces of lath, 1,300,000 shingles, 50,000 feet of square timber, and 2,000 logs. The three establishments reported in the 1850 census produced 6,500,000 board feet of lumber and 2,500,000 pieces of lath; other smaller operations may have added to this total. By 1852 the fifteen mills on the Chippewa River cut 20,000,000 feet of lumber or approximately one tenth of the annual product of the Wisconsin pineries.[4]

During the 1850's the Chippewa Valley became a focus of much greater exploitation and settlement. Increasing land sales within the Eau Claire Land District indicated the growing interest in lumbering. Up to 1851 land sales had amounted to 2,548.64 acres. In 1854, however, purchases for that year alone totaled 80,207.23 acres. Entrepreneurs who were formerly content to cut timber from government tracts now found it expedient to own land along

---

[3] Randall, 35, *Chippewa County, Past and Present*, 1: 234.
[4] U.S. Senate, *Executive Documents*, 30 Cong. 1 Sess. (1847), Doc. 5, p. 71; J. Gregory, 83–84; *De Bow's Review*, 15 (1853), 334, citing the Owen Report; *Hunt's Merchants' Magazine*, 27 (1852), 310; *Watertown Chronicle*, Feb. 25, 1852; MCSW, Chippewa County, 1850.

the river if they wanted to stay in business. Sales continued to grow until the depression of the late 1850's restricted economic activity.[5]

Settlers followed in the wake of the lumbermen. Chippewa County, which had a population of 615 in 1850, had at least 3,625 inhabitants five years later, while in 1860 there was a minimum of 10,179 settlers.[6] These settlers included farmer-loggers who worked in the lumber mills and farmed in the off season, local businessmen, professionals and their families, as well as timber merchants and lumber workers. By 1860 the Chippewa River Valley was beginning to show signs of activity other than the mere exploitation of lumber.

In 1856, in the midst of a land sales boom and increased settlement, Eau Claire was set off as a separate county from Chippewa.[7] Located in the heart of the northwestern pineries, this county had a copious supply of valuable timber. It was also well placed with respect to transport, for the Eau Claire and Chippewa rivers flowed into the main southward route of the Mississippi. (Map 1.) Given these resources, the antebellum economy of the county focused on the sawing and planing of lumber. Indeed in 1860 this branch of industry provided 81.7 per cent of Eau Claire's value added and employed 89.8 per cent of the working force. Other processing industries, namely flour milling, brewing, and construction materials, contributed in a small way; the household-craft consumer group — represented by only two branches, boots and shoes and tinware — accounted for less than 5 per cent of the county's aggregate. (Table 18.) Eau Claire, in fact, had a monolithic manufacturing economy with virtually no diversification. Lumber and lumber alone was the pivot of industrial activity.

In this respect manufacturing in Eau Claire was more heavily

[5] Fischer, 36, 42-47, 62.

[6] It is difficult to obtain comparable population figures. The area called Chippewa County in 1850 had become Chippewa, Dunn, Eau Claire, and Pepin counties as well as part of Barron (Dallas), Buffalo, and Clark counties by 1860. The first four named counties provided the minimum figures quoted, but to this should be added an unknown percentage of Buffalo's 832 inhabitants and Clark's 232 inhabitants in 1855 and Barron's thirteen, Buffalo's 3,865 and Clark's 769 inhabitants in 1860.

[7] Eau Claire County was given a land area of 649 square miles. *Origin and Legislative History of County Boundaries*, 77; William Bailey (ed.), *History of Eau Claire County, Wisconsin* (Chicago, 1914), 30.

concentrated than was usual. Most Wisconsin counties had two
industries which contributed the major share of their manufacturing output; the average value-added figures for the two leading
industries of all fifty-five counties in 1860 was 70.4 per cent. But
Eau Claire had one industry which accounted for over 80 per
cent of the county aggregate. Thus it overstated the Wisconsin
mean in the same way that Milwaukee County, by its diversified
spread of industries, understated the mean. Yet Eau Claire was
still typical of northern parts of Wisconsin, where the only known
natural resource was lumber and most industrial activity centered
on the saw mill. Other northwestern counties had even higher
proportions of their value added in lumber planed and sawed
than did Eau Claire; Chippewa had 99.1 per cent, Clark 91.1 per
cent, and Dunn 97.9 per cent.

The emphasis on primary lumber processing in Eau Claire had
several consequences for the manufacturing economy of the county. In the first place, it meant that this was the only industry in
which Eau Claire contributed to Wisconsin's manufacturing economy to any sizable degree, though this contribution was sizable
only in comparison to the other industries within Eau Claire, for
3.2 per cent could hardly be called of major importance. However, considering the small population of the county — 3,164 people, or 0.5 per cent of the Wisconsin total — the lumber contribution might be called significant.

In the second place, lumber processing attracted relatively large
amounts of money to the four Eau Claire banks. Eau Claire had
the second-highest assets of any county in Wisconsin after Milwaukee, namely 7.5 per cent of the state aggregate, compared to Milwaukee's 23.0 per cent and Racine's 3.3 per cent.[8] This situation
probably reflected the substantial capital brought into the region
for the lumber industry rather than the availability of financial
reserves for the development of other manufacturing.

A third noteworthy consequence of the concentration on primary lumber processing was that Eau Claire diverged from the
norm in the size of its manufacturing establishments. In 1860
the mean Wisconsin firm employed 5.4 men, while the mean Eau
Claire firm employed 18.3 men. This high figure was due solely

[8] "Semi-Annual Reports," Banking Commissioner, State of Wisconsin, July, 1860,
in the State Historical Society of Wisconsin.

TABLE 18

MANUFACTURING IN EAU CLAIRE COUNTY, 1860

(Value Added in Current $'s.)

Industry	Value Added	Per Cent of Total	No. of Workers	Per Cent of Total
Processing Industries				
Lumber	81,700	81.72	247	89.82
Flour	5,150	5.15	5	1.82
Liquors	1,960	1.96	3	1.09
Construction Materials	7,790	7.79	12	4.36
Aggregate	96,600	96.62	267	97.09
Household-Craft Consumer				
Boots and Shoes	1,949	1.95	5	1.82
Tin, Copper etc.	1,428	1.43	3	1.09
Aggregate	3,377	3.38	8	2.91
Eau Claire County	99,977	100.00	275	100.00

[SOURCE: Manuscript Census for the State of Wisconsin, 1860. Eau Claire County.]

to the five lumber enterprises, which had an average of 49.4 workers each. Indeed the firm of Chapman & Thorp alone employed 54.5 per cent of the county's entire manufacturing labor force, a marked contrast to Winnebago County, where the largest firm, the Menasha Wooden Ware Company, employed only 13 per cent of the county's workers. The remainder of Eau Claire's industries, however, were small operations of the craft and pioneer processing variety.

Eau Claire was thus by no means industrialized as the crude figures of firm size might seem to indicate. To be sure, three of the sawmills were very large, employing 150, fifty-one, and thirty-five laborers each; but for the most part these men performed only seasonal and unskilled work. Two of the firms were in operation for only five months of the year; the smallest firm was in operation for only three months of the year. The low value added per worker in the large plants, namely $311, indicated that labor was for the most part unskilled, especially as this figure was lower than the average of $476 per worker in the Wisconsin lumber industry. Certainly the lumber mills in Eau Claire seemed to be abreast of modern technology; rotary saws, which were quicker and used less labor than the traditional mulley and double edger, were in use, as well as gang saws and shingle machines. Moreover all lumber firms used steam power. But the productivity figures were still low. Any division of labor was only on a semiskilled or unskilled basis, namely foreman, cook, clerk, chopper, sawyer, skidder, swamper, teamster, and possibly a scaler to measure logs. Most men were casual laborers with no special training, although many did come from the lumbering regions of New England, New York, and Canada.[9]

Although lumber processing was the predominant branch of manufacturing, the antebellum industrial economy of Eau Claire cannot be judged by the criterion of lumbering alone. About 20 per cent of the county's value added was produced by small firms using hand power and crude tools, and most often working on a custom basis. These were the types of establishments — flour mills, shoe shops, and hardware shops — traditionally associated with a frontier or self-sufficient economy, and they arose in response to local demand. This demand was of a servicing nature, namely job work and repairs, for a strong tradition of importing merchandise had early been established in the Eau Claire region. The tendency for the small-scale and craft artisans to be ancillary to the merchants who imported mass-produced goods, and even foodstuffs, was probably more strongly marked in Eau Claire than in many other Wisconsin counties. But the small custom trade added another dimension to the virtually monolithic frontier exploitation of lumber resources.

Lumber Planed and Sawed

Primary lumber processing in Eau Claire was carried out by relatively few enterprises. In 1860 the census listed five lumber

[9] MCSW, Eau Claire County, 1860; Merk, 69–71; Fries, 26, 61; *Eau Claire Free Press*, Sept. 23, 1858; Aug. 29, 1859; Frank Hartman, "Life in a Lumber Camp," *La Crosse County Historical Sketches*, Series 3, 1937, p. 1823; Ruth Stoveken, "The Pine Lumber-Jacks in Wisconsin," *Wis. Mag. Hist.*, 30 (1947), 322–326; Thomas J. Vaughan "Life of the Wisconsin Lumberjack, 1850–1870" (unpublished M.S. thesis, University of Wisconsin, 1951), 60–93, *passim*; Bernice P. Landaal, "Early Lumbering Communities in Northern Wisconsin" (unpublished M.Phil. thesis, University of Wisconsin, 1934), 93–105.

firms, three of which were large, having a value added of $39,599, $20,500 and $13,500 respectively, and two of which were small, with a value added of $7,000 and $1,200 respectively.[10] This was a sharp contrast to lumber processing in Winnebago County in 1860, where twenty-four mills provided 50 per cent of the county's value added, but none of which could individually rival the large Eau Claire mills. Eau Claire lumber manufacturing was dominated by big enterprises, and an analysis of the functions and problems of the individual firms illustrates the development of the industry both in the county itself and as representative of other parts of northwestern Wisconsin.

Nelson C. Chapman and Joseph G. Thorp, owners of the largest lumber operation in Eau Claire in 1860, were relatively new arrivals to the area. Giving up their merchandising business in Chenago County, New York, and joining with two brothers-in-law named Gilbert, in the spring of 1856 they bought land and the mill property of Gage & Read, at the mouth of the Eau Claire River, for $42,000. The following year, using a small downpayment, they purchased Carson & Eaton's mill, more land, water power, and booming privileges on the Eau Claire River.[11] Obviously the new firm had ample capital and sound credit. When Chapman & Thorp bought the establishment of Gage & Read they paid $29,000 of the purchase price, leaving only $13,000 to be mortgaged. On their arrival in Eau Claire they were reputed to be worth some $20–30,000 in capital, while the Gilberts were also supposed to have large assets. Further finances were to be realised from the sale of town lots. Given such a sound financial backing, the firm had invested in property which had great potential.[12]

Success now depended on two main factors, namely the entrepreneurial skill of the two resident partners and the future status of the lumber market, which, in 1857, was depressed. Chapman

---

[10] There were actually six firms processing lumber, but J. F. Stone & Co. of Bridge Creek ran a combined saw- and gristmill. As the value of flour was higher than that of lumber, this firm was classified as a gristmill.

[11] D. & B. vol. 8: 3; Randall, 1: 190–191; Hotchkiss, 482; Bailey, 373–374; Kleven, 335–337.

[12] D. & B. vol. 8: 3; This estimate of the company's wealth differs from that made by Randall, who seemed to think that the partners had $250,000 when they came to Eau Claire. However, the two sources agree on the purchase price of the Carson & Eaton lots at about $125,000.

and Thorp were quick to assert their managerial capacity. They began improvements to their property almost immediately by building a large steam sawmill and flouring mill costing some $10–15,000. The steam mill was initially equipped with a mulley saw, a siding saw, a rotary saw, and a lath saw, combining the older, slower machinery with more modern machinery. Then in the fall of 1858 a slabber and stock gang saw were added which increased the capacity of the mill by some 35,000 feet per day. The following February improvements were made to the piers, the rafting slides, and the boom. By January, 1860, Chapman & Thorpe had three sawmills, one steam- and two water-powered, a flour mill, and control of the water power on the Eau Claire River. By January, 1861, they had also started to build a large dam on the Eau Claire River. Moreover the partners were not content to stay only in the lumber business; they also ran a large store and a boardinghouse and engaged in farming to supplement local food supplies.[13]

The partners also skillfully survived the depression of the late 1850's by drawing on capital reserves at the same time as they laid foundations for an extension of their market threshold. As early as January, 1857, Chapman went to St. Louis to supervise the downstream marketing operations of the company. The price of lumber was very low in 1858 and the partners had difficulty in meeting all their liabilities. They managed, however, to get an extension on their debts, and when the downriver prospects improved in the spring of 1859, consequent on new building in St. Louis, they quickly took advantage of the situation. By the summer of 1859 they were doing a heavy business for the times. The lumber market held fairly steady in the next two years and the firm increased its output and profit; indeed it was considered the most reliable firm in the Chippewa area. A combination of solid financial assets, good credit, and managerial competence both in improving plant and in increasing sales explained this success.[14]

The other two major lumber companies in Eau Claire in 1860

[13] D. & B. vol. 8: 56; *Eau Claire Free Press,* Sept. 23, 1858; Feb. 24, 1859.

[14] D. & B. vol. 8: 56; A. M. Dole to Ingram & Kennedy, Sept. 23, 1858; John Whitehall & Co., to Ingram & Kennedy, Sept. 3, 1860; I. Plume, to Dole, Ingram & Kennedy, Oct. 1, 1860, Ingram Papers, State Historical Society of Wisconsin; Randall, 1: 190; Bailey, 374.

revealed business characteristics similar to those of Chapman & Thorp. The firm of Shaw & Bullen, which had the second highest value added in 1860 was also of recent origin. Daniel Shaw, formerly of Maine, and Allegheny County, New York, where he had a substantial business, came to Wisconsin to look over the Chippewa pineries in 1855. The following year he bought a large tract of pineland on the Chippewa River near the outlet at Half Moon Lake.[15]

Although wealthy himself, Shaw still needed additional finances and the co-operation of other businessmen in order to succeed in the late 1850's. This aid was forthcoming in several ways. He borrowed money from George Bradstreet of Maine at 7 per cent interest.[16] He persuaded his brother-in-law Charles Bullen, who had technical knowledge of lumbering, to join the business. Then, to facilitate the movement of logs from river to lake, he co-operated with other lumber firms in securing a special charter from the state legislature granting permission to excavate a canal from the Chippewa River to Half Moon Lake. When the canal was completed, a sheer boom was built across the river to divert the logs into the lake for storage. This undertaking would have been too expensive for a single firm, but working in conjunction with other establishments, Shaw was able to improve his business facilities.[17]

The Shaw Lumber Company, again like Chapman & Thorp, was willing to build new plant and use modern equipment. Daniel Shaw got his cousin Noah, the superintendent of his New York sawmill, to go to Eau Claire and design a frontier sawmill. In order to ensure the high quality of the operation, Noah Shaw imported the machinery for the mill and the equipment with which to build the mill from New York. By 1858 the steampowered mill, containing a large rotary saw, a siding saw, one edger, one slab saw, one shingle machine, one drag saw, and two

[15] D. & B. vol. 8: 8; Randall, 1: 187–188; Arthur R. Reynolds, *The Daniel Shaw Lumber Company: A Case Study of the Wisconsin Lumbering Frontier* (New York, 1957), 7; Forester, 388; Bailey, 375; Willard F. Miller, "A History of Eau Claire County During the Civil War" (unpublished M.S. thesis, University of Wisconsin, 1954), 9.

[16] Miller, 9, citing the Northwest Lumber Company records; D. &. B. vol. 8: 8 states that Constant Cook, president of the Bank of Bath, New York, was involved in the firm.

[17] Bailey, 375; Randall, 1: 78–79.

lath saws, was producing 14,000 feet of lumber, 8,000 shingles, and 8,000 pieces of lath a day.[18]

Despite these arrangements the Shaw Company had to struggle to survive the depressed economic conditions of the late 1850's intact. In mid-1858 there was doubt about their credit reliability and their capacity to meet their debts. The partners managed to stay in business, but not until mid-1861 were they able to meet some of their liabilities, and not until early 1863 were they considered to be financially sound. This predicament did not seem to stem from poor sales tactics, for like other firms in the Chippewa River Valley, Daniel Shaw & Co. had a traveling agent who looked after sales in the downriver towns.[19] Marketing procedures may not have been as efficient as those of rival firms, but the main reason for the difficulties was the condition of the lumber market rather than the internal structure of the firm. When the price of lumber was low, as it was in the late 1850's, and payments on shipments were slow in being made, then the Shaw Company lacked the financial reserves to carry on smoothly. The company did not have capital reserves to draw upon in slack times, and thus its expansion was determined by the condition of the lumber market, which in turn reflected general economic conditions. This was in contrast to Chapman & Thorp, which seemed to command the assets for growth even in hard times.

The third large lumber company in Eau Claire County in 1860, Dole, Ingram & Kennedy, was also a new concern, established in 1857. All three partners came from Canada, where they had managed lumber firms, though Ingram had also worked in New York lumber mills prior to going to Canada. Although well qualified for the lumbering business, they were not well endowed with capital, having only some $10–15,000 between them. In fact Dole remained in Canada to work, in order to secure some $6,000 for purchasing timber lands. Even then over $30,000 had to be borrowed from various sources to buy land and build a mill. The strictest economy was needed to see them safely through not only the first year, but also the rest of the 1850's.[20]

[18] D. & B. vol. 8: 8; *Eau Claire Free Press*, Sept. 23, 1858; Reynolds, 7.
[19] D. & B. vol. 8: 8; Miller, 8; Reynolds, 105.
[20] D. & B. vol. 8: 7; A. M. Dole to O. H. Ingram, May 30, 1857; A. M. Dole to Ingram & Kennedy, Oct. 8, 1857; Feb. 6, 1858; Oct. 8, 1859, Ingram Papers; Kleven, 343; Randall, 1: 197; Miller, 6–8; Forester, 423.

Tight finances notwithstanding, the company did not skimp in the construction of their sawmill. This mill, built in the fall of 1857, started operations the following spring, and by September two gang saws, a mulley saw, a double edger, and a butting saw cut, on the average, 15,000 feet a day. Early in 1859 further improvements were made on the boom, thus easing shipments of logs. In 1859, also, the firm opened lumber yards at Reeds Landing, Minnesota, and at Dubuque, Iowa, to improve the retail and marketing side of the business. By 1860 more lumber yards were opened at McGregor, Iowa, and East St. Louis, Illinois, to take greater advantage of the downstream trade.[21]

Shortage of capital was one element retarding progress, but of equal importance was the poor market for lumber. Lumber prices rose slowly from a low of $8 per thousand in 1858 to some $12 by 1860. Such prices meant meager returns. The market was better for secondary processed wood such as lath, shingles, sashes, and doors; but even these sales were made on a long-term payment basis of from six to nine months, which further inhibited growth. Then the election of Abraham Lincoln and the threat of sectional troubles slowed down the lumber trade, and in 1861 the price of lumber fell to $6 as business in St. Louis drew to a standstill. It was not until 1863 that wartime business conditions gave the firm increased trade and enabled Dole, Ingram & Kennedy to make large profits.[22]

In 1860 three major lumber firms in Eau Claire shared certain characteristics which were necessary for survival, if indeed not for success, in antebellum northwestern Wisconsin. The entrepreneurs were all newcomers to the region about 1856–57, and thus had not had to struggle through the late 1840's and early 1850's. They were experienced in industrial management, and usually, though not necessarily, in the lumber business. They all had partners or agents in the downriver towns to supervise the retail side of the business and, most important of all, they had capital to

[21] D. & B. vol. 8: 7; A. M. Dole to Ingram & Kennedy, Sept. 26, Oct. 8, Nov. 11, 1857; Sept. 7, 10, 24, 1859; O. H. Ingram to D. Kennedy, Nov. 12, 1860, Ingram Papers; *Eau Claire Free Press*, Sept. 28, 1858; Kleven, 343; Miller, 6–8, 20–21.

[22] D. & B. vol. 8: 7; O. H. Ingram to D. Kennedy, Aug. 3, 11, 1859; Nov. 17, 1860; A. M. Dole to Ingram & Kennedy, Aug. 29, Sept. 29, 1859; R. Mussey & Co., to Dole Ingram & Kennedy, Feb. 11, 1861; W. H. Pardee to Dole, Ingram & Kennedy, May 14, 1861, Ingram Papers; Miller, 20–21.

spend, either on improving their plant and equipment or in buying more timber land. It might not be entirely correct to conclude that success had a direct correlation with a firm's available capital, for entrepreneurial skill, seasonal hazards, poor sales, and slow payments for lumber were significant variables; but it seems probable that the less capital a firm had, so its chances of survival decreased.

The crucial importance of capital can be attested to by reference to three other important lumber firms in the area.[23] Time of arrival in the Chippewa Valley was not necessarily critical, for Carson & Eaton, which became Carson & Rand in 1860, and Knapp & Co., survived the 1850's to emerge as large corporations in the 1860's. Business experience of some kind, often in lumbering, was common in most firms; William Carson, John Knapp, and Hiram S. Allen all had long experience in lumbering in the Valley itself. Attention to retail sales was necessary; all large firms employed agents downriver, and most operated their own lumber yards in order to reduce business costs. But capital was vital. Both Carson & Eaton and Knapp Stout & Co. had large assets which enabled them to make improvements to their property and to survive the shocks of the late 1850's with very little trouble. But Hiram Allen of H.S. Allen & Co., and later of the Chippewa Falls Company, seemed unable to obtain sufficient funds to meet his commitments. Flood damage in the summer of 1855, followed by poor sales in late 1857, further flood damage in 1858, the poor state of the lumber market in 1858 and 1859, and financial chicanery within the firm in 1859 impeded the two companies' growth.[24]

The small companies which did not survive the economic turmoil of the late 1850's presented a sharp contrast to the large, successful enterprises. Information on these firms is difficult to obtain, but it seems that they were essentially local operations. Lack-

---

[23] The firms of H. S. Allen & Co., Chippewa Falls; Carson & Eaton, Eau Galle; and Knapp Stout & Co., Menomonee, were all major lumber enterprises in the Chippewa River Valley, having respective value added and employment figures of $90,000 and 250 workers; $53,140 and 124 workers; and $71,700 and 250 workers.

[24] D. & B. vol. 8: 1, 11, 30, 36, 48, 51, 166, 167; John H. Knapp Diaries, 1848, 1859, 1860, 1861, and John H. Knapp, Daily Memorandum Book, 1851, Knapp Papers, State Historical Society of Wisconsin; Hotchkiss, 477–478, 490–491; Kleven, 329, 355; Randall, 1: 52–53.

ing substantial financial resources, they could not meet the problems posed by poor lumber prices, delayed payments, seasonal flooding, older machinery, and the cost of paying downriver agents. They thus concentrated on neighborhood rather than regional markets.

Three small Eau Claire firms reported in the 1860 census were typical. D. Kendall operated his mill only three months of the year and hired only one workman. He concentrated on the jobbing business. Smith *et al.* operated throughout the year and employed ten laborers, but only produced 200,000 feet of lumber or 1.3 per cent of the county total. The third firm, J.F. Stone & Co., employed three workers and produced 300,000 feet of lumber. However, the proprietor obtained a larger income from his flour mill, suggesting that his enterprise catered to neighborhood needs. These three firms thus resembled pioneer village sawmills in the less well-endowed areas of Wisconsin.

Lumber manufacturing in antebellum Eau Claire County consisted both of very large and very small operations, with the former taking by far the leading role. Entrepreneurial skill was definitely important in the big firms, for slack sales and low prices meant that it was essential to know what kinds of lumber were in demand, at what times of the year, and at which particular locations downriver. But business ability itself was of little avail without money to keep the establishment working. Capital in large quantities was needed for the construction of the mill, dams, and piers, for the importation of machinery, for constant repairs, and for the regular payment of labor. When the lumber market was slow, the firms whose operations were geared to the downriver markets simply had to have financial reserves. Lacking plentiful capital they would probably collapse.

Secondary Lumber Processing

In 1860 three firms were engaged in the secondary processing of construction materials in Eau Claire County. In comparison to the sawmills, they were small enterprises, having an average capital invested of $5,433 and an average value added of $2,997. These firms seemed to cater mainly to a local market, and they found difficulty in competing with the lower transport costs of the larger establishments for the downstream trade in lath, pickets, sashes, and doors.

Adin Randall, the largest of the three, offered a wide variety of construction materials and in 1859 was prepared to supply goods anywhere on the Mississippi River between Eau Claire and St. Louis. But when the firm changed hands in 1860, its trade seems to have contracted, for the partners advertised their sashes, doors, and blinds mainly to farmers from whom they would take wheat as payment. The other two firms, A. Kendal *et al.* and J. & P. McNear, employed fewer workers and enjoyed less profit, suggesting a more restricted clientele.[25]

Secondary lumber processing in antebellum Eau Claire County was not a well developed industry. The main economic concern in the county was to produce lumber for sale in the downriver prairie markets. If more refined processing of lumber would bring a higher profit, the large mills were willing to undertake that function themselves rather than turn it over to other firms. Therefore the cost of purchasing rough lumber, processing it into construction materials, and then transporting it downstream proved too high for small independent firms. Their market was local, and, in view of the small population in Eau Claire County in 1860 — namely 3,164 — was correspondingly restricted.

Other Manufactures

The remainder of the manufacturing establishments in Eau Claire in 1860 contributed some 10 per cent of the county's value added. (Table 18.) These manufactures were a composite of processing branches such as flour milling and brewing, and of household-craft consumer branches such as boots, shoes, and tin-smithing. They were, for the most part, small firms, the largest among them having a capital of $8,000, producing goods either on a custom basis or for limited sales.

The two gristmills ground grain to order. J.F. Stone ran a combination grist- and sawmill, and the smaller mill was part of the lumbering complex of Dole, Ingram & Kennedy. This establishment made a very small profit. Presumably it was run to process wheat grown on the company lands. These two mills, together

---

[25] MCSW, Eau Claire County, 1860; *Eau Claire Free Press,* Feb. 17, 1859, adv.; Feb. 23, Sept. 20, 1860, advs.

with establishments which might have been adjuncts to the larger lumbering operations and others too small to be included in the census, did not meet the needs of the local population. The general merchandise stores imported flour from downstream, indicating the lack of local wheat and local flour mills.[26]

Brewing was a comparatively new venture in antebellum Eau Claire. Schaefer & Leinenkugel built the North Eau Claire Brewery late in 1858. Although the proprietors hoped to sell their lager to a wide area, the value of the product in 1860 indicated that the market was both local and restricted. Another brewery established in Eau Claire late in 1859 was either too small to be classified as a manufacturing establishment or had collapsed prior to the taking of the 1860 census.[27]

Household-craft consumer goods were usually made on a custom basis both by artisans and by merchant-manufacturers. These articles, however, were also imported for sale by general merchandise stores. For example, boots and shoes were made to order by John Betz, but they were also retailed by merchant-manufacturers like T.U. Rowath and in the general store of Dole, Ingram & Kennedy. Tinware was made in the town of Eau Claire by Richards & Teaksley, but it was also sold in the hardware store of N.J. Bridges. Ready-made clothing was retailed by William Newton, but dressmaking establishments were located in Eau Claire. Fanning mills were made by A. Hendershott, and J.W. French, a blacksmith, made plows, wagons and sleighs. Yet J.I. Case's threshing machines, Blake & Eliot's fanning mills, and McCormick's reapers and mowers were advertised by local agents.[28] Most household consumer goods were certainly not made in establishments with a value of product over $500. Some items were probably produced by craftsmen who commanded a very small trade or who worked part-time as lumbermen or farmers. But prior to the Civil War most articles seemed to be imported either upriver from

[26] A. M. Dole to Ingram & Kennedy, Jan. 25, 1858, and Jan. 25, 1860, Ingram Papers; *Eau Claire Free Press*, Sept. 23, 1858, adv.

[27] MCSW, Eau Claire County, 1860; *Eau Claire Free Press*, Jan. 6, Dec. 29, 1859, advs.

[28] D. & B. vol. 8: 6, 9, 10, 63; MCSW, Eau Claire County, 1860; A. M. Dole to Ingram & Kennedy, Jan. 25, 1860, Ingram Papers; *Eau Claire Free Press*, Oct. 21, 1858, adv.; Aug. 4, 11, Dec. 1, 1859; Apr. 19, June 7, Sept. 12, Oct. 31, adv., 1861.

St. Louis or later by rail from Milwaukee and then upriver from Prairie du Chien or La Crosse.

Conclusion

The manufacturing structure of pioneer Eau Claire County was essentially monolithic, focusing on the sawing and planing of lumber from the readily accessible pineries. By contrast, Winnebago County in northeastern Wisconsin had developed a broader-based industrial economy, using not only nearby lumber resources but also agricultural resources. Moreover other branches of manufacturing provided some of the building and household needs of a larger local population. Eau Claire manufacturing was highly concentrated on lumber processing done by large firms, moving ahead of a settled population. Yet even in the hard times of the late 1850's, these substantial firms had to struggle to survive. Insofar as other industries were established, they were usually too small to be reported in the census. Eau Claire manufacturing was only getting off the ground in the antebellum years.

CHAPTER SIX

Racine County: Sophisticated Pioneer Manufacturing in the Wisconsin Wheat Belt

RACINE COUNTY, located in the heart of the fertile prairie belt spanning southeastern Wisconsin and northeastern Illinois, had potential for developing industries focused on agricultural production. As in Jefferson County, accessible raw materials provided the inputs for primary processing industries, notably flour milling, and, to a lesser extent, tanning, meatpacking, brewing, and wool carding. But in addition, agriculture also functioned as a market incentive to manufacturing in Racine, owing to the more southerly and lakeshore location and to the early settlement which supplied an initial advantage.[1] The high demand for specialized farming equipment created a fairly sophisticated agricultural implements industry, with ancillary iron and wagon branches. With their forward and backward linkages, these in turn acted as growth sectors for servicing industries. By 1860 Racine County had developed a mature range and scale of manufacturing activities, hertofore unexpected in a recently settled farming area.

Indeed the demands of commercial prairie farming and its lakeside site appear to have combined in Racine County not only to stimulate certain branches of manufacturing, but also to encourage the development of an urban center as a focus of these activities. For Racine city, with approximately 40 per cent of the

---

[1] For details on the early settlement of the county, see Schafer, *Four Wisconsin Counties*, 56–139; *History of Racine and Kenosha Counties, Wisconsin* (Chicago, 1879), *passim*; *Racine, Belle City of the Lakes and Racine County, Wisconsin* (Chicago, 1916), *passim*; Michael N. Margosian, "Town Promotion in Early Day Racine" (unpublished M.S. thesis, University of Wisconsin, Milwaukee, 1966), *passim*.

county's population in the antebellum years, was responsible for some 90 per cent of the county's manufacturing, measured either by value added or by number of workers.[2] Racine city served not only as the county supply center, but also as the locus of state and perhaps regional markets in at least one branch of manufacturing. With one in 11.5 persons employed in industry in 1860, compared to one in thirteen for Milwaukee at the same date, Racine already appeared to have attained a predominantly manufacturing economy.[3]

Though proportionately the city of Racine may have been more industrialized than the city of Milwaukee, yet neither Racine nor Racine County could rival its larger neighbor in its share of the Wisconsin manufacturing aggregate. Racine County provided only 10.5 per cent of the state's manufacturing by value added in 1850, and 4.5 per cent in 1860, in contrast to Milwaukee's contribution of 22.8 per cent and 27.3 per cent. Although increasing the absolute value added by some 37 per cent to $545,344 in 1860, and maintaining its position as the second leading industrial county in Wisconsin, Racine did not have the necessary local urban market nor the labor threshold to develop economies of scale and high productivity in a variety of industries.

The one branch of manufacturing in which Racine made an outstanding contribution to the Wisconsin total was that of agricultural implements, producing approximately one third of the state's farm machinery in both 1850 and 1860. The contribution of iron products, which often provided machinery and castings for the agricultural industries, increased from 5.8 to 13.7 per cent of the state's aggregate during the 1850's. But in other industries,

[2] This tendency becomes stronger after Racine County was reduced in size from 610 square miles to 337 square miles, following the establishment of Kenosha County in 1850. *Origin and Legislative History of County Boundaries in Wisconsin*, 164. Racine city had a population of 3,647 in 1847 or 18.7 per cent of the county total; 5,880 in 1850 or 39.7 per cent of total; 9,520 in 1855 or 46.1 per cent of the total; and 7,831 in 1860 or 36.7 percent of the total. "Census of Wisconsin From the Year 1836 to 1860 Inclusive. Compiled from Official Sources for the *Wisconsin State Journal*," by H. A. Tenney, *Census of Wisconsin* (pamphlet, n.p. n.d.).

[3] Richard L. Brown, "An Economic Base Study of Racine, Wisconsin" (unpublished M.S. thesis, University of Wisconsin, 1952), 8, suggests that the transition from commerce and handicrafts industry to manufatcuring as the dominant economic activity was achieved when manufacturing employed one in ten of the population. (The figures quoted are a ratio of number of hands employed, in industries having an annual value of over $500, to the total city population.)

most notably flour milling, Racine County lost relative status in
the ranking of Wisconsin's leading counties. For example, Racine
produced 11.3 per cent of Wisconsin's flour in 1850, but only 3.1
per cent in 1860; the county produced 17.4 per cent of the state's
boots and shoes in 1850, but only seven per cent in 1860; or 12.4
per cent of Wisconsin's furniture in 1850, but only 3.1 per cent
in 1860. The settlement of new areas in central and northern
Wisconsin augmented the state's manufacturing activities and
reduced the relative contribution of the older regions. Racine
County was only able to maintain its leading or a high position
in industries for which it had locational or initial advantages of
production.

As might be expected of the second-ranking county, Racine's
manufacturing establishments were larger than the average Wisconsin firm, employing six men in 1850 compared to 4.8 for Wisconsin, and 6.3 in 1860 compared to 5.4 for the state. This average
figure for the county was a combination of factories and establishments employing three or four hands. The self-employed operator
and the very small firm were few in number. However, the Racine firms did not increase as rapidly in the 1850's as their Wisconsin counterparts, having only a 6 per cent growth rate compared to
a 12 per cent rate for the state. But, unlike firms in Milwaukee
County, they did expand during the decade; and furthermore the
Racine city firms, dominated by the agricultural implements
branch, increased by 16 per cent, so that by 1860 they employed
7.3 men each — making them larger than the average Milwaukee
city establishment with its 6.1 hands. Though minute in comparison to the lumber firms in the northern counties, the Racine
establishments were in the forefront of the older areas of the southeast, where manufacturing was centered on agriculture, and they
compared favorably with the urban manufacturing complex of
Milwaukee.

Yet the average size of Racine manufacturing operations did
not necessarily indicate sophistication in the methods of production. Increasing size was only one prerequisite of industrialization.
Motive power, machine technology, output per worker, division
of labor, capital investment, and entrepreneurial initiative were
other critical variables. With respect to motive power, however,
Racine was in the Wisconsin vanguard, even if by default rather
than by choice. The county, unlike Winnebago, Jefferson, or

even Grant, was unable to boast of its abundant water resources and thus had to look for alternatives at an early date. In the city of Racine, steam power was used in flour mills, foundries, and agricultural works by 1850, if not sooner. The dependence on steam, which in the long run was more stable and efficient (though initially more expensive) than water, may have encouraged technological and managerial innovations which were not so readily adopted in plants driven by water. Use of steam power was mainly confined to Racine city, making any comparison of steam and water power an urban-rural comparison, which may not take into account economies of scale resulting from an urban and port environment. Yet it should be noted that flouring mills scattered throughout the county yielded a higher net gain if driven by steam.[4] Furthermore the leading establishments did use steam power in some capacity, which seems to imply some direct — though not necessarily causal — relationship between size and steam.

The overall average value added per worker in Racine was higher than in Wisconsin, the respective figures being $672 and $609 in 1850, and $698 and $656 in 1860. But, as with firm size, the rate of increase in value added per worker in the county during the 1850's was slower than in the state. This narrowing of differential growth did not stem solely from the use of different base levels. Racine definitely lagged behind the state in productivity in the household-craft consumer group in 1860, having an average value added per worker of $422 as compared with $477. There was also a notable drop in the value added per worker in the processing group, from $930 in 1850 to $786 in 1860, although the county still maintained a higher average than the state. These declines may, however, be interpreted in a positive light with respect to industrial sophistication; namely that craft work was dying out and neighborhood processing was giving way as transportation widened market horizons.

---

[4] Milling was the only industry in which the two kinds of motive power could be effectively compared. In other branches of manufacturing, such as agricultural implements or machinery, the comparison was in terms of horse and hand as opposed to horse and steam. The four flour mills powered by water in 1850 had an average value added of $9,035, while the two powered by steam had an average value added of $33,992. In 1860 the five mills running on water had a value added of $3,606 each, while the two running on steam had an average value added of $21,918. MCSW, Racine County, 1850 and 1860.

But though worker productivity in Racine County was relatively high, division of labor was minimal. Even in the large heavy-goods establishments such as J.I. Case's reaper factory, A.P. Dickey's machine shop, and T. Falvey's machine works, craftsmen used their individual skills within separate departments.[5] Little attempt was made to obtain any cost advantage by reducing the quality or quantity of labor required, although some benefit was obtained from the assemblage and fabrication of raw materials in a central location and from greater managerial supervision. In large shoe and clothing establishments employing fifteen or more workers, the situation was less progressive, for all the work was done by hand. At most the large firms in Racine could be called well-developed manufactories; at least they were merely functional gatherings of craftsmen.

This lack of sophistication in organization and production may in part have resulted from meager local supplies of capital. In 1860 the three banks in Racine the city reported a net worth of only $500,084, or 3.3 per cent of the assets available in Wisconsin. Furthermore these finances were not readily available for loan to manufacturers, but tended to be given for agricultural or railroad development. This situation was made worse by the fact that there was proportionately less capital attracted to Racine for launching manufacturing ventures than there was to the city of Milwaukee or to the lumbering industry. Certainly some entrepreneurs came with money or had Eastern connections, but many others appear to have had little, if any, ready cash or credit, and thus had to attain the rank of manufacturer with limited assets.[6] The Racine environment may well have been conducive to the rapid development of manufacturing branches focused on agriculture, but most businessmen could look forward to little or no local financial aid.

That many entrepreneurs succeeded in expanding their enterprises, despite the stringent conditions of the late 1850's, attests to their managerial initiative and competence. On the supply

[5] *Racine Advocate,* Nov. 6, 27, 1854; Apr. 1, 1857; March 27, 1861; Reynold M. Wik, "J. I. Case: Some Experiences of an Early Wisconsin Industrialist," *Wis. Mag. Hist.,* 35 (1951–52), 6.

[6] R. E. Ela to Abigail Ela, July, 1836; R. E. Ela to his father, Sept. 4, 1838; William G. Ela to R. E. Ela, Nov. 1841, Ela Papers, State Historical Society of Wisconsin; D. & B. vol. 47: 10, 17, 18, 19, 27, 41, 47, 53, 83, 94, 120.

side they often exchanged or sold materials and finished goods to each other. With production, quality control and efficiency were stressed rather than mechanization. In marketing, however, manufacturers were ready to take more risks by adopting and innovating techniques suitable to the agricultural Midwest. Sales were made on a credit basis; agents were sent throughout the county and even the state to sell merchandise; and newspapers and journal advertisements were used extensively. A favorable sellers' market was exploited to best advantage.[7]

Manufacturing Activities in Racine County

The industrial structure of antebellum Racine County evolved from that of a pioneer self-sufficient economy through transitional phases to develop a wide range of manufactures and a leading agricultural implements sector. In 1840, about four years after initial settlement, manufacturing was understandably focused on lumber planed and sawed and house construction; these two branches accounted for approximately two thirds of the total value of product of $64,520. Other limited activities, such as tanning and making furniture, bricks, and wagons likewise catered to the basic needs of recently arrived settlers.

By 1850 manufacturing had both widened in scope and increased in output, attaining a value added of $397,003. (Table 19.) Over one quarter of this total was contributed by flour milling; agricultural implements supplied another 15 per cent, indicating the important backward and forward linkages of commercial prairie agriculture. There was a broad scatter of other industries both of the processing variety and the craft-consumer variety, all of which catered mainly to domestic household needs.

Ten years later, in 1860, the industrial profile had rounded out, and each of the four manufacturing groups contributed at least one sixth of the county aggregate. (Table 20.) This distributional change was due primarily to the decline in flour milling, which now supplied only 11.3 per cent of the county value added,

[7] *Racine Advocate,* July 2, 1851, adv.; March 16, 1853, adv.; Nov. 6, 1854; July 2, adv., July 9, Nov. 24, 1856; Apr. 1, 29, 1857; June 16, 1858, adv.; July 13, 1859, adv.; Jan. 16, 1860; March 27, 1861, adv.; *Wisconsin Farmer,* 2 (1850), adv.; 3 (1851), adv.; 5 (1853), adv.; "Old Notes, Receipts, Orders for Machines," 1850's, and letters from J. I. Case to his wife, 1849–1853, both in the J. I. Case Papers; also miscellaneous correspondence, 1840's and 1850's, in the Ela Papers.

TABLE 19

MANUFACTURING IN RACINE COUNTY, 1850

(Value Added in Current $'s.)

Industry	Value Added	Per Cent of Total	No. of Workers	Per Cent of Total
Processing Industries				
Lumber	13,300	3.35	24	4.06
Flour	108,117	27.23	27	4.57
Cooperage	14,805	3.73	41	6.94
Liquors	3,850	0.97	1	0.17
Leather	21,236	5.35	32	5.41
Construction Materials	16,424	4.14	54	9.14
Meat Packing	18,360	4.62	31	5.25
Minerals	9,030	2.27	16	2.71
Soap and Candles	10,596	2.67	6	1.02
Aggregate	215,718	54.33	232	39.27
Household-Craft Consumer				
Boots and Shoes	30,660	7.73	52	8.80
Clothing	7,749	1.95	50	8.46
Furniture	19,601	4.94	38	6.43
Blacksmiths	8,588	2.16	18	3.05
Confectionery	3,350	0.84	8	1.35
Tin, Copper etc.	10,188	2.57	20	3.38
Aggregate	80,136	20.19	186	31.47
Agricultural Industries				
Agricultural Impls.	59,476	14.98	77	13.03
Wagons	19,439	4.90	46	7.78
Aggregate	78,915	19.88	123	20.81
Other Industries				
Iron	11,207	2.83	21	3.55
Paper	6,483	1.63	22	3.72
Miscellaneous	4,544	1.14	7	1.18
Aggregate	22,234	5.60	50	8.45
Racine County	397,003	100.00	591	100.00

[SOURCE: Manuscript Census for the State of Wisconsin, 1850. Racine County.]

and the increase in agricultural implements and iron products. Within this grouping agriculture still supplied the main stimulus to manufacturing, but the emphasis had shifted from providing raw materials to providing markets. Again, as in 1850, other industries either catered to limited household needs or supplied services for the agricultural branches.

Antebellum Racine County was thus distinctive within the Wisconsin industrial framework because of its wide range of activity and the relatively small percentage of county output supplied by the leading industry — flour milling in 1850 and agricultural implements in 1860. These branches contributed 27.2 and 26.8 per cent respectively, compared to 57.6 and 54.8 per cent for the leading industry in the average Wisconsin County. Racine also fell below the average county figure when the contributions of its two leading industries are taken together. Outputs of 42.4 per cent in 1850 and 41.8 per cent in 1860 were lower than the Wisconsin figures of 71 and 70.4 per cent for the same years. The Racine pattern thus contrasted markedly with that of the northern counties, where lumber processing provided the bulk of manufacturing. But several counties in southern and south-central Wisconsin also had less than 30 per cent of their value added in any one industry and approximately 40 per cent in their two leading industries. Racine was more typical of the diversified manufacturing style of the older settled and more heavily populated areas of Wisconsin.

AGRICULTURAL INDUSTRIES

Agricultural Implements

The rapid growth of wheat production in the western portions of the Old Northwest during the 1840's and 1850's was a response both to improved market conditions at home and abroad, and to better transportation networks which opened the national and international markets to interior farmers. But an equally decisive factor in this spread of wheat culture was the introduction and improvement of agricultural equipment suitable to prairie farming.[8] Plows to break the tough prairie sod and survive the climate

_____

[8] For discussions of the various factors involved in the growth of large-scale commercial farming in the Midwestern prairies, see W. N. Parker and J. L. Klein, "Productivity Growth in Grain Production in the United States, 1840–1860 and

TABLE 20

MANUFACTURING IN RACINE COUNTY, 1860

(Value Added in Current $'s.)

Industry	Value Added	Per Cent of Total	No. of Workers	Per Cent of Total
Processing Industries				
Lumber	2,000	0.37	6	0.77
Flour	61,764	11.33	33	4.23
Cooperage	11,090	2.03	35	4.48
Liquors	14,594	2.67	15	1.92
Leather	43,069	7.90	34	4.35
Construction Materials	17,268	3.17	48	6.15
Meat Packing	25,591	4.69	20	2.56
Wool	2,405	0.44	14	1.79
Minerals	6,736	1.24	23	2.94
Tobacco	2,120	0.39	8	1.02
Soap and Candles	365	0.07	2	0.26
Aggregate	187,002	34.30	238	30.47
Household-Craft Consumer				
Boots and Shoes	34,139	6.26	94	12.04
Clothing	29,457	5.40	79	10.12
Furniture	13,025	2.39	18	2.30
Blacksmiths	4,325	0.79	8	1.02
Confectionery	4,565	0.84	10	1.28
Tin, Copper etc.	9.527	1.75	16	2.05
Aggregate	95,038	17.43	225	28.81
Agricultural Industries				
Agricultural Impls.	146,090	26.79	179	22.92
Wagons	9,340	1.71	27	3.46
Aggregate	155,430	28.50	206	26.38
Other Industries				
Iron	81,970	15.03	49	6.27
Paper	9,621	1.76	35	4.48
Gas	4,541	0.83	4	0.51
Miscellaneous	11,742	2.15	24	3.08
Aggregate	107,874	19.77	112	14.34
Racine County	545,344	100.00	781	100.00

[SOURCE: Manuscript Census for the State of Wisconsin, 1860. Racine County.]

intact, time- and labor-saving threshers and separators, reapers and harvesters, grain cultivators, broadcast sowers, harrows, and seed drills were all available for purchase at midcentury.[9] Although few Midwestern farmers bought specialized machines such as planters, most owned a plow and fanning mill, and a steadily increasing number purchased threshers and reapers. The market for agricultural implements in southern Wisconsin and northern Illinois in the 1840's and 1850's was potentially large.

Racine County was well placed for the development of a farm machinery industry focused on the prosperous wheat-growing region of the newer Old Northwest. The market was readily accessible; so were the raw materials. Wood could be brought from several parts of Wisconsin and iron imported by water from Pennsylvania. All that was needed to take advantage of the location were competent entrepreneurs to exploit first the local and then the regional market. Ready capital could ensure more rapid success, but it was not imperative. In the wheat growing boom of the late 1840's and early 1850's, hard work backed by managerial skill seemed to be a substitute for ample money supplies. To be sure, there had to be some capital on which to fall back in times of crisis; but in an expanding market, a little would go a long way.

Ambitious entrepreneurs were quick to realize the potential of Racine County as an agricultural implements center. As early as 1838 Richard E. Ela had made arrangements for establishing a fanning mill shop at Rochester. Although the region was badly hurt by the depression of the late 1830's, and cash was still scarce in 1840, Ela still expected to sell fifty mills at $25 each in 1841. By 1842 he was making 100 fanning mills a year and was branch-

1900–1910," in *Output, Employment and Productivity in the United States after 1800* (National Bureau of Economic Research, *Studies in Income and Wealth*, Vol. 30, New York, 1966), 523–546; George R. Taylor, *The Transportation Revolution, 1815–1860* (New York, 1951), 1–102; Paul W. Gates, *The Farmers Age: Agriculture, 1815–1860* (New York, 1960), 156–196; Paul A. David, "The Mechanization of Reaping in the Ante-Bellum Midwest," in Henry Rosofsky (ed.), *Industrialization in Two Systems* (New York, 1966), 3–39; Leo Rogin, *The Introduction of Farm Machinery in Its Relation to the Productivity of Labor in the Agriculture of the United States During the Nineteenth Century* (Berkeley, 1931), *passim;* J. F. Clark, *passim;* Fishlow, *passim.*

[9] Rogin, *passim;* R. L. Ardrey, *American Agricultural Implements* (Chicago, 1894), 5–146; *Wisconsin Farmer*, 1–15 (1849–1863), *passim.*

ing out into the manufacture of plows and wagons.[10] Thus, despite economic crises in a newly settled area, a promising start had been made.

The 1840's witnessed a steady growth of the agricultural implements industry, especially in threshing equipment. Jerome I. Case, who moved from Rochester (in Racine County) to Racine city in 1844, soon had many orders for his threshers. Three years later he needed to build a three-story shop to cope with increased demand; three years later, in 1850, he produced approximately 100 threshing machines. Lucius Blake, who came to Racine village as a carpenter in 1839, began manufacturing fanning mills in 1844. The business proved so remunerative that he and his partner James Eliot made between 100 and 300 mills a year. Albert P. Dickey started making fanning mills in Racine in 1845. Using his eleven years experience and capital gained in this business both in New York and Chicago, he ran a very profitable enterprise. By 1850 he was making about 625 fanning mills annually. The proprietors of the Racine Foundry were prepared to manufacture agricultural implements as well as specialized mill castings in the 1840's; by 1850, H. F. Cox of this foundry was annually producing fifty threshing machines.[11]

Other types of farm machinery were also manufactured in Racine County in the 1840's. Edwin Putnam specialized in steel clipper plows, and in 1850 produced 250 plows of various kinds. By 1848 Sexton & Puynamere were making "Superior and Improved Clippers" and "Michigan Steel Polished Plows." In the middle and late 1840's, Richard E. Ela was also selling several types of plows in addition to numerous fanning mills; and at midcentury he was making 300 plows per year.[12]

[10] R. E. Ela to his father, Dec. 18, 1838; March 16, 1840; Sept. 1841, Ela Papers; Ida L. Ela, "Early History of the Town of Rochester, Racine, Wisconsin," 37–39, State Historical Society of Wisconsin; Stewart H. Holbrook, *Machines of Plenty: Pioneering in American Agriculture* (New York, 1955), 29.

[11] *Racine Advocate,* Feb. 15, 1843, adv.; Dec. 17, 1844, adv.; Jan. 19, 1848, adv.; D. & B. vol. 47: 12, 119; MCSW, Racine County, 1850; E. W. Leach, "Pioneer Facts and Folks," clippings from the *Racine Journal News,* 1936, p. 17; *History of Racine and Kenosha County,* 466; *Portrait and Biographical Album of Racine and Kenosha Counties, Wisconsin* (Chicago, 1892), 417–418, 992; *Wisconsin Farmer,* 2 (1850), 213, adv.; Lydia P. Wallis, "The Man America Made," 27, J. I. Case Papers; *USDB,* 190–192; Holbrook, 30–36.

[12] *Racine Advocate,* Feb. 23, Dec. 13, 1848, advs.; MCSW, Racine County, 1850. Journal of Accounts, 1847–1849, 1849–1854, Vols. 11 and 12, Ela Papers.

The expansion of the agricultural implements industry in Racine County was so great that Ela was probably not exaggerating when he claimed that 500 or 600 threshing machines, 400 to 600 steel plows, plus some cast-iron plows, and 4,000 to 5,000 fanning mills and other implements had been produced in various Racine machinery shops by 1851.[13] Obviously these articles were not sold only to the farmers of Racine and neighboring counties. Even before the advent of railroads in Wisconsin the market for Racine's farm implements was definitely regional. For several years in the late forties J. I. Case himself peddled his machines in southern Wisconsin and northern Illinois. By midcentury R. E. Ela had branch shops in Waterloo in Jefferson County and at Waupun in Fond du Lac County. He also employed agents to sell machinery in Waukesha, Walworth, Jefferson, and Rock counties, and in northern Illinois.[14] The explanation for this wide sales area was the existence of a sellers' market. The cost of transporting the finished article was evidently insufficient to stimulate competition from other local centers, especially if — as in the case of A. P. Dickey's fanning mills — the implements were made so that they could be taken to pieces and reassembled in a few minutes by anyone competent to use them.[15]

The position of the agricultural implements industry in Racine county was improved during the 1850's despite increased competition from Eastern and other Midwestern establishments and the nationwide depression. By 1860 the four firms recorded in the census employed 179 men to make at least 315 threshers, 550 reapers, 100 cultivators, and sixty corn shellers valued at $230,970. If account is also taken of A. P. Dickey's machine shop, the output would be increased by 720 fanning mills and thirty threshers. If still further account is taken of the large but unknown number of

[13] WSAS Trans., 1 (1851) 208.
[14] J. I. Case to his wife, Oct. 30, 1849; Nov. 12, 22, 1850; Nov. 4, Dec. 4, 1851; Feb. 24, Apr. 10, 14, Sept. 1, 5, 1852, typewritten copies in the J. I. Case Papers. G. W. Bly to R. E. Ela Sept. 3, 1848; March 27, Aug. 20, 1849; March 20, 1850; R. E. Ela to A. Van Aanam, May 11, 1849; A. Van Aanam to R. E. Ela, Apr. 20, 1849; I. N. Ostrunder to R. E. Ela, July 13, 1850; G. B. Dickinson to R. E. Ela, Jan. 29, 1850; J. O'Reilly to R. E. Ela, Sept. 19, 1850; Fergusson & McNish to R. E. Ela, Oct. 11, 1850; H. J. Sawyer to R. E. Ela, Dec. 4, 1850; W. A. McCommel to R. E. Ela, Oct. 23, 1850; A. P. Goodrich to R. E. Ela, Nov. 15, 1850; W. Bowman to R. E. Ela, Dec. 25, 1850, all in the Ela Papers.
[15] USBD, 202–203.

mills and plows sold by R. E. Ela, and of other equipment built by local craftsmen, Racine County could be considered a major center for manufacturing farm machinery.[16]

Not only did the output of farm machinery increase in the 1850's; production methods were also improved. Racine manufacturers, with one exception, used steam power. J. I. Case installed a large steam engine in 1855. Lucius S. Blake purchased a fifteen-horsepower engine for his new shop in 1856. Thomas Falvey made steam engines in his foundry, so steam power was readily available when he extended his business to reapers and mowers in 1857. A. P. Dickey used steam power for the manufacture of implements soon after he bought H. F. Cox's foundry in 1853. Nor was it only the Racine city manufacturers who were aware of the advantages of steam power. In 1854 A. P. Dickey completed a six-horsepower engine for Sawyer & Barnes, plow manufacturers at Burlington, and another one for R. E. Ela of Rochester.[17]

Along with the use of steam power, manufacturers also extended their plant layouts. Expansion did not simply consist of additional buildings; it made some headway towards vertical integration. When J. I. Case added to his shop in 1854-55, he also built a furnace to ensure quality control over his supply of castings. By 1857 he combined all the processes involved in manufacturing threshers and plows under one roof. Case also took on new staff to deal with the management and labor side of the business, which had grown too large for him to handle personally. In 1852 he employed Massena B. Erskine, a skilled engineer, to superintend the mechanical department of the thresher works. Five years later he hired John R. Davis, a foundryman, to make more reliable castings. In 1858 his brother-in-law Stephen Bull was made his personal assistant, and in 1860 Robert Baker was appointed agent and general collector in charge of the selling side of the business. Case thus went far beyond the stage of running a local enterprise.[18]

---

[16] MCSW, Racine County, 1860; D. & B. vol. 47: 46. Thompson & Ela, "Journal of Account," 1854-1860, Vol. 16; "Notes of Sales," 1856-1860, Vol. 17, Ela Papers.

[17] *Racine Advocate*, March 16, 1853, adv.; Feb. 3, Nov. 6, 1854; July 18, 1855; Nov. 26, 1856; Apr. 15, 1857; MCSW, Racine County, 1860; D. & B. vol. 47: 12, 52; A. P. Dickey to R. E. Ela, Jan. 31, Feb. 4, March 2, 1854, Correspondence, Ela Papers.

[18] *Racine Advocate*, Nov. 6, 1854; July 9, 1856; Apr. 1, 1857; D. & B. vol. 47: 33;

Other agricultural implements manufacturers in Racine did not attain a like degree of sophistication, but they strived to emulate Case's efficiency. In 1856 Lucius Blake purchased a new building which he turned into a departmentalized shop in which he could supervise his employees. In 1854 A. P. Dickey successfully combined the fanning mill and thresher side of his business with a foundry. He arranged the building space to expedite the production of all types of machinery. Though he encountered financial difficulties in the late 1850's, this setback was temporary, and by early 1861 he was employing forty men and had an annual output worth at least $20,000. Thomas Falvey likewise found economies of scale in production when in 1857 he added an agricultural implements shop to his foundry. Indeed by 1861 most of his seventy employees and at least 60 to 70 per cent of his profit were tied up in reapers and cultivators, while the foundry appeared to have taken on the ancillary function of supplying raw materials and making some castings.[19]

A corresponding increase in the sales of farm machinery matched the modernization of the large Racine city firms. This expansion, however, was more noticeable in the territorial extent of sales rather than in sales techniques. The firms still relied on a small downpayment at the time of delivery succeeded by installments over a period of from six to eighteen months.[20] This sales method was, in fact, the only way to conduct business with farmers who were dependent on harvesting crops for their supply of ready cash. Yet installment buying led to serious difficulties, particularly in the late 1850's, when the farmer sometimes fell two or three years behind with his payments, if indeed he paid at all. S. M. Moulton, who made fanning mills in Rochester, gave up his business in the late 1850's. A. P. Dickey got into so much debt that he had

---

"Articles of Agreement, J. R. Davis and J. I. Case," Oct. 15, 1855; "Case Chronological History: Personnel and Associates," J. I. Case Papers; "Massena B. Erskine," Biographical Material. Vol. 1, E. W. Leach Papers, State Historical Society of Wisconsin; Portrait and Biographical Album of Racine and Kenosha Counties, 261, 284, 572–573; USBD, 174–175, 190–193.

[19] Racine Advocate, Feb. 12, 1851; May 15, Nov. 27, 1854; Feb. 8, 1855; Aug. 6, Nov. 26, 1856; Apr. 15, 29, 1857; June 16, 1858, adv.; March 27, 1861; D. & B. vol. 47: 12, 28; MCSW, Racine County, 1860.

[20] "Notes of Sales, 1856–60," Vol. 16; Thompson & Ela, Journal of Accounts, 1854–60," vol. 17, Ela Papers; Sales of Machinery, 1859, 1862, J. I. Case Papers.

to sell out temporarily in 1857. Other entrepreneurs were financially embarrassed, and they managed to survive only by going deeply into debt or using the barter system of negotiation[21]

The market for Racine agricultural implements had been extended during the early and middle 1850's when wheat cultivation boomed in the Middle West. It was consolidated in the later years of the decade despite the general economic conditions. Indeed the farm machinery entrepreneurs seem to have confirmed their status as regional producers. R. E. Ela sold his machinery mainly in southern Wisconsin, northern Illinois, and eastern Iowa, but occasionally also in northern Wisconsin. He also set up a branch shop at Marion, Iowa, in 1856. Lucius Blake sold his fanning mills in Illinois, Iowa, and Minnesota as well as in Wisconsin. A. P. Dickey had agents in western Wisconsin, northern Illinois, and eastern Iowa; Thomas Falvey sold his reapers in Wisconsin, Illinois, Iowa, and Minnesota. J. I. Case, as the largest manufacturer, outstripped his local rivals. By the mid-1850's his threshers were known throughout the West, especially in Iowa and Minnesota, and in 1860 he even shipped six machines to California.[22]

The manufacture of agricultural implements in Racine County was one of the most highly developed industrial activities in antebellum Wisconsin. In monetary terms of net profit, this branch was outstripped only by the lumber industry in several northern counties and by several Milwaukee industries. And industrial development cannot be judged by the criterion of profit alone. Lumber firms were only involved in the primary and secondary processing of wood; they did not fabricate articles from various raw materials. The manufacture of agricultural implements involved a much greater use of skilled labor and machinery. Milwaukee's industrial outputs were usually contributed by both very small shops and large establishments, and they were often absorbed locally by the city population. None of the Racine manufacturers of farm equipment were artisans doing

[21] D. & B. vol. 47: 12, 28, 58, 81, 118; Holbrook, 43–44; William T. Hutchinson, *Cyrus Hall McCormick* (2 vols., New York, 1935), 2: 67–76.

[22] *Racine Advocate*, May 30, adv., July 18, 1855; July 9, 1856; Apr. 29, 1857; June 16, 1858; Aug. 31, 1859; Jan. 18, 1860; March 27, 1861. "Journal," 1847-54, Vol. 12; "Journal of Accounts," 1855–61, Vol. 13; G. W. Thompson to R. E. Ela, spring and summer, 1856, Correspondence, Ela Papers.

a custom trade. They produced machinery for a nonlocal market, which entailed a degree of sophistication in the production and selling sides of their enterprises. The Milwaukee foundries and machine shops also catered to a western regional market and suffered from the competition of Eastern and other Midwestern firms. But the Racine implements manufacturers seem to have been more aggressive in their sales policies and their use of specialized production methods. Indeed the Racine farm machinery branch of manufacturing may well have been the apex of industrial development in antebellum Wisconsin.

Wagons and Carriages

By contrast the other branch of agricultural industries in Racine County, namely wagons and carriages, always had a limited market and was even declining in output in the later 1850's. (Table 19 and Table 20.) Wagonmakers had certainly established shops early in the settlement of the county, for the 1840 census reported that five workers produced articles valued at $2,000. But this branch of manufacturing did not grow rapidly. There was no carriagemaker in Racine city until 1842, and the only other establishment in the early 1840's was in Burlington. The second half of the decade was more encouraging. By 1850 at least six craftsmen were making buggies as part of their output. For example, Richard E. Ela made wagons in his agricultural implements shop, while O. S. Taylor operated both a smithy and a wagon shop. But business was limited; most work was in repairing and most wagons were custom made.[23]

Although there was a dramatic increase in the number of wagon- and carriage-makers in the 1850's — for at one time during the decade there were at least twenty-eight different shops in operation — these artisans had a short life span. Most of them did repair work or job work and were unable to survive the late 1850's.[24] Indeed Henry Mitchell, the leading carriage maker in

[23] *Racine Advocate*, Dec. 28, 1842; Feb. 15, 1843; "Pioneer Facts and Folks," 21, quoting the *Southport Telegraph*, 1845; MCSW, Racine County, 1850; *The Racine Register, Business Directory and Advertiser, 1850*, adv. [hereinafter cited as *RCD*]; "Industry and Invention," 13, 34; Box 4, Leach Papers.

[24] *Racine Advocate*, Dec. 6, 16, 1853, advs.; Oct. 9, 1854; Feb. 8, June 20, adv., 1855; *RCD, 1858–59*, 92, 111–112; MCSW, Racine County, 1850 and 1860; *Hunt's Merchants' Magazine*, 26 (1852), 556; "Industry and Invention," 13, Box 4, Leach Papers; D. & B. vol. 47: 22, 25, 33, 36, 47.

Racine, was himself in embarrassing financial straits in 1858–59. Unable to enforce payments for either his wagons or his plows. he was only able to employ fifteen men in 1860, and it was not until 1861 that his situation improved.[25]

Wagonmaking in antebellum Racine County was neither a leading nor a flourishing industry. It was still carried out mainly on a craft basis for local customers or as ancillary to agricultural implements manufacturing and blacksmithing. Some entrepreneurs were trying to extend their sales, but they still produced individually styled vehicles. Limited in scope and in market threshold, this branch of manufacture was severely crippled by the panic and ensuing depression and had not recovered much momentum before the outbreak of the Civil War.

OTHER INDUSTRIES

Iron Foundries and Machine Shops

The iron industry grew from a position of minor significance in the Racine County manufacturing output in 1850 to become the second-leading branch in 1860. This expansion was in part due to the lakeshore location which facilitated the import of raw materials at a much cheaper cost than to any interior rival center in Wisconsin. But of more importance, the industry was stimulated by the complementary growth of the agricultural implements branch, which required castings and machine parts.

The pioneer iron foundry appears to have been built at Rochester, Racine County, in the late 1830's, but apparently it did little business, for it was not working in 1840. The first successful foundry was established in Racine city in 1844 by J. B. Wilson and G. C. Burgess. These entrepreneurs did not limit their trade to castings but also made hardware and farm machinery and did smithing work. Yet in spite of their diversified activities and the addition of two more partners in 1847, the firm collapsed before the end of the decade, probably because local competition was too strong. In 1845 Russell Skinner established a foundry and machine shop to make castings, farm ma-

---

[25] *Racine Advocate*, Aug. 6, 1855; May 14, Aug. 30, adv., 1856; March 27, 1861; MCSW, Racine County, 1860; D. & B. vol. 47: 12; "Industry and Invention," 13, Box 4, Leach Papers.

chinery, mill wheels, and tools as well as doing turning and finishing work. Also in the late 1840's England & Co. operated a foundry producing a variety of castings and machinery.[26] Since these competing foundries did not concentrate on the production of castings, they likewise met with competition from agricultural implements manufacturers and, to some extent, from blacksmiths.

These meager beginnings notwithstanding, the iron industry increased rapidly in the early and middle 1850's and the value of iron products reported by the Racine Board of Trade in 1855 was $181,400. This expansion centered on the three foundries of Albert P. Dickey, Thomas Falvey, and Russel Skinner, and on the machine shops of the Racine, Janesville and Mississippi Railroad Company. A. P. Dickey, who had long experience in the manufacturing of fanning mills, entered the foundry business in 1853. Although he soon acquired a considerable trade and insisted on calling his works a foundry and machine shop, most of his output was still in agricultural implements. Thomas Falvey tripled the value of his foundry property from $4,000 or $5,000 to some $15,000 in the early years of the 1850's. Like Dickey, he made farm implements, but the bulk of his trade lay in foundry and machine products. Russel Skinner continued to operate his foundry, though he was not doing a substantial business in the early 1850's. Much of the heavy castings work was done in the car shops of the Racine, Janesville and Mississippi Railroad Company, which employed some thirty men in the production of platform and freight cars in 1854 and 1855.[27]

The expanding trade of the iron foundries and machine shops was cut short by the Panic of 1857 and the ensuing depression. In 1857 A. P. Dickey was forced to sell his foundry to Orlando Jennings. Although Jennings started off well and sold his horse powers and steam engines in many parts of the West, he too got so far in debt that he had to give up his business in 1859. Thomas

---

[26] *Racine Advocate*, Dec. 17, adv., Dec. 24, 1844; March 11, June 24, adv., 1845; Jan. 19, 1848, adv.; Feb. 12, 1851, adv.; *Sixth Census, 1840, Compendium*, 347–353; MCSW, Racine County, 1850; "Industry and Invention," 8, Box 4, Leach Papers; Ida L. Ela, "Early History," 35; *Racine, Belle City of the Lakes and Racine County, Wisconsin*, 169.

[27] *Racine Advocate*, Feb. 3, 10, adv., May 15, Oct. 30, 1854; Feb. 8, 19, March 19, adv., 1855; Aug. 6, 1856; D. & B. vol. 47: 12, 28, 38; A. P. Dickey to R. E. Ela, Jan. 31, Feb. 4, March 2, 1854, Correspondence, Ela Papers.

Falvey kept his works in operation throughout the hard times, but he was very straitened, and his partner Riley quit in 1859 because of their poor financial standing. Russel Skinner also managed to survive the late 1850's but he had a very poor credit rating. Indeed, the only foundry which did not seem to be badly crippled by the panic was part of the large manufacturing complex of Jerome I. Case.[28]

Nevertheless, despite the financial difficulties of the late 1850's, the Racine city foundries and machine shops still managed to produce goods to the value of $116,631 in 1860. This output may not have been as large as that achieved in 1855, but it still represented 14.1 per cent of the Wisconsin iron industry. Entrepreneurs had seized the advantage of a lakeport site to establish an industry which had a large potential for supplying the county's farm implements works as well as for selling castings and other machinery. A promising start had been made.

THE PROCESSING INDUSTRIES

Flour Milling

Flour milling was the most important processing industry in Racine County during the antebellum period. It had also been the leading industry until the early 1850's when it was surpassed first by the agricultural implements branch and later by foundries and machine shops. Millers were unable to maintain their pre-eminence in Racine manufacturing owing to the changing nature of the flouring industry in Wisconsin. Although the county mills had relatively easy access to raw materials, had sufficient supplies of water or steam power, and were conveniently close to both urban markets and Lake Michigan, these advantages only lasted a short time. When the center of wheat cultivation in Wisconsin moved northward, and when the railroads lowered transportation costs, the flouring industry gradually became centralized in Milwaukee. By the late 1850's Racine mills were becoming less able to compete with the economies of scale practiced by their larger Milwaukee counterparts.

Pioneer gristmills were built early in the settlement of Racine

---

[28] *Racine Advocate,* Apr. 29, 1857; July 13, 1859; D. & B. vol. 47: 28, 38, 53, 58, 118; MCSW, Racine County, 1860.

County. By 1837 a primitive establishment, containing no bolting apparatus and requiring the customer to sift his own grain, was located on the water power near Racine village. In 1838 a frame mill with three run of stone, two for grinding wheat and one for corn, was built at Burlington; by 1839 a third mill with two run of stone had been erected at Waterford.[29] Such establishments were necessary parts of frontier farming life.

It was not long, however, before mills in Racine County were being constructed for commercial as well as custom flouring. Rochester men were early aware of the potential market for flour. By 1844 a large mill with four run of stone, designed to carry out an extensive business both for export and home consumption, was nearing completion. Waterford had two flour mills in operation by late 1844. Burlington had only one such mill in 1845, but the following year Pliny M. Perkins built a larger establishment designed to accommodate both the increase in local population and in grain output. Racine city had two steam flouring mills in operation by 1848, and both appeared to be more interested in the merchant than in the custom trade.[30] Indeed the six mills reported in the 1850 census produced not only custom work, but also some 71,000 barrels of flour which yielded a net return on operations of $108,117. Such an output made Racine the second-leading county in Wisconsin, with 11.3 per cent of the state's aggregate.

Racine, however, was unable to maintain this position either relatively or absolutely. During the 1850's production first increased and then decreased, leaving the county with an output of some 52,000 barrels of flour and custom work in 1860. This total only created a value added of $61,764, making Racine the tenth-ranking county in Wisconsin. Racine was in the process of readjustment. During the early part of the decade the milling industry in the county continued its earlier growth. In 1851 seven large mills reputedly produced some 95,050 barrels of flour. But

[29] *Racine Argus*, March 10, 1838; "Biographical Material," Vol. 1, Leach Papers; E. W. Leach, *Racine: An Historical Narrative* (Racine, 1920), 36; Stone, 128, 158; *History of Racine and Kenosha Counties*, 471–472, 482–483.

[30] *Racine Advocate*, Oct. 24, 1843; May 7, Nov. 12, adv., 1844; Apr. 22, Dec. 9, 1845; Apr. 14, 1846, adv.; July 12, Sept. 13, 1848; D. & B. vol. 47: 172; "Racine Facts and Folks," 21, citing the *Racine Advocate*, 1843, and the *Southport Telegraph*, 1845; *History of Racine and Kenosha Counties*, 471–472, 485.

this trend did not continue. Newspaper editorials bemoaned the lack of active flour mills in 1853 and the statistics of manufacturing for the city of Racine in 1854 failed to report any flour. Though milling capacity increased in the late 1850's with the addition of new mills in Racine city, Burlington, and Waterford, these new plants were hit badly by tight economic conditions.[31]

The panic struck sharply at the stability of the Racine flour mills in 1857–58. Even solid and reliable millers like the Hurlburt Brothers, who had been doing a good business and were even exporting some of their flour to Boston, did not have sufficient capital to survive the hard times. So it was not surprising that when entrepreneurs like the Titus Brothers or James Scott built new mills in 1858, they were either forced out of business or were not considered responsible. The new Racine steam flouring plant, opened by Hart and Glass in 1859, was also unable to operate at full capacity. The panic which crippled many medium-sized operations in Wisconsin was doubly shattering to the Racine flour industry because several enterprises were new and had not been able to build up sufficient capital reserves to meet the stringent conditions.[32]

But the increasingly poor standing of the Racine mills cannot be attributed solely to new enterprises and hard times. These mills were also suffering side-effects from the initial stages of the centralization of the Wisconsin flouring industry. In the 1840's and early 1850's this industry was widely dispersed in many small establishments, usually situated on rivers and driven by water power. Such mills often processed wheat grown in their own neighborhoods either for sale locally or on a custom basis. But by the middle and late 1850's the railroads were bringing wheat to one or several central locations where larger enterprises achieved economies of scale in milling flour. Milwaukee benefited most from the chaneling of railroad receipts of wheat. By 1860 that city was producing 26 per cent of Wisconsin's value added in flour, in contrast to 10.4 per cent in 1850. Racine city, which alone in Racine County had relatively good port and rail-

[31] WSAS Trans., 1 (1851), 208; Racine Advocate, Aug. 9, 1853; Aug. 29, Oct. 31, 1855; July 13, 1859; Burlington Gazette, May 31, 1859.

[32] Racine Advocate, Jan. 8, 1855; Nov. 1, 1857; June 2, 1858, adv.; July 13, Nov. 9, 1859; March 27, 1861; Burlington Gazette, Nov. 22, 1859; D. & B. vol. 47: 27, 63, 89, 120.

road facilities, had not yet shown any marked tendency to develop commercial milling on a competitive scale. Only the steam-powered mill of Hart & Glass, with its output of some 30,000 barrels of flour in 1861, could rival some of the Milwaukee firms; yet this establishment was exceptional.[33] Racine flour millers were generally unable and unwilling to invest the capital needed to build up enterprises which could operate within a market economy on a regional scale. Despite the spurt of new building in the later fifties, they failed to make much impact on either Racine County or Wisconsin.

Leather Processing

Leather processing was another pioneer branch of manufacturing in Racine County. In 1840 the census reported a value of product of $3,725, which presumably entailed the existence of a tannery if not also a saddlery or a leathergoods shop. Such enterprises were small, using the limited supply of raw materials and catering to a custom trade. They increased in number in the 1840's with the growth of population. But some entrepreneurs also wished to enlarge the scope of their activities, and made hesitant steps towards integrating the several processing stages in a general leathergoods establishment. For example, in 1845 Edward Gould opened a leather store in conjunction with his tannery. Later he entered a partnership with Charles Herrick, who had been in the meatpacking business and could still probably obtain a ready supply of hides. Or again, McDonald and Roby, who became partners in 1849, added a tannery to Roby's shoe shop so as to have a better supply of raw materials.[34]

By midcentury the census noted five leather and leathergoods firms producing articles valued at $40,555. These establishments, all located in Racine city, contributed some 14 per cent of the Wisconsin value added in leather — a proportion which was maintained in the next decade. Racine firms, increasing both in size and in number in the 1850's, were able to hold their rank within the state industry. The reasons for this

[33] *Racine Advocate*, Nov. 9, 1859; March 27, 1861; D. & B. vol. 47: 120; MCSW, Racine County, 1860.
[34] *Racine Advocate*, Feb. 15, 1843; Jan. 9, 1844; Nov. 11, 1845, adv.; June 2, 1846, adv.; Jan. 19, June 7, 1848; D. & B. vol. 47: 9, 171; MCSW, Racine County, 1850.

success, minor though it may be in comparison to the county's overall manufacturing development, lay mainly in the lakeside location of Racine city. Most of the larger firms were located in the city where they could take advantage of port facilities for obtaining supplies of tanbark from northern Wisconsin and for exporting surplus hides.[35]

Most of the larger firms were also tanneries, as distinct from saddleries and harness shops. The latter establishments were small and were usually run by craftsmen doing a custom trade and a considerable amount of repairs. The size of their businesses did increase by some 15 per cent in the 1850's but this was only sufficient to cope with part of the local demand for leather goods.[36] The tanneries, by contrast, did a more thriving business. With the exception of Jacob Kawelti, who only began manufacturing in 1859, their individual outputs were some four or five times higher than those of the leather shops. True, there had been a considerable turnover in tanning personnel in the 1850's; but this did not appear to have affected the industry's growing prosperity.[37] The tanneries were able to supply the local demand for hides, either directly to their own leathergoods establishments or for sale to independent harnessmakers, trunkmakers, and cobblers; and they were also able to export their product if a surplus existed.

Leather processing in antebellum Racine County was in a relatively good position within both state and county because it could still exist as a local industry not unduly subject to pressures of economies of scale and specialization. Though none of the firms, not even the tanneries, could match the output of the large Milwaukee establishments, there was still sufficient local demand to absorb a large proportion of the hide output. Too, the lakeport facilitated the export of surplus hides. But of equal importance with the fluid market situation was the ease of obtaining raw ma-

[35] Charles E. Schefft, "The Tanning Industry in Wisconsin. A History of Its Frontier Origins and Its Development" (unpublished M.A. thesis, University of Wisconsin, 1938), 18–42.

[36] *Racine Advocate*, Feb. 12, 1851, adv.; Aug. 12, 1853, adv.; May 15, Dec. 18, 1854, adv.; July 13, 1859, adv.; MCSW, Racine County, 1850 and 1860; D. & B. vol. 47: 53.

[37] *Racine Advocate*, June 10, 1857; Aug. 23, 1858; D. & B. vol. 47: 9, 10, 115; MCSW Racine County, 1860.

terials, both tanbark from northern Wisconsin and cattle from southern Wisconsin and northern Illinois.

Meat Packing

The tannery industry thus had backward linkages to the meat-packing industry, which began on a small scale when cattle and hogs were brought to Racine city for slaughter. Additional incentive was given to the business by the prospects of Eastern markets, for pork was exported in the early 1840's. Yet this incentive was not strong enough to stimulate a major effort, especially in the 1850's when the railroad carried most cattle and hogs destined for the export trade directly to Milwaukee. In this instance the centralizing tendencies of the processing industries, consequent on improved transportation, worked to the disadvantage of Racine.

The early packing industry in Racine County was run by butchers who killed cattle in the town markets and sold the carcasses immediately. The jointing, curing, and preserving of meat was an added refinement to the basic step of slaughtering; but this secondary stage was soon taken up, for by 1842 some 350 barrels of pork and 100 barrels of beef were exported from the port of Racine. Obviously the potential of sales in Eastern markets attracted the attention of all three packing firms — Charles Herrick and his various partners, Killip & Clough, and Norton & Mosher — active in Racine in the 1840's. Indeed a considerable proportion of their output must have been exported, for the city directory claimed that 4,125 barrels of beef and 2,385 barrels of pork had been shipped to Eastern markets in 1849.[38] Yet the export market could not provide the incentive to encourage growth on any permanent basis. This trade was a peculiar feature of the 1840's, when small towns with access to both water transport and cattle were able to take advantage of the high meat prices offered in cities like New York and Boston.

The Racine packers expanded their business in the early 1850's. But increasingly they had to look to the local markets not only for the sale of hides, skins, tallow, and lard, but also for the

[38] *Racine Advocate,* Nov. 12, 1844, adv.; July 1, adv., Sept. 23, adv., Nov. 4, 1845; Dec. 2, 1846; Feb. 23, 1848, adv.; *RCD, 1850,* 19; "Biographical Material," Box 1, Leach Papers; *History of Racine and Kenosha Counties,* 368.

sale of most of their meat product. When the railroads ensured a relatively quick and steady supply of cattle from the wider hinterland of southern Wisconsin and northern Illinois, the export trade in the southern lakeshore region became concentrated in Milwaukee and Chicago. This squeeze on the position of the Racine packing industry was made tighter by the depression of the late 1850's, which not only reduced profits but also prevented further investment in a business which at best was seasonal and always tended to fluctuate. By 1860 the industry appeared to have reverted to catering mainly to the local urban market. All six firms then in operation were small, the largest among them employing only five men on a seasonal basis, and between them they only packed 800 barrels of beef and 545 barrels of pork.[39]

Other Processing Industries

The remaining processing industries — lumber, cooperage, liquors, construction materials, wool, minerals, soap, and tobacco — all provided a small share of the antebellum Racine manufacturing profile. (Table 19 and Table 20.) In relative terms their overall contribution dropped from 17.1 per cent in 1850 to 10.4 per cent in 1860, thus reflecting a slower increase in these processing branches than in manufacturing in general. In absolute terms the lumber, cooperage, minerals, and tobacco branches were on the decline. These industries were fading both as a result of the depletion of natural resources and the general constriction of trade in the late 1850's. For example, Racine County was not well endowed with timber, and thus the early sawmills soon used up local lumber in meeting building demands. By 1860 the one reported planing mill in Racine processed wood brought in by lake from the northern pineries. The decline in stone quarrying seemed to be a consequence of the hard times, which curtailed building projects and directly hit lime and stone contractors.[40] But more generally the other processing industries were never well established, and gradually they went out of existence or shrank to very small or part-time enterprises.

[39] *Racine Advocate,* March 16, 1853; Riley, 123–129; MCSW, Racine County, 1860.
[40] D. & B. vol. 47: 83; MCSW, Racine County, 1850 and 1860.

HOUSEHOLD-CRAFT CONSUMER INDUSTRIES

The household-craft consumer industries in antebellum Racine County revealed traits similar to their group behavior in the state as a whole. Though usually increasing in absolute value throughout the period, they declined in relative standing within the county industrial stratum. Unable to withstand the growing competition from imported mass-produced goods, and lacking a sufficiently large urban base to manufacture many ready-made goods locally, these branches had to rely on an increasingly specialized custom trade and on repair work. They were therefore limited in potential.

Boots and Shoes

Cobblers were among the first artisans to establish shops or to work as journeymen in the pioneer villages of Racine County in the 1830's and 1840's. These craftsmen generally made shoes for the custom trade and took in repairs. With the improvement of roads and the consequent ease of importing goods they often had to compete with footwear sold by general merchants. But only the more ambitious entrepreneurs, such as George Chapman or William Buckingham, who were located in Racine city, became merchant-manufacturers and themselves imported supplies of shoes from the East. Village cobblers tended to remain small-scale, even part-time artisans.[41]

Shoemakers managed to hold both their relative and absolute positions within the Racine manufacturing profile, though with greater difficulty in the fifties. The availability of local hides and leather certainly eased the supply side of the trade, but the market side was cramped. Shoe retailers were more active, especially in the larger urban centers. Moreover several shoemakers were becoming merchant-manufacturers and were emphasizing their imported merchandise rather than their own ready-made or custom-made articles. While the panic and depression of the late 1850's may have further impeded local manufactures, it would seem that the Racine shoe industry, like that in most parts of Wisconsin, was entering the transitional stage between the decline

---

[41] *Racine Advocate*, Nov. 28, 1842; adv.; Feb. 13, 1843, adv.; Apr. 22, 1845; Dec. 2, 1846, adv.; Jan. 19, 1848, adv.; D. & B. vol. 47: 19, 23, 176; *RCD, 1850*, n.p.; *Racine, Belle City of the Lakes and Racine County, Wisconsin*, 135–137.

of traditional craftsmen and the predominance of mass-produced goods.[42]

Clothing

The Racine County clothing industry also illustrated many of the characteristics common to craft manufacturers in Wisconsin. Pioneer tailors and dressmakers custom-made articles of clothing either for cash or for produce. But they early had to compete for their trade with general merchandise shops, and several tailors therefore took on retailing functions. Chauncy Hall, for example, came to Racine as a journeyman tailor about 1847, but shortly thereafter became a merchant-manufacturer. James E. Lockwood also became a merchant-tailor by 1848. Both Moore & Jones and Elminger & Keidel sold ready-made clothes as well as catering to the custom trade. By midcentury the larger establishments reported in the census were run by merchant-manufacturers. The making of clothing, especially men's clothing, was being undercut by the retail trade, which in turn was probably boosted by the lakeshore location and by close proximity to Milwaukee.[43]

The clothing industry expanded in both number of establishments and output in the 1850's, but many of the new firms were small enterprises or jobbing departments of merchants' stores. If those firms reported in the census were typical, then there was a decline in size from 8.3 employees per establishment in 1850 to 5.3 in 1860. But such figures included merchant-manufacturers like Keidel and Elminger, both of whom now employed several workmen. More likely the average tailor's shop consisted of the proprietor and his one or two apprentices.[44]

The growth in the output of the Racine clothing industry was accountable in terms of a larger population, but the two increases were not proportionate. Craftsmen were only catering to that small section of the population which could afford to have its clothes individually styled. Most of the clothing business, at least

[42] *Racine Advocate,* July 28, 1852, adv.; Dec. 16, 1853, adv.; Aug. 12, 1854, adv.; June 5, Oct. 17, adv.; 1860; D. & B. vol. 47: 10, 19, 20, 23, 47, 55, 63, 176; *RCD, 1858–59, passim;* MCSW, Racine County, 1850 and 1860.

[43] *Racine Advocate,* Nov. 23, Dec. 14, 1842, advs.; Feb. 15, 1843, adv.; Jan. 9, adv., Oct. 29, 1844, advs.; Jan. 7, 1845, adv.; D. & B. vol. 47: 10, 17, 21, 32; *RCD, 1850,* adv.; MCSW, Racine County, 1850.

[44] D. & B. vol. 47: 8, 17, 21, 32, 121; MCSW, Racine County, 1850 and 1860.

in men's wear, was carried out by the merchants' stores. A higher proportion of women's clothing was fashioned in dressmakers' shops, but much female apparel was still made at home.

Furniture

Cabinetmaking was another craft occupation which became less visible and less significant in antebellum Racine County. Often originating as carpenters and joiners, cabinetmakers would generally turn out any article of woodwork or construct most wooden buildings. During the 1840's they gradually became more specialized. Orin White of Rochester made chairs, tables, and bedsteads; J.D. Pulcifer of Southport concentrated on chair making. But most artisans were still willing to make any kind of furniture, either for cash or produce.[45]

However, even as early as 1842 cabinetmakers found their trade threatened by retail sales, for in that year some 850 tons of furniture, valued at $95,000, were imported to Racine. To build up a reasonable business it was necessary to compete with imported merchandise, and often the best way to do this was either to become a merchant-manufacturer or to seek employment as a craftsman in a merchandise shop. Those artisans who did not wish to become involved in retailing, either directly or indirectly, could only run a small, select enterprise, and they often had to do joinery and undertaking as well as make furniture. During the booming years of the early 1850's these craftsmen were able to expand their business, but the panic reduced their trade considerably and undermined their already weak position.[46]

Tinsmiths and Blacksmiths

Racine County tinsmiths and blacksmiths, like the cabinetmakers, were on the wane both relatively and absolutely. (Table 19 and Table 20.) Tinsmiths were always challenged by the competition of ready-made hardware. As early as 1842 Racine city's two stove stores made sales valued at $10,000, while the two craft

---

[45] *Racine Argus*, Apr. 14, 1838; *Racine Advocate*, Feb. 18, 1845, adv.; Feb. 23, 1848, adv.; "Reminiscences," an autobiography of Hannibal Lugg, as told to Frances R. Green, 1909, p. 6, State Historical Society of Wisconsin, Ida L. Ela, "Early History," 43, 44; *Racine, Belle City of the Lakes and Racine County, Wisconsin*, 124.

[46] *Racine Advocate*, Dec. 28, 1842; March 16, Dec. 16, 1853, advs.; D. & B. vol. 47: 29, 41, 51; MCSW, Racine County, 1850 and 1860.

shops only produced $5,000 worth of goods. This rivalry between craftware and ready-made goods increased, usually to the detriment of the tinsmith, whose manufacturing consisted of repairs or job work, often carried out as the ancillary side of a hardware store.[47] The tinsmith seemed to be less well equipped than any of his artisan contemporaries to cope with the influx of mass-produced articles.

Blacksmiths in Racine County, as in other parts of Wisconsin, were ceasing to be regarded as manufacturers. They either took on general service and repair functions or began to specialize in some aspect of their diverse business. Active early in village life in taking care of horse shoeing, tool making, the manufacture of wagons, carriages, and sleighs, as well in making general repairs, the smiths were unable to continue such a variety of functions as population increased and its demands became more specialized. Some therefore turned to custom work, horse shoeing, and repairs. The more ambitious turned to other craft trades, such as making plows or wagons.[48]

Conclusion

Manufacturing in antebellum Racine County was quite distinctive when compared to other counties or to Wisconsin as a whole. A moderate urban base coupled with a lakeshore location encouraged a wide range of industrial activities; but within this range a strong emphasis was placed first on flour milling and then on agricultural implements and iron products. While resembling the diversified pattern of manufacturing in the older and more heavily populated southern and southeastern counties, Racine was noteworthy in developing an industry with regional potential. Yet, unlike the northern counties whose lumbering activities also had regional significance, Racine's major industry was not a primary processing branch. Nor did the production of agricultural implements dominate the county's manufacturing in the same way in which the lumber industry dominated the manufacturing profile of Eau Claire or even Winnebago County.

[47] *Racine Advocate*, Nov. 23, Dec. 28, 1842; Feb. 12, Oct. 25, 1851; Aug. 12, 1853; D. & B. vol. 47: 14, 21, 32; *RCD, 1850*, adv.; MCSW, Racine County, 1850 and 1860.
[48] *Racine Advocate*, Apr. 22, 1845; Dec. 4, 1854; *Burlington Gazette*, Apr. 4, 1860; *RCD, 1850*, adv.; D. & B. vol. 47: 22, 47; MCSW, Racine County, 1850 and 1860; "Industry and Invention," 33–35, Box 4, Leach Papers.

Racine County manufacturing was also distinctive in the way in which it manifested the transitional stages of manufacturing found in the antebellum Middle West. It was a sort of microcosm in which industrial activity was present in its various evolutionary forms, ranging from the household to the craft shop, the mill, the manufactory, and even the factory. The family system of manufacturing had not entirely disappeared, having a $0.44 per capita value in 1860; but it was limited to the farm. The craft shop, the merchant-manufacturer, and the mill, all supplying neighborhood demands, were numerically the most common types of industrial organization both before and after the arrival of the railroad. Alongside these more traditional establishments, however, flourished the manufactory and the factory, using division of labor and some machinery, and supplying a county, statewide, and sometimes a regional market. These larger enterprises were limited to the agricultural machinery and the foundry branches of manufacture — trades for which the county was well located in relation to changing currents of supply and demand. But they indicated an awareness of the need for specialization in an expanding market. Thus Racine, Wisconsin's second-ranking county in manufacturing outputs, illustrated the various stages and modes of industrial growth in the antebellum Midwest.

CHAPTER SEVEN

Milwaukee County:
The Urban Industrial Frontier

MILWAUKEE, the commercial entrepôt of antebellum Wisconsin, was also the center of industrial activity.[1] Taking advantage of the hinterland resources of lumber, minerals, and farm produce, the water power of the Milwaukee canal, a growing urban complex, its lakeside location for access to other parts of Wisconsin, the Middle West, and the Eastern seaboard, the city of Milwaukee had made solid progress in encouraging manufacturing activities by 1860. Despite the uncertainties of a new settlement and the hindrances of periodic panics, depressions, and credit inflations, Milwaukee had burgeoned from the wilderness village of the 1830's with a few mills and some craftsmen into an aspiring city, manufacturing goods valued at $6,871,689.

This growth placed Milwaukee in the forefront of industrial developments in Wisconsin. By midcentury Milwaukee County contributed 22.8 per cent of the state's value added, a percentage that had increased to 27.3 a decade later. One quarter of Wisconsin's manufacturing was localized in a very small area of the state — in fact in its major urban settlement — for some 90 per cent of the county manufacturing took place in Milwaukee city. With a population of 20,061 in 1850 and 45,286 in 1860, Milwaukee had

[1] For the most comprehensive history of antebellum Milwaukee, see James S. Buck, *Pioneer History of Milwaukee* (4 vols., Milwaukee, 1876–1886). For the commercial history of the city, see Bayrd Still, *Milwaukee: The History of a City* (Madison, second edition, 1965), 168–199; William E. Derby, "A History of the Port of Milwaukee, 1835–1900" (unpublished Ph.D. dissertation, University of Wisconsin, 1963), 135–248; Milwaukee Board of Trade, *Annual Reports of Commerce* 1854–1856 [hereinafter cited as Board or Trade, *A.R.*]; Milwaukee Chamber of Comerce, *Annual Statements of Trade and Commerce*, 1858–1863 [hereinafter cited as Chamber of Commerce, *A.R.*].

6.6 per cent and 5.8 per cent of the Wisconsin aggregate respectively and in 1860 it was over six times the size of its nearest urban rival.[2]

Within this urban industrial sector certain branches of manufacturing were more highly developed both in relation to the Milwaukee and to the Wisconsin aggregates. In Milwaukee the processing industries contributed more to the total output than did any other group. In 1840, four to five years after initial settlement, 80 per cent of the reported capital of $63,450 was invested in mills.[3] In both 1850 and 1860 approximately half of the county's value added came from this group. Flour milling was the leading processing industry, producing 11.4 per cent of the Milwaukee value added in 1850 and 16.7 per cent in 1860. Construction materials and liquors were each responsible for some 6 to 8 per cent of the Milwaukee total. However, clothing, boots and shoes, and furniture in the household-craft consumer group and iron products in the other group were each individually as important as construction materials and liquors, contributing some 6 to 10 per cent of the county's total. (Table 21 and Table 22.) Easy access to natural resources and a port location could not alone account for the development of all of Milwaukee's major industries. The domestic demands of the urban population and the ability to provide goods for a wider state market also carried considerable weight in determining the diversified character of the Milwaukee industrial profile.

This degree of diversification, in addition to the aggregate county production, made Milwaukee doubly peculiar within Wisconsin. In 1850 six branches of manufacturing — flour milling, clothing, construction materials, iron, furniture, and boots and shoes — were responsible for half the county's value added. A decade later, five branches — flour milling, iron products, clothing, liquors,

[2] The ten largest cities in Wisconsin in 1860 were: Milwaukee, 45,286; Racine, 7,831; Janesville, 7,703; Oshkosh, 6,847; Madison, 6,601; Fond du Lac, 5,447; Watertown, 5,302; Beloit, 4,090; Kenosha, 3,989; and La Crosse, 3,865. "Census of Wisconsin From the Year 1836 to August, 1860, Inclusive. Compiled from official sources for the *Wisconsin State Journal*," by H.A. Tenney, *Census of Wisconsin, 1836–1880* (pamphlet, n.p. n.d.); *Ninth Census, 1870, Population*, Vol. 1. 287–295.
[3] The statistics in *Sixth Census, 1840, Compendium*, 347–353, are incomplete, though capital invested is more fully reported than either value of product or number of workers. The census did not distinguish between the individual outputs of gristmills, sawmills, or oil mills.

TABLE 21

MANUFACTURING IN MILWAUKEE COUNTY, 1850

(Value Added in Current $'s.)

Industry	Value Added	Per Cent of Total	No. of Workers	Per Cent of Total
Processing Industries				
Lumber	12,440	1.44	25	1.57
Flour	98,864	11.42	48	3.01
Cooperage	29,726	3.43	66	4.14
Liquors	54,517	6.29	52	3.26
Leather	44,655	5.16	74	4.64
Construction Materials	75,770	8.75	230	14.44
Wool	22,500	2.60	10	0.63
Minerals	20,650	2.38	39	2.45
Soap and Candles	18,975	2.19	19	1.19
Tobacco	41,639	4.81	42	2.63
Aggregate	419,736	48.47	605	37.96
Household-Craft Consumer				
Boots and Shoes	59,230	6.84	144	9.03
Clothing	76,950	8.88	293	18.38
Furniture	61,099	7.05	123	7.73
Blacksmiths	19,195	2.22	34	2.13
Confectionery	16,372	1.89	34	2.13
Tin, Copper etc.	27,745	3.20	36	2.26
Aggregate	260,591	30.08	664	41.66
Agricultural Industries				
Agricultural Impls.	7,025	0.81	8	0.50
Wagons	46,630	5.38	102	6.40
Aggregate	53,655	6.19	110	6.90
Other Industries				
Iron	67,652	7.81	104	6.52
Paper	9,160	1.06	18	1.13
Miscellaneous	55,330	6.39	93	5.83
Aggregate	132,142	15.26	215	13.48
Milwaukee County	866,142	100.00	1,594	100.00

[SOURCE: Manuscript Census for the State of Wisconsin, 1850. Milwaukee County.]

and boots and shoes — provided half the output. This spread contrasted sharply with many Wisconsin counties, which had over 50 per cent of their value added in one industry alone; and it contrasted even more markedly with the northern counties, which had some 80 to 90 per cent of their value added in lumbering. The diversification was even more remarkable in comparison to the pattern of manufacturing found in the more heavily populated counties of southern and south-central Wisconsin. These counties generally had less than 30 per cent of their value added in any one industry and approximately 40 per cent in their two leading industries. But Milwaukee, with only 20 per cent of its aggregate in two industries in 1850 and 26.6 per cent in 1860, was not typical of these areas. It was in fact unique, and could claim the distinction of having the most well-balanced industrial structure in the state.

Those industries which contributed the largest share to the Milwaukee aggregate also contributed a substantial amount of that particular Wisconsin industry, though not necessarily in the same proportions. Milwaukee only processed 10.4 per cent of Wisconsin's flour in 1850 when the milling industry was very localized and the southern and southeastern counties were equally well placed as producing centers. A decade later, however, Milwaukee processed 26 per cent of Wisconsin's flour. By 1860 the new railroad network brought increasing amounts of grain to the commercial center of Milwaukee, and city millers took advantage of the bulk supply to practice economies of scale. This tendency towards centralization was also marked in meatpacking and, on a lesser scale, in leather processing.[4] It was also seen in the iron products branch, which increased its share of the Wisconsin iron industry from 32.5 per cent in 1850 to 51.3 per cent in 1860. Here the lakeport, which facilitated the import of raw materials, combined with the urban concentration to stimulate an industry serving a statewide community.

Those leading Milwaukee industries in the household-craft consumer group — namely, clothing, boots and shoes, and furniture,

---

[4] It is impossible to estimate the increasing proportion of the Wisconsin meatpacking industry which was carried out in Milwaukee, because the census marshals failed to provide the necessary figures in 1850 and may well have only given a partial coverage in 1860. Using the reported statistics, Milwaukee had 72.4 per cent of the state's industry in 1860.

TABLE 22

MANUFACTURING IN MILWAUKEE COUNTY, 1860

(Value Added in Current $'s.)

Industry	Value Added	Per Cent of Total	No. of Workers	Per Cent of Total
Processing Industries				
Lumber	35,335	1.14	40	1.09
Flour	516,228	16.67	105	2.87
Cooperage	105,628	3.41	199	5.43
Liquors	240,505	7.77	149	4.07
Leather	100,701	3.25	134	3.66
Construction Materials	205,968	6.65	439	11.98
Meat Packing	149,162	4.82	140	3.82
Wool	1,200	0.04	2	0.05
Minerals	47,348	1.53	87	2.37
Soap and Candles	56,565	1.83	29	0.79
Tobacco	51,800	1.67	140	3.82
Aggregate	1,510,440	48.78	1,464	39.95
Household-Craft Consumer				
Boots and Shoes	205,975	6.66	329	8.98
Clothing	293,433	9.48	636	17.35
Furniture	171,456	5.54	152	4.15
Blacksmiths	18,598	0.60	43	1.17
Confectionery	39,468	1.27	61	1.66
Tin, Copper etc.	36,415	1.18	77	2.10
Aggregate	765,345	24.73	1,298	35.41
Agricultural Industries				
Agricultural Impls.	25,810	0.83	62	1.69
Wagons	69,258	2.24	100	2.73
Aggregate	95,068	3.07	162	4.42
Other Industries				
Iron	306,219	9.90	205	5.59
Paper	103,869	3.35	123	3.38
Gas	40,660	1.31	36	0.96
Miscellaneous	274,448	8.86	377	10.29
Aggregate	725,196	23.42	741	20.22
Milwaukee County	3,096,049	100.00	3,665	100.00

[SOURCE: Manuscript Census for the State of Wisconsin, 1860. Milwaukee County.]

but especially clothing — also cornered a large share of the total Wisconsin product from the late 1840's onwards. Milwaukee boot and shoe manufacturers provided 33.6 per cent of the Wisconsin aggregate in 1850 and 42.1 per cent in 1860; Milwaukee furniture makers provided 38.6 per cent of the Wisconsin aggregate in 1850 and 41.2 per cent a decade later; and clothing manufacturers provided 67.1 per cent of the state total in 1850 and 63.7 per cent in 1860. These three industries benefited from an urban environment large enough to supply both the initial market and later the labor force needed to stimulate a trade catering both to sections of Milwaukee city and to smaller towns in Wisconsin.

Several other Milwaukee branches of manufacturing were remarkable because they were either very poorly or very well developed within the state framework. With respect to primary lumber processing, for example, Milwaukee County had little or no local timber to exploit, and the industry was thus marginal. Few agricultural implements were produced in the county owing to the locational advantages of the southeastern counties. In other industries, such as soap and candle making or tobacco processing, Milwaukee dominated the Wisconsin output to the extent of 89 and 73 per cent respectively; but these branches were of relatively slight importance in the Wisconsin manufacturing economy as a whole.

As might be expected of the leading industrial county, Milwaukee's manufacturing establishments were larger than the average Wisconsin firm, employing 6.8 men in 1850 compared to 4.8 for Wisconsin, and 6.5 in 1860 compared to 5.4 for the state. This average county figure was a combination of factories and manufactories and very small enterprises. Several large firms in the clothing, footwear, leather, and construction branches each employed from fifty to eighty workers, often using machinery to fabricate articles for mass consumption. But at the other extreme there was a proliferation of shops run by owner-operators or craftsmen and their one apprentice. Indeed the slight decline in firm size in Milwaukee in the 1850's was due to the increasing number of such small shops. The artisan appeared able to survive the Panic of 1857 and the depression; or if he did not survive intact, at least he started again on a smaller footing.

The structural profile of antebellum Milwaukee manufacturing thus presented a dual face, consisting of a sophisticated quasi-factory sector and a much more traditional craft and shop sector. Thus any attempt to measure industrial organization in Milwaukee by using general county figures, such as the average number of hands employed in the various manufacturing branches, often fails to give an accurate assessment of scale and use of machine technology. Even the construct "average value added per worker" blurs the distinction between the contribution of skilled artisans producing for a high-class market and that of unskilled machine operators producing ready-made articles. For example, the household-craft group of industries lagged behind the county as a whole in both 1850 and 1860, having an average value added per worker of $392 compared to $543 in the earlier year and $590 compared to $845 for the later year. The Milwaukee craft group also lagged behind its Wisconsin counterpart in 1850 — the figures being $392 and $737 respectively — though it had pulled ahead by 1860, the respective figures being $590 and $477. Yet the household-craft group in Milwaukee contained those large manufactories producing ready-made clothes and footwear.

Division of labor is probably an improved measure of industrial maturity in Milwaukee County, though this category applies only to the larger establishments. The small firms with less than six employees were basically craft shops. By the mid-1850's most iron foundries and machine shops had organized the various production functions into specialized departments which were supervised by a foreman. Among the processing industries most of the larger breweries employing some eight or ten workers, the larger flour mills, employing ten to twelve workers, and the tannery and leather works of Pfister & Co. all had separate stories for housing the machinery required for the different stages of manufacture, a development which indicates some rudimentary specialization.[5]

Machinery was used in the production of ready-made goods in the leading establishments of the household-craft consumer industries, but the degree of division of labor was not always clear. In the clothing industry, especially, there was little evidence to show whether the employees made whole garments themselves or wheth-

[5] MCSW Milwaukee County, 1850 and 1860; *Milwaukee Sentinel*, July 6, 1849; July 18, Sept. 22, 23, 24, Oct. 15, 1853; Apr. 16, 1859; Apr. 29, May 15, 1862; Sept. 1, 1866; *The Conservator*, Dec. 29, 1859; *Milwaukee City Directory, 1847–48*, advs. [hereinafter cited as *MCD*]; *Wisconsin Farmer*, 13 (1861), 236.

er they concentrated on producing only parts of garments; in other words, whether they merely took over the tailor's role or whether they accelerated production by making only one piece of clothing. Those large establishments in the household industries which employed a minimum of fifteen workers might more realistically be described as manufactories rather than factories, while the smaller firms worked in the traditional way with hand power.

Use of newer modes of motive power was also confined to the larger firms. However, the presence of steam-driven machinery in such enterprises was not necessarily an indication of industrial leadership. The construction of the dam on the Milwaukee and Rock River canal in 1842 had provided a relatively cheap and accessible source of water power in the 1840's and early 1850's; the canal was advertised as one of the city's advantages as an industrial location.[6] But intermittent legal wrangles over payment for use of the water, and the seasonal hazards of floods and droughts, encouraged an increasing number of large firms with available capital to install steam power in the 1850's. Steam power was necessary in the foundry and machinery industry; but it also came to be regarded as a more reliable form of energy in some of the leading flour mills, the major breweries, and the brickyards.[7] Reliability, rather than specific cost factors, was responsible for the introduction of steam power in Milwaukee.

The dichotomy present in the industrial organization of Milwaukee firms was reflected not only in machine technology and division of labor, but also in the availability of capital for manufacturing. Local finances for starting industrial enterprises in Milwaukee were always in short supply. Although the six city banks controlled some 23 per cent of Wisconsin's banking assets, or about $3,533,084 in 1860, their loans, in the antebellum years,

[6] *Milwaukee Commercial Herald*, Aug. 25, 1843; *Milwaukee Courier*, Sept. 6, 1843; Sept. 9, 1844; *Milwaukee Sentinel*, July 4, 1849; March 28, 1853; Jan. 24, 1860; *De Bow's Review*, 17 (1854), 531; *MCD, 1847-48*, 68; Chamber of Commerce, *A.R.*, 1861, p. 4; Increase A. Lapham, *Wisconsin: Its Geography and Topography* (Milwaukee, 1846), 113-114.

[7] MCSW, Milwaukee County, 1860; *Milwaukee Sentinel*, Aug. 20, 1849; Sept. 22, 28, Oct. 15, 1853; Aug. 9, 1854; Feb. 16, Aug. 10, 1858; Jan. 24, 1860; Aug. 27, 1861; *Milwaukee Courier*, Jan. 20, 1847; *The Conservator*, Dec. 29, 1859; Chamber of Commerce, *A.R.*, 1856, p. 29; 1859, p. 12; *MCD, 1847-48*, advs.; Buck, vols. 1-4, *passim*; Thomas C. Cochran, *The Pabst Brewing Company: The History of An American Business* (New York, 1948), 28.

usually went to the visibly more remunerative commercial and railroad enterprises. Whatever remaining capital was available usually went to large industrialists who had already brought much of their own capital to Milwaukee, or who had Eastern credit and were thus considered to be fairly safe risks. Craftsmen with little tangible financial security faced serious problems in trying to obtain capital for the expansion of their businesses. The polarization in the size of firms thus tended to be reinforced.

Antebellum Milwaukee revealed the most highly developed example of industrial growth in Wisconsin in terms of grass output and diversified production. The city contributed approximately one quarter of the state's aggregate and had a wide range of leading industries, in contrast to most areas in Wisconsin which tended to concentrate on one product. The port location, the availability of natural resources, a growing urban population, and an improving transportation network encouraged Milwaukee to forge ahead in Wisconsin manufacturing and become the leading sector. Indeed these locational assets also encouraged structural change in part of Milwaukee's industry, for they attracted a certain amount of fluid capital which facilitated technical innovations and subsequent economies of scale. A small number of large firms increasingly became modernized and moved towards factory production. But the bulk of industrial enterprises run by craftsmen remained small and catered to the needs of segments of the local community. Milwaukee thus displayed many of the traditional and transitional stages of antebellum manufacturing.

THE PROCESSING INDUSTRIES

Flour Milling

Flour milling was the leading industry in Milwaukee throughout the antebellum period. Originating in the need to serve the pioneer community, local gristmills soon turned to commercial flouring as well as to custom work. The advantage of a port location offered the incentive of sales in Eastern markets, and as plank roads and then railroads increased the radius of the wheat-producing hinterland, city millers were able to expand their output.

As with most frontier settlements, gristmills were early built to supply the wants of pioneer Milwaukee residents. By 1840 the census reported that eight such mills were in operation in Milwaukee County. They must, however, have been primitive, since flour was still imported until 1845. Only in the mid-1840's did entrepreneurs start to construct larger mills on the water power of the canal. The first flour mill was built on the canal in 1843; two more were constructed the following year and a fourth in 1846. By 1849 five mills, one driven by steam power, were each reputed to have a capacity of eighty or a hundred barrels of flour daily, and in 1850 they produced 96,291 barrels of flour in addition to custom work.[8]

These mills were taking advantage of the ready supply of wheat shipped to Milwaukee from the grain-producing counties of Wisconsin. Though the agricultural hinterland from which the city could draw wheat supplies in the 1840's was limited by the high cost of transportation, Milwaukee's mills did not suffer from a shortage of raw materials.[9] Indeed in the late 1840's more wheat was exported than was processed locally despite the steady rise of flour exports from 15,756 barrels in 1846 to 136,657 barrels by 1849.[10] The availability of wheat supplies grew in the 1850's along with the expansion of the city's agricultural hinterland. Increased shipments of wheat came not only by wagon from neighboring counties, but also by railroad both from other parts of Wisconsin and from trans-Mississippi areas. By 1860 one third of Milwaukee's wheat receipts of 9,108,458 bushels originated in Illinois, Iowa, and Minnesota.[11]

[8] *Milwaukee Courier*, Oct. 29, 1844; *Milwaukee Sentinel*, July 4, 1849; Thomas Whitney, "An Address at the Opening of the New Chamber of Commerce Rooms in the City of Milwaukee," Feb. 1863, *Milwaukee Pamphlets*, vol. 4, no. 6, p. 16; Frank A. Flower (ed.), *A History of Milwaukee, Wisconsin* (Chicago, 1881), 1117, 1177, 1178, 1179, 1181; Howard L. Conrad (ed.), *History of Milwaukee* (3 vols., Chicago, 1895), 1: 282, 284; 2: 19; John G. Gregory, *History of Milwaukee, Wisconsin* (4 vols., Chicago, 1931), 1: 532; Buck, 2: 164, 175, 264, 278; *Sixth Census, 1840, Compendium*, 353; *MCD, 1848–49*, 19; MCSW, Milwaukee County, 1850.

[9] Derby, 137, suggests that wagon transportation cost as much as one third of the wheat price in the lakeshore markets; Sophie A. Boe, "Lars Davidson Reque, Pioneer," Norwegian American Historical Association, *Studies*, 6 (1931), 43–44, claims that in the 1840's Milwaukee was the nearest wheat market for the settlers of Koshkonong, Jefferson County, but that the eighty-mile trip usually consumed all the farmers' profits.

[10] It is impossible to estimate the proportions of Milwaukee flour which were consumed locally or sold in Wisconsin and those which were exported. The flour exported from Milwaukee included some which was not processed in the city mills, but the reports of the Chamber of Commerce do not show the origins of this flour.

[11] J.G. Clark, 266–267; Thompson, 115–116; Chamber of Commerce, *A.R.* 1860, p. 12.

The Milwaukee millers gradually took more advantage of the enlarged flow of wheat through the port. During the second half of the 1850's the number of flour mills increased from five to thirteen and the commercial milling output rose to some 300,000 barrels by 1860. About half of the city mills manufactured flour for sale in both Eastern and foreign markets. The Eagle Mills, producing some 200–250 barrels of flour daily by 1860, specialized in Eagle brand flour. The Empire Mills, reputed to be the largest establishment of its kind in Wisconsin in 1858, made "superior" flour, under the brand name Stone, which commanded a high price in both local and Eastern markets. The Phoenix Mill of Edwin Sanderson produced a high output; the Kilbourn Mill, owned by Amos Sawyer, also made flour which sold at top prices in the Buffalo market. The new steam-powered flouring mill of Nichols, Britt & Co., with its 135-horsepower engine, already had the highest individual output — 80,000 barrels — in Milwaukee in 1860. Other smaller mills like the City, the Curtis, the Upper, and the Cherry, and the mills of the towns of Wauwatosa, Oak Creek, and Greenfield, had a more limited output and appeared mainly to supply the local market.[12]

This increased output of flour in Milwaukee placed the city and indeed the county firmly in the forefront of Wisconsin's second-leading industry. In the 1840's when the flouring industry was dispersed in numerous small mills catering to local communities, Milwaukee was merely one of several manufacturing centers. In fact in 1850, both Racine and Rock counties contributed more to the state total than did Milwaukee County, having outputs of 14.7 per cent and 11.3 per cent respectively as compared to 10.4 per cent for Milwaukee. But in the 1850's Milwaukee began to rise above the status of a local center by processing part of the wheat shipments brought in by the growing railroad network. In 1860 the county produced over a quarter of the state's total, mainly in large city establishments with a capital over $10,000.

Yet even this output, remarkable as it was in contrast to other parts of Wisconsin, was small in comparison to the total wheat

[12] *Milwaukee Sentinel*, May 25, 1850; Sept. 12, 1853; Nov. 21, 1854; Apr. 24, 1856; May 19, Aug. 10, 1858; Jan. 24, 1860; *The Conservator*, Dec. 29, 1859; MCSW, Milwaukee County, 1860; Board of Trade, *A.R.* 1854, p. 5; 1855, p. 10; 1856, p. 29; Chamber of Commerce, *A.R.* 1859, p. 12; 1860, p. 19; *Wisconsin Farmer*, 13 (1861), 235; D. &. B. vol. 36: 17, 39, 88; *USDB*, 640; Buck, 3: 85; 4: 335; Flower, 1149, 1158, 1177.

shipments through the port of Milwaukee. By 1860 some 7,568,608 bushels of wheat were being sent eastward, while only 1,407,600 bushels were consumed directly in the city mills. The cost of shipping wheat by the Great Lakes, or after 1858 by railroad, was not much higher than that of shipping flour.[13] Given a minimal price differential in carrying charges, the commission and forwarding merchants in Milwaukee preferred to export the bulk of the wheat and only looked to the local manufacturers to absorb a small proportion of the total. Furthermore, fluctuations in the price of wheat and periodic interruptions of milling due to floods and droughts tended to diminish the financial security of flouring.[14] The Milwaukee milling industry was thus not exploited to its full potential.

Construction Materials

Construction materials, which in Milwaukee consisted of the famous cream-colored bricks as well as the secondary lumber products of sashes, doors, blinds, shingles, and lath, comprised the second-leading branch in the processing group in terms of value added and the leading branch in numbers of men employed. (Table 21 and Table 22.) In an expanding city there was a constant demand for materials for houses and commercial, service, and recreational buildings. Although Milwaukee County was soon depleted of lumber resources, the harbor facilitated the import of pine from northern Wisconsin. Turning and planing mills in Milwaukee were then able to process the rough-sawed lumber into finished shapes. The material for bricks was readily available in the huge clay beds found within the city limits.

Carpenters, joiners, turners, sawmill operators, and brickmakers working either on a full-time or a part-time basis were essential to the development of a village community. In Milwaukee a dam and sawmill had been built on the river at Humboldt as early as 1833–34 when settlers numbered but a dozen or so. By mid-1836 there were two other sawmills further up the river, at least two carpenters' shops, and numerous handymen working on the fifty houses then being built. But even the earliest buildings in Mil-

---

[13] Chamber of Commerce, *A.R.* 1858–1868, *passim.*
[14] *Milwaukee Sentinel,* Jan. 24, 1860; June 3, 1866; *Wisconsin Farmer,* 13 (1861), 235; Chamber of Commerce, *A.R.* 1859, p. 8; Buck, vols. 1–4, *passim;* Merk, 132.

waukee were not completely wooden; their chimneys were some-times made from brick such as that produced by the Olin Brothers and Isaac Loomis in the spring of 1835.[15]

The growth of the frontier village was retarded by the Panic of 1837, which impeded all improvements but especially those in the West. Building did not halt altogether during the depres-sion, and the census in 1840 noted the existence of eight sawmills and three brick kilns in the county. But growth was slow, and it was not until the spring of 1841 that the business outlook became more promising. Then the presence of at least sixteen boss car-penters and three principal brick masons in Milwaukee indicated a resurgence of building activity. Two years later, in 1843, this expansion was confirmed as three new brickyards were opened and improvements on the new water power included a sawmill, a planing mill, a wood-turning shop, and a sash, door, and blind factory.[16]

Throughout the remainder of the 1840's local mills and shops processed increasing amounts of wood, often imported from other parts of Wisconsin. Of the twenty-five industrial establishments located on the water power in 1848, eleven were turning mills or sash, door, and blind factories. In 1849 planed lumber, shingles, sashes, doors, and blinds made in Milwaukee city were valued at $99,200. A year later the census reported that the value added in both primary and secondary lumber processing in the county reached $47,181. As the local market expanded, so most of the shops and mills made construction materials in bulk for quick sale as well as catering to the custom trade.[17]

Brickmaking was an industry of only slightly smaller dimensions than lumber processing. The three brick kilns in operation in 1840 were soon overworked, for bricks were increasingly used to erect complete buildings and even blocks of buildings in the early 1840's. By 1843 three new yards had been opened, and in the

[15] Enoch Chase, "Reminiscences," 1876, State Historical Society of Wisconsin; Buck, 1: 41, 43; 2: 27; Andrew C. Wheeler, The Chronicles of Milwaukee (Milwau-kee, 1861), 1–72, passim; Rudolf A. Koss, Milwaukee (Milwaukee, 1871), 1–71, pas-sim; "Milwaukee Notes and Stories" (Milwaukee, 1946), typewritten, p. 17.

[16] Milwaukee Courier, March 2, 1842; Buck, vol. 1, passim; Wheeler, 73–128, passim; Flower, 189–192; Koss, 72–184, passim.

[17] Milwaukee Democrat, Jan. 26, 1844, adv.; Milwaukee Courier, Oct. 9, 1844; American Freeman, Aug. 18, 1846, adv.; Milwaukee Sentinel, July 4, 1849; MCD, 1847–48, pp. 68–69; MCSW, Milwaukee County, 1850.

following year the Burnham Brothers, later to become the leading brickmakers in Milwaukee city, began production. The distinctive creamy yellow of the finished article, which so infuriated early brickmakers, was now adding to its sales potential. By 1847 some 125 men and twenty-four teams of horses were employed in manufacturing 8,788,000 bricks, of which 300,000 were exported to Chicago and other lakeports. Three years later, in 1850, eleven brick years employed ninety-five men in the manufacture of 11,550,000 bricks.[18]

During the 1850's the manufacture of construction materials increased from an aggregate value added of $75,770 in 1850 to $205,968 in 1860. This rise was more rapid in the first half of the decade, for the eight brickyards in operation in 1856 employed about 300 laborers producing 35,000,000 bricks, whereas the eight yards of 1860 only employed 214 men producing 23,500,000 bricks. The Panic of 1857 and the depression of the late 1850's restricted the output of the building industry. Yet the overall growth during the decade was more substantial than the corresponding 126 per cent rise in the city's population. Some of this differential in the increases may have resulted from the building of shops, warehouses, mills, churches, and recreational facilities in addition to houses, as well as from the export of some brick.

Most wooden building materials manufactured in Milwaukee in the 1850's were for use in the city, though some sashes, doors, blinds, and shingles may have been sold to master builders who had contracts in the county where materials and mechanics were not so easily procured. At any rate these materials were probably not exported a great distance, since several Milwaukee lumber merchants were importing shingles and lath in the early 1850's. These imports might have been intended for the re-export trade within Wisconsin, but this is doubtful. Milwaukee lumber merchants involved in the re-export trade appeared to be more interested in sending large quantities of sawed and planed lumber to Chicago and other Lake ports. Then too, Wisconsin towns often had their own local resources of lumber or could import planed timber directly from the pineries, especially after the advent of

---

[18] Chase "Reminiscences," 28; *MCD, 1847–48,* pp. 8–9; MCSW, Milwaukee County, 1850; Flower, 1505; J.G. Gregory, 1: 512, 513; Buck, 1: 183; 2: 164.

the railroads. They thus had no need to obtain construction materials from Milwaukee.[19]

Most of the brick manufactured in the factories on the Menominee River were also sold in Milwaukee city and environs. The exotic cream color stimulated an export market which could afford to absorb the high cost of transportation, but local demand was usually too heavy to allow much trade. Of the three large brickyards in operation in 1853, the two belonging to the Burnham Brothers sent approximately one third of their output to Chicago, Green Bay, and Michigan City; but C.B. Kindler sent out only a small amount. The output of the smaller kilns was all consumed in the city. In 1856, despite the steady increase in output — from a total of 12,900,000 bricks in 1853 to some 35,000,000 — only about 1,000,000 were exported. The export market must have declined further during the late 1850's.[20]

The manufacture of shingles, lath, sashes, doors, blinds, bricks and other building materials remained essentially a local industry oriented to the expanding needs of Milwaukee city and vicinity. The cost of transporting construction materials from Milwaukee was too expensive to absorb, if, as was the case with most Wisconsin towns and lakeshore ports, it was possible to import lumber directly from the pineries, or if there were timber resources near at hand. The only product which could overcome the high cost of transportation and create an export demand was the distinctive Milwaukee brick, but its supply was conditioned by the local market.

Brewing

The liquor industry, which in Milwaukee in 1860 meant the manufacture of lager beer, was the third-leading processing industry in the county in the antebellum years and indeed was the fourth-leading industry in Wisconsin. Its origin and steady growth lay not so much in the accessibility of agricultural crops such as

[19] MCD, 1851–52, adv.; 1856–57, p. 92; Milwaukee Sentinel, Aug. 10, 1858, adv.; Board of Trade, A.R. 1855, p. 11; Chamber of Commerce, A.R. 1858, p. 21; 1859, p. 19; 1860, p. 43; 1862, p. 29; Harrison Ludington Papers, Box 1, scattered correspondence, late 1850's and early 1860's, State Historical Society of Wisconsin.

[20] Milwaukee Sentinel, Sept. 28, 1853; Jan. 24, 1860; Board of Trade, A.R. 1854, p. 3; 1855, p. 8; 1856, p. 29; MCD, 1854, p. 5; 1855, p. 10; 1857–58, p. 12; MCSW, Milwaukee County, 1860.

barley and hops, but rather in the presence of an ethnic group —
the Germans — both as producers and consumers. To be sure,
a supply of pure water, malt, hops, and yeast was essential; but
it was primarily the foreign-born workers, most notably the Germans, who played the critical role in developing a product for
which Milwaukee was later to become famous.

Remarkably enough, the first brewery in Milwaukee, the Lake,
made ale. Opened in 1840 by three Welshmen — Owens, Pallet,
and Davis — this establishment supposedly produced enough beer
and ale to last eastern Wisconsin for two years. The first German
lager brewery, the South Side, was built the following year by a
Würtemburger, Herman Reutelshofer. The product sold well,
but the proprietor lacked the necessary capital for the venture
and sold out to J.B. Meyer. The second lager brewery, the Empire, opened by Jacob Best in 1842, was more successful. Run as
a family concern along with a vinegar and distillery plant, the
several members did all the work, including making the barrels.
Other concerns, each with a limited output of from 250 to 300
barrels a year, were started in the 1840's to serve the demands of
an increasing number of Germans in Milwaukee. By midcentury
there were ten breweries in the city producing some 18,820 barrels and 33,000 bottles of beer valued at $82,812.[21]

The brewing industry expanded rapidly in the early 1850's. By
1853 breweries were making some 33,900 barrels of beer, an output
which increased to 47,207 barrels the following year and to 50,578
barrels in 1855. In the latter year, 240 men were employed in
the twenty city establishments. The industry was highly profitable
and most brewers received sound credit ratings. Growth continued until 1858 when the severe effects of depressed business
conditions began to be felt. Indeed 1857, with its output of
75,000 barrels of beer from twenty-six establishments employing
some 500 men, probably marked the ceiling of prosperity for
Milwaukee brewers for nearly a decade ensuing. Certainly the
1860 production of 45,800 barrels was down on the 1855 total
even though twenty breweries were still in operation.[22]

[21] MCD, 1847–48, p. 67; MCSW, Milwaukee County, 1850; Cochran, 11–28; Koss,
passim; Buck, 2: 116; 4: 343–349; Flower, 1456–1463; "Milwaukee Notes and
Sketches," 45–48.
[22] Board of Trade, A.R. 1854, p. 3; 1855, p. 8; 1856, p. 29; Chamber of Commerce,
A.R. 1860, p. 40; Milwaukee Sentinel, Jan. 24, 1860; MCD, 1857–58, p. 12; MCSW,
Milwaukee County, 1860; Cochran, 28; D. & B. vol. 36: 27, 55, 68, 101, 107, 186.

The increase in brewing capacity before 1857 was contemporaneous with the increase in railroad mileage in Wisconsin. There was, however, no direct connection between the two, although shipments of barley were more readily available if sent by rail rather than wagon. There may, however, have been some relationship between Milwaukee's lager beer production and the new markets accessible by improved transportation. As early as 1852 Milwaukee brewers shipped 645 barrels of beer to Chicago and other more distant cities. A hot summer soon depleted Chicago's own supply during the seasonal closure of lager breweries in 1854, and the completion of the Chicago and North Western Railway in 1855 gave a further boost to the export of the Milwaukee product. Possibly 25-35,000 barrels of beer were shipped from Milwaukee in 1857, though this total must have dropped in the immediate prewar years. In view of this export potential, transportation networks providing easier access to a wider market may have encouraged the expansion of Milwaukee breweries in the early and middle 1850's.[23]

But the local Milwaukee market was of far greater significance in explaining the rapid increase of new breweries. Consumption of lager beer was high among the working class of Milwaukee, and especially among the German element, which formed about one third of the city's population. Despite the temperance sentiments of the Yankees, the increase in the market for beer and the popularity of the beverage was probably far greater than even the German population figures suggested. Other ethnic groups, notably the Irish, had a drinking tradition. Moreover, during the 1850's, German drinking habits spread to other groups by way of social gathering places such as beer halls and beer gardens.[24]

Equally as important as the German consumer in the success of the antebellum Milwaukee brewing industry was the German producer. Most of the successful brewers were German mainly because they were experienced in the business and because they often possessed a little capital which could be used for the initial venture. For example, Jacob Best owned a brewery and winery in Mettenheim, Rheinhessen, before he came to Milwaukee in

[23] Board of Trade, *A.R.* 1855, p. 8; 1856, p. 29; Chamber of Commerce, *A.R.* 1860, p. 40; *Milwaukee Sentinel,* Aug. 24, 1860; Cochran, 31.
[24] Cochran, 29-35; "Milwaukee Notes and Sketches," 48.

1842. His son Philip had learned the trade in Germany and France. A small amount of capital was probably obtained from the sale of the business in Mettenheim. Valentine Blatz, who started his enterprise in Milwaukee in 1851 with a capital of $500, was likewise a skilled craftsman. He had served an apprenticeship in his father's plant and then gained further experience in other large German breweries. Franz Falk had also worked in several German breweries before emigrating to the United States. He accumulated capital for his business by working as foreman in C.T. Melms' brewery for seven years. Such entrepreneurs, using their native training and a little capital, were virtually assured of success in the 1840's and 1850's when they were catering to a sellers' market. Even during the hard times of the late 1850's few brewers went out of business. Trade was more restricted, but was still adequate for survival, if not for prosperity.[25]

Tanning and Leather Products

Tanning and the production of leathergoods such as saddles, harnesses, and trunks was another important processing industry in antebellum Milwaukee. The Wisconsin towns on Lake Michigan were well placed for the manufacture of leather, for they had access to local supplies of hides and pelts, and could import tanbark from northern Wisconsin. Furthermore they could take advantage of the lake route to export products to Eastern markets. Milwaukee, in addition, benefited from a growing urban market and a ready labor supply, and quickly took a commanding position in Wisconsin, manufacturing 30.2 per cent of the state's leather and leathergoods in 1850 and 33.1 per cent in 1860.

The initial supply of leather products in early Milwaukee was sold or exchanged for produce in two retail shops owned by Ezra Dewey and Street & Scott, the latter firm claiming to have had their merchandise manufactured at their Albany, New York, shop expressly for the Milwaukee market. Other leathergoods shops were opened in 1841 and 1843 by William McKillip and William Lee. But the early trade was not confined to retailing and repairing. The census of 1840 reported the manufacture of leather-

---

[25] D. & B. vol. 36: 55, 68, 101, 107, 131, 186, 320; *USDB*, 19, 25–26, 196–197, 376–377, 382, 670–673; Cochran, 1–19; Flower, 1456–1472; Buck, 3: 348–49; 4: 343–348; Conrad, 2: 36, 185, 327, 336–337.

goods valued at $5,000, and a contemporary observer noted that Milwaukee had four saddle-and-harness makers and two tanneries in 1842.[26]

Daniel Phelps had started Milwaukee's first small tannery in 1842 and was followed shortly thereafter by Christopher Doerfler, who tanned deerskins. These two were joined in 1844 by Trumbull & Hotchkiss, who built their establishment on the canal water power. By the mid-1840's Milwaukee was becoming a center for the Wisconsin leather industry. The Allen brothers opened their shop in Milwaukee in 1846, though their actual tanning operations were done at Two Rivers in Manitowoc County. Frederick Vogel built a tannery on the Menominee River in 1847. In the same year Guido Pfister opened his Buffalo Leather Store and George Dyer began manufacturing saddles and harnesses. Two years later R. Suhm & Co. and Willard B. Johnson began tanning leather in the city. Most of these operations were small scale; they either supplied craftsmen, especially shoemakers, with leather, or produced custom-made leather goods. The exception were the tannery of Guido Pfister, which accounted for some 50 per cent of the Milwaukee leather industry in 1850, and the leather store of Allen & Allis, which was supplied from Two Rivers.[27]

Apparently there were two extremes of scale. On the one hand there was the skilled craftsman and the merchant-manufacturer like Herman Zöhrlaut or Albert Trostel and August Gallum. These small operators, who were quite often native Germans, usually had a capital of about $2,000 and employed three or four workers. While increasing in size in the 1850's, they still did a limited business as practical artisans and supplied a local demand for hides and finished goods.[28]

On the other hand, there was the industrialist of regional if

[26] *Milwaukee Advertiser*, Sept. 16, Dec. 9, 1837, advs.; *Milwaukee Sentinel*, Sept. 14, 1842, adv.; *Milwaukee Semi-Weekly Gazette*, Jan. 23, 1846; Flower, 189–190; Buck, 2: 84, 147, 156, 175.

[27] *American Freeman*, Feb. 14, 1845, adv.; Sept. 1, 1846, adv.; D. & B. vol. 36: 14, 53, 70; MCSW, Milwaukee County, 1850; Schefft, 22–27; Buck, 3: 187, 420; J.G. Gregory, 1: 536; Conrad, 1: 330; 2: 303, 308, 318; Flower, 1438; *The Century Club of Business in Milwaukee*, reprinted from the *Milwaukee Sentinel* (Milwaukee, 1966), 28.

[28] D. & B. vol. 36: 42, 57, 66, 70, 99; MCSW, Milwaukee County, 1860; Schefft, 15–16; Flower, 1438–1443.

not national repute. Two Milwaukee firms, Pfister & Vogel and the Wisconsin Leather Company, clearly fell into this category.[29] These firms were in the forefront of the Wisconsin leather industry mainly because they were able to command ample capital. Many of the other Milwaukee tanners, saddlers, and harnessmakers had practical business experience, and all benefited from the locational advantages of proximity to raw materials, a lakeshore site, and a local urban market; but Pfister & Vogel and the Wisconsin Leather Company started business already well endowed and had the financial assets to build up establishments of major importance.

Guido Pfister and Frederick Vogel had both previously worked in the Buffalo tannery of J.F. Schoelkoff, a cousin of Vogel. While neither had large assets, Schoelkoff, who remained in Buffalo, was willing to put up $12,000 and supply the Milwaukee enterprise with any required goods. By 1857, when the tannery was prospering, Schoelkoff sold his interest for $45,000. Edward Allis and William Allen, who came from Cazenovia, New York, were even better endowed financially. Allis' father was estimated to have made about $20,000 from his tanning business; Allen's father had made double that amount. The Milwaukee establishment — or, more aptly, the Milwaukee branch — was to be supplied from Cazenovia. The finances of these two entrepreneurs were further strengthened when the Wisconsin Leather Company was formed in 1851, with a capital of $30,000, and Rufus Allen, the father, became one of the partners.[30]

Pfister & Vogel and the Wisconsin Leather Company both used their capital well in developing a lucrative and extensive business. Their large tanneries, built at great cost in 1849 and 1851, were constructed to facilitate the swift but high-quality processing of leather. Attempts were then made to control the supply of raw materials. In the early 1850's Pfister & Vogel had imported some of their skins from as far off as New Orleans and had obtained hemlock bark from Michigan and northern Wisconsin. But later

[29] The Wisconsin Leather Company of R. Allen, C.W. Allen, E.P. Allis, W.T. Allen, and C. Whitcomb had its extensive tannery at Two Rivers, Manitowoc County, and its leather store in the city of Milwaukee. It was not until 1870 that economies of scale encouraged the relocation of the tannery in Milwaukee.

[30] D. & B. vol. 36: 14, 53; *The Century Club*, 28–29; Conrad, 2: 308.

in the decade they bought land in Manitowoc County, Wisconsin, in order to obtain bark, while their supply of hides was improved by the opening of the railroads to the Mississippi in 1857 and 1858. The Wisconsin Leather Company was able to obtain tanbark from its own grounds at Two Rivers, and, like Pfister & Vogel, gained a steadier supply of hides by using the railroads.

Both firms were active in sales arrangements, for they were looking to Eastern as well as Western markets. Even in 1852 the Wisconsin Leather Company estimated that it would ship 200,000 pounds of rough leather to the East, over and above that large stock of finished leather sold in the Milwaukee store. By the mid-1850's the two firms were clearly enterprises of high standing, and though the general economic conditions of the late 1850's were not conducive to rapid growth, both firms survived the panic and depression with little trouble. Pfister & Vogel even added to their premises in the late 1850's, though the Wisconsin Leather Company waited until 1861 before building another tannery.[31]

Success in the leather industry in Milwaukee did not depend upon location and access to raw materials alone. Certainly these were basic ingredients, but training in leather work, whether obtained in Germany or in the United States, was an additional asset. Most Milwaukee tanners and leathergoods manufacturers, whatever the size of their businesses, had had some previous experience in leather or an allied trade. Moreover, to establish a large firm in antebellum Wisconsin, it was also essential to command abundant capital to spend on plant construction, raw materials, and marketing arrangements.

Meat Packing

The antebellum meatpacking industry in Wisconsin, more so than any other major processing industry, was dominated by Milwaukee. By 1860 the city was responsible for approximately three quarters of the state's value added. Other towns in Wisconsin usually butchered cattle and hogs on a small scale for local consumption. Milwaukee, however, not only served the city and its

[31] *Milwaukee Sentinel*, Apr. 28, July 25, 1851; July 27, 1852; Jan. 5, Oct. 15, 1853; Apr. 16, 1859; Jan. 24, 1860; *Watertown Chronicle*, Jan. 12, 1853; *Oshkosh Democrat*, Nov. 15, 1851; D. & B. vol. 32: 251; vol. 36: 53; Buck, 3: 420–422; Flower, 1438–1439; *The Century Club*, 28–29.

environs, but also exported meat northward to the lumber camps and eastward to urban markets. This Wisconsin industry was being centralized.

Prior to 1851 the amount of pork and beef packed in Milwaukee for eastern shipment was very limited — perhaps not exceeding a total of 8,000 barrels, an amount which fell below that packed in contemporary Racine. Possibly the receipt of cattle and hogs from the local hinterland did not greatly exceed the consumption demands of Milwaukee. The character of the industry was certainly one of butchering rather than slaughtering and packing. For example, August Greulich had a butcher's shop as early as 1840. John Layton and his son Frederick started in the butchering business in 1842, and in 1845 they opened a meat market to supply hotels and boardinghouses. A year earlier, in 1844, John Plankinton had opened a butcher's shop and packed pork in the winter, using animals killed on local farms.[32] Conditions in pioneer Milwaukee were not really conducive to the large-scale development of meatpacking. Owing to the lack of good all-year transportation and refrigeration, nearly every Wisconsin town was a center for its own locality. Furthermore, as most packing had to be done during the three-or-four-month winter season when the lake was frozen, the export trade to the East was hampered.

It was not until midcentury that packing was started on a commercial basis by more enterprising butchers such as Layton and Plankinton, and by commission merchants who regarded it as a side-line for using their warehouses in the winter.[33] In 1849 John Plankinton expanded his butcher's shop and went into the business of slaughtering cattle. Layton's meat market was doing an increasing trade in 1850. In 1851 Thomas and Edward Roddis built a large packing establishment on the Menominee River, which they enlarged the following year to slaughter 125 head of cattle and between 300 and 400 hogs a day. In 1852 Frederick Layton formed a partnership with John Plankinton and, using capital acquired in their businesses and borrowed from

[32] "Records of the Milwaukee Board of Trade, 1849–1853," Box 1, Vol. 1, p. 19, Milwaukee Grain Exchange Collection, State Historical Society of Wisconsin; Whitney, 28; Milwaukee Writers' Project, *History of Milwaukee County* (Milwaukee, 1947), 535; Koss, 128; Buck, 2: 131, 211; J.G. Gregory, 1: 535; Conrad, 1: 284.
[33] D. &. B. vol. 36: 68, 151, 295, 311; *MCD, 1851–52, passim;* Riley, 58–61; Still, 186–187; Flower, 1216; Conrad, 2: 425; Buck, 2: 210.

the local bankers Marshall & Illsley, they also built a slaughter
and packing house in the Menominee Valley. Plankinton erected
another large packing house in the next year. Following this construction there was a rapid increase in the packing industry. Outputs grew from a total of some 2,500 barrels of beef and 4,000
barrels of pork in 1851 to 10,151 barrels of beef and 23,707 barrels
of pork in 1853. Beef packing remained stable for the next two
seasons, but 43,404 barrels of pork were packed in 1855.[34]

The output of meat packed fluctuated in the second half of
the 1850's. Dropping to a low point of 10,000 hogs slaughtered
in 1857-58, the industry recovered and increased its product to
reach a total of 25,755 barrels of pork and 18,888 barrels of beef
in 1860. To some extent this fluctuation stemmed from the seasonal nature of the industry. But of much more importance in
the late 1850's was the changing supply-and-demand situation and
the general economic condition of the country. On the one hand
the expanding railroad connections in Wisconsin meant that cattle and hogs could be brought to Milwaukee alive for slaughtering.
Theretofore packing had been mainly restricted to hogs already
dressed and brought in by the farmer by road. The improved
railroad network also made available an all-year route to the
East, where much of the meat packed in Milwaukee by 1860 was
sent. These favorable conditions, however, were partially offset
by the hard times following the Panic of 1857.[35]

Not only did the output of the packing industry fluctuate, but
the number of firms involved also rose dramatically. In 1855
there were three main packing houses in Milwaukee. Two years
later, in the 1857-58 season, only two firms had any considerable
business. In 1858, however, the number of pork packing establishments had grown to six; in 1859 it was seven; by 1860 it had
risen to twelve. The number of firms in beef packing remained
fairly stable at two or three. There was in fact a hard core of
two large firms, namely Layton & Plankinton and Roddis Bros.,

[34] "Records of the Milwaukee Board of Trade, 1849-1853," Box 1, Vol. 1, p. 62;
Milwaukee Sentinel, Nov. 23, 1850; Oct. 15, 1851; Sept. 16, Oct. 23, 1852; March
8, July 13, 1853; *De Bow's Review,* 17 (1854), 533; Board of Trade, *A.R.* 1855, p.
10; 1856, p. 29; *MCD, 1851-1852,* adv.; Conrad, 1: 284; Buck, 2: 210; J.G. Gregory,
1: 535.
[35] *Milwaukee Sentinel,* Jan. 24, 1860; Board of Trade, *A.R.,* 1855, p. 10; Chamber
of Commerce, *A.R.,* 1858, p. 19; 1859, p. 29; 1860, pp. 37, 39; 1861, p. 20.

which slaughtered some 95 per cent of the cattle and 60 to 70 per cent of the hogs. There was also a varying number of butchers producing limited quantities of meat for local consumption. In good seasons several of these small firms were regarded as packers rather than as butchers.[36]

The packing industry, like the leather industry, was structurally divided between larger regional producers and small local enterprises. Unlike the major tanning firms, however, the leading packing establishments were apparently self-financed. Layton and Plankinton were each reputed to have made money in the trade as early as 1853, while T. R. Roddis was worth over $30,000 in 1855. Having obtained an early hold on the local market, they thus acquired the capital necessary for expansion and for weathering the unstable market conditions of the late 1850's. Moreover they did not limit their business interests to meatpacking. Both firms made practical use of meat by-products to make tallow and lard. John Plankinton built a large candle factory in 1854. He had also earlier entered the hotel business, and T. R. Roddis was building stores in 1855.[37]

The antebellum meatpacking industry in Milwaukee was basically a development of the 1850's. The early and more limited butchering trade provided some entrepreneurs with sufficient capital to take advantage of the increased railroad shipment of cattle and to develop large packing plants. Increasingly these manufacturers participated in a regional and even a national trade. Other Milwaukee meatpackers, or more accurately butchers, catered to a localized trade.

Other Processing Industries

The six other processing industries in Milwaukee County — lumber, cooperage, wool, minerals, soap and candles, and tobacco — were together responsible for 16.9 per cent of the aggregate value added in 1850 and 9.6 per cent in 1860. (Table 21 and Table 22.) Of these, cooperage contributed a steady relative pro-

[36] Board of Trade, *A.R.*, 1856, p. 29; Chamber of Commerce, *A.R.*, 1858, p. 20; 1859, p. 30; 1860, pp. 20, 37, 39; 1861, pp. 19, 20; Conrad, 2: 425.

[37] *Milwaukee Sentinel*, Oct. 15, 1851; Dec. 26, 1859; Board of Trade, *A.R.*, 1856, p. 29; Chamber of Comerce, *A.R.*, 1858, p. 20; 1859, p. 30; 1860, pp. 20, 37, 39; 1861, pp. 19, 20; D. & B. vol. 36: 1g, 30, 68, 80, 84, 311; MCSW, Milwaukee County, 1860.

portion of the total, as it was ancillary to three other processing industries: flour milling, brewing, and packing. The other branches did not have a substantial resource base and though they increased in absolute value in the 1850's, they faded relatively in comparison to the better-endowed and more profitable branches.

HOUSEHOLD-CRAFT CONSUMER INDUSTRIES

The household-craft consumer industries, which catered to the domestic needs of the local population, were better able to maintain their standing in antebellum Milwaukee County than elsewhere in Wisconsin. The size of the local market — Milwaukee County had a population of 62,564 in 1860 — and the availability of a large labor force encouraged the output of ready-made goods in the clothing, footwear, and even furniture branches of manufacture. These factory or manufactory products were able to compete more effectively with imported mass-produced articles than were the higher-quality goods fabricated by local craftsmen. Thus these three consumer industries in particular, in contrast to the other three household-craft branches of blacksmithing, tinsmithing, and confectionery, were able to sustain a growth rate similar to that of the county as a whole.

Clothing

Clothing, which included ready-made ware, tailoring, dress-making and millinery goods, was the leading branch of the consumer group of industries in antebellum Milwaukee both in terms of value added and number of hands employed. (Table 21 and Table 22.) Moreover Milwaukee County, which in this case was synonymous with Milwaukee city, dominated the clothing industry in Wisconsin, contributing two thirds of the aggregate value added in both 1850 and 1860. The city industry benefiting from a large local market and available labor supplies was able to practice economies of scale impossible elsewhere in the state.

The clothing industry in early Milwaukee was run by tailors and dressmakers who cut, fitted, and sewed clothes for the custom trade and did repair work. Tailors were among the first craftsmen to establish shops in the frontier village in 1836, and by 1837 several were advertising their wares in the local newspapers.

But even at this date they did not monopolize the market, for drygoods and general stores imported ready-made "Yankee" clothes. Moreover several tailors were merchant-manufacturers and themselves imported a miscellaneous stock of clothing. It is impossible to ascertain the proportion of clothes made locally, but even in the early 1840's artisans appeared to be catering to only a limited clientele.[38]

Certainly by the mid- and late 1840's merchant-tailors dominated the locally-made clothing trade, and their large shops were already taking on certain aspects common to manufactories. Entrepreneurs like William S. Wells, Henry Newhouse, and Solomon Adler were active in the drygoods and retail clothing business, but they also employed craftsmen to make clothing for their ready-made stock and to cater to the jobbing trade. As their general business expanded, they also extended their facilities for manufacturing men's clothing. By midcentury these three employed forty, thirty-two and twenty workers respectively, tailoring clothes by hand.[39] There were at least five other merchant-tailors with clothing manufactories of similar size.[40]

These merchant manufacturers continued to dominate the Milwaukee clothing industry, producing at least 70 per cent of the output made in establishments with an annual value of product over $500.[41] During the boom years of the early 1850's, when the value of clothing increased from $179,000 in 1850 to some $600,000 in 1856, they did a prosperous business in both Milwaukee and other parts of Wisconsin. Some firms, for example Friend Bros., not only sent traveling salesmen through the state but also established branch houses at Watertown and Jefferson. Although they ran into financial difficulties in the late 1850's they were usually able to draw on their capital reserves and still

[38] *Milwaukee Advertiser,* July 1, Dec. 9, 1837, advs.; *Milwaukee Democrat,* Dec. 20, 1843, adv.; *American Freeman,* March 27, 1844, adv.; Sept. 15, 1846, adv.; *Milwaukee Courier,* Feb. 19, May 14, 1845, advs.; *Milwaukee Semi-Weekly Gazette,* Feb. 17, 1846, adv.; Buck, 1: 43, 45; 2: 100, 121, 130, 175; Flower, 190.

[39] *Milwaukee Courier,* May 14, 1845, adv.; *MCD, 1847,* pp. 21, 38, 48, 49, 69, advs.; MCSW, Milwaukee County, 1850; D. & B. vol. 36: 5, 8, 11, 47, 72, 87, 230; Buck, 2: 130; 3: 134, 146–147, 309–310.

[40] MCSW, Milwaukee County, 1850; D. & B. vol. 36: 11, 13, 72.

[41] These estimates are based on figures reported in MCSW, Milwaukee County, 1850 and 1860. They are probably conservative, because some merchant-manufacturers were not listed in the census.

emerged as large firms in 1860. At that date William Wells was employing eighty workers while D. J. Adler employed sixty-five.[42]

The increasing market for ready-made clothes in both Milwaukee and Wisconsin doubtless contributed to the success of these large firms. But the available market by itself is an insufficient explanation, for Milwaukee-made clothes had to compete with clothes imported from other parts of the country. An important factor stimulating the growth of men's clothing manufactories in frontier Milwaukee was the presence of entrepreneurs able to take on the roles of both merchant and manufacturer. Often these men began in the retail trade and were familiar with the commercial aspects of sales, such as bargaining and market contacts. Seeing the need to build up the jobbing side of their business, they also employed or took in craftsmen as partners. Gradually the manufacturing side, which was able to cater more specifically to local demand, became more important than the retailing aspects of the enterprise, and some merchant manufacturers even abandoned retailing to concentrate on the wholesale and manufacturing trade.[43]

The Milwaukee clothier was able to draw on capital gained in retailing to finance his manufacturing. In this respect Jews, and particularly German Jews, played a significant role. Of the eight leading firms in Milwaukee in 1850, at least four were Jewish, and these firms, with the exception of Henry Newhouse, expanded in the 1850's and were joined by more smaller Jewish firms. Certainly Jews did not monopolize the clothing business, for the large firms of W. S. Wells, J. Magee, the Mullen Brothers, and G. Tracy produced some 45 per cent of the clothes made in Milwaukee in 1860. But their importance should not be underestimated, for they had relatives and friends in the same business in the East, and they had a heavy financial commitment to the clothing industry.[44]

[42] MCSW, Milwaukee County, 1860; Board of Trade, *A.R.*, 1856, p. 29; D. & B. vol. 36: 5, 8, 11, 13, 47, 72, 87, 109, 117, 133, 171, 175, 219, 230, 267; *USDB*, 294–95; 372–75.

[43] Wooster, "Manufacturer and Artisan," *passim;* D. & B. vol. 36: 5, 8, 11, 13, 47, 72, 75, 87, 109, 117, 133, 152, 171, 175, 219, 230, 267; *USDB*, 294–95, 372–376; Flower, 1240–1248; Buck, 2: 130–131; 3: 134, 146–147, 309–10; Conrad, 2: 438.

[44] D. & B. vol. 36: 8, 11, 13, 87, 99, 109, 117, 133, 171, 291; Still, 277; Conrad, 2: 234; Louis J. Swichkow, "The Jewish Community in Milwaukee, Wisconsin, 1860–1870," American Jewish Historical Society, *Publications,* 47 (1957), 34–58.

Entrepreneurial initiative and ready capital were essential to the growth of large-scale clothing manufacture in Milwaukee. Economies of scale were also of some importance. The big establishments produced about two thirds of the total output of clothes, and they were able to sell garments cheaper than the small tailors' shops because their work forces facilitated division of labor. Not only were sewing machines used in some major firms in the 1850's, but the semiskilled or skilled workers seem to have concentrated on making one article or part of an article of clothing, thereby speeding up the production process. Although there was little difference between the value added per worker in the manufactories, namely $458, and that in the numerous small tailoring and dressmaking shops, namely $461 per worker, it appears that the worker in the large firm produced more or contributed to producing more articles each.[45]

The clothing industry in Milwaukee was thriving in the antebellum years. But expansion in output centered on the larger merchant-manufacturers, for though the number of small tailoring and dressmaking establishments rose dramatically in the 1850's, these shops only catered to a limited market. Utilizing the largest urban center in Wisconsin and an accessible labor force, the leading clothing manufacturers had developed manufactories producing ready-made goods for both Milwaukee city and other Wisconsin markets.

Boots and Shoes

Footwear, like clothing, was an important branch of manufacturing in antebellum Milwaukee. In both 1850 and 1860 boots and shoes contributed some 6.8 per cent of the county's value added. However, the city only cornered about one third of the state's output. Milwaukee shoe manufacturers were not able to gain the same control over this industry as were their counterparts in clothing manufacture. Despite the increasing output of mass-produced shoes made in Milwaukee manufactories, the cobblers in other parts of Wisconsin maintained a stronger position in their own localities.

Shoemaking in Milwaukee started off on a repairing and custom basis, and most enterprises remained small craft shops until the

[45] MCSW, Milwaukee County, 1850 and 1860.

Civil War. Cobblers were among the first artisans to come to Milwaukee in the mid-1830's, but, as with tailors, these men had to compete against general stores for the local trade. Several therefore became involved in retailing, either as merchant-manufacturers or as craftsmen looking after the jobbing trade of a retail store. For example, Charles Bradley and William Metcalf, who came to Milwaukee from New York City in 1843 with a stock of ready-made boots and shoes, soon started to make their own large assortment of footwear. Ambrose Ely, who stressed his own products in 1844, was calling attention to his Boston-made products by 1846. Such merchant-manufacturers came to dominate the output of shoes, though numerically the industry was dominated by artisans employing some two or three apprentices.[46]

The merchant-manufacturers in the footwear industry were similar to those in the clothing industry in having adequate if not ample financial assets. This capital might come from personal or family wealth or from mercantile activity. Bradley and Metcalf certainly had sufficient means in 1844, and by 1847 they were reputed to be worth some $10–12,000. Metcalf's marriage to the daughter of an Eastern businessman strengthened the credit of the establishment by allying it with a reputable Eastern firm. Then increasing trade in the early 1850's created new sources of money and by 1855 the business was worth at least $50,000. Albert Atkins and Chester Steele came from Hartford, Connecticut, with a good reputation and sufficient money to open a wholesale and retail shoe store in Milwaukee in 1848. By 1850 they had a capital of $5,000 and a large inventory valued at $12,000. The firm expanded, and by 1855 they felt confident enough to start manufacturing over and above the jobbing trade. Both firms weathered the economic conditions of the late 1850's in reasonable condition, and by 1860 they employed seventy and sixty workers respectively and produced some $240,000 worth of goods or 65 per cent of the Milwaukee total.[47]

[46] *American Freeman*, Sept. 18, 1844, adv.; Dec. 22, 1846, adv.; *Milwaukee Sentinel*, July 27, 1841; Jan. 13, 1844, adv.; March 8, 1845, adv.; *MCD, 1847-48*, pp. 21, 58; MCSW, Milwaukee County, 1850; D. & B. vol. 36: 10, 69; Buck, 1: 41–43; 2: 118–131, 153–154.

[47] Bradley and Metcalf, "Articles of Agreement," Jan. 2, 1843, State Historical Society of Wisconsin; *Milwaukee Sentinel*, Jan. 13, 1844, adv.; March 8, 1845, adv.; Jan. 24, 1856; MCSW, Milwaukee County, 1850 and 1860; D. & B. vol. 36: 4, 10; Buck, 2: 153–54; 3: 130–31; Flower, 1448; Conrad, 2: 361.

The merchant-manufacturers in the shoe industry were distinctive, however, in being relatively few in number. While 30 per cent of the Milwaukee clothing firms employed over fifteen workers each in 1850, and 21 per cent employed over fifteen in 1860, only 20 per cent of the shoe firms employed that number of operatives in 1850 and only 6 per cent in 1860.[48] The shoe industry was slower than the clothing industry in moving from the craft shop to the merchant-manufacturer's shop and then to the manufactory stage of production. It was not until midcentury that ready-made shoes were shaped for left and right feet, and many customers had their footware custom-made for some years. Moreover the installation of machinery in a shoe factory was more expensive than for a clothing factory, and Wisconsin capital for investment in manufacturing was in short supply.

The Milwaukee shoe manufacturers were also notable because they were clearly benefiting from economies of scale. In 1860 the three leading firms had a value added per worker of $932, in contrast to $365 per worker for the forty-eight small firms. Not only did the large firms use machinery; division of labor also reduced the cost of their production process.[49] Thus the smaller shops in Milwaukee, even those which had backward linkages with the tanneries and leather goods firms, were less able to withstand the competition of locally mass-produced goods.

The successful boot-and-shoe manufacturers in antebellum Milwaukee were those who came with capital and who had or gained experience in the retail trade. By contrast, James Campbell, who had an excellent custom work business and was described as "the genteel Boot maker of the City," employed only eight workers in 1850 and eleven in 1860. He possessed little capital, having but $500 invested in his shop in 1850 and $1,000 a decade later. Yet he was the leading craftsman in his line.[50] Obviously it was more profitable to mass-produce shoes for the medium

[48] These figures are taken from MCSW, Milwaukee County, 1850 and 1860. They may well understate the number of merchant-manufacturers in the footwear industry.

[49] MCSW, Milwaukee County, 1860, reported no use of machinery in the large boot-and-shoe establishments, but a vistor to the Bradley & Metcalf plant in 1861 claimed that the latest and most approved machinery was employed there. See Wisconsin Farmer, 13 (1861), 236.

[50] D. & B. vol. 36: 124; MCSW, Milwaukee County, 1850 and 1860.

value market than it was to fashion customware for sale in a small shop or to individual clients.

Furniture

Furniture manufacturing was the third expanding branch of the household-craft consumer industries in antebellum Milwaukee, and as such it shared similar characteristics with the clothing and footware branches. Contributing 7 per cent of Milwaukee's value added in 1850 and 5.5 per cent a decade later, the industry held a leading position in the state, manufacturing some 40 per cent of Wisconsin's cabinetware. This preponderance was, for the most part, dependent on the contribution of a small number of manufactories which produced ready-made goods for popular consumption. This core of large firms was surrounded by many small craft shops, but these shops were not as numerous as those in either the clothing or the boot-and-shoe industries.

Pioneer furniture makers in Milwaukee, as elsewhere in Wisconsin, tended to be carpenters and joiners who were prepared to make tables, chairs, bureaus, and sofas when they were not occupied in building construction. They were among the earliest craftsmen and journeymen in the frontier village, for their services were basic to the establishment of most households. Even in 1836 there were at least two full-time carpenters and two cabinet shops in Milwaukee. By the early 1840's craftsmen were being distinguished from the more general handyman, and in 1843 Milwaukee business statistics specified seven cabinetmakers. With the influx of more artisans in the mid-1840's further distinctions were drawn between cabinetmakers who took cash or produce and who also made coffins, and manufacturers of furniture who were doing a larger specialized business and who often participated in the retail trade.[51]

A dichotomy within the organizational structure of the industry was apparent by the mid-1840's. Small-scale entrepreneurs with a capital of some $500, and employing two or three journeymen, kept a fair stock of their own cabinetware, would make

[51] *Milwaukee Advertiser*, July 1, Dec. 9, 1837, advs.; *Milwaukee Democrat*, Feb. 16, 1844, adv.; *American Freeman*, March 27, 1844, adv.; *Milwaukee Courier*, May 14, 1845, adv.; *Milwaukee Sentinel*, Dec. 16, 1843, adv.; Sept. 14, 1844, adv.; Buck, 1: 41, 43; 2: 175, 208, 210, 266; 3: 30–32.

furniture to order, and would also do repairing. They were practical workmen doing a limited trade.[52] The larger-scale manufacturers of furniture were in fact merchant-manufacturers. John Birchard came from New York City in 1845 to establish a business as a manufacturer of, and wholesale and retail dealer in, furniture bought in New York. Although he had only a small capital, he was doing fairly well in the late 1840's and by mid-century he ran the second-largest firm, employing twenty-four workers. Alonzo D. Seaman also arrived from New York about 1846 to take up the manufacture and retailing of furniture. By 1849 he had established extensive show rooms for the sale of his stock and a manufactory which employed thirty men arranged in specialized departments. A year later he employed thirty-nine men to make some $40,000 worth of articles. Indeed Messrs. Birchard and Seaman between them produced 62 per cent of the Milwaukee furniture manufacture.[53]

The structural division in the Milwaukee furniture industry continued in the 1850's. The two merchant-manufacturers prominent in the 1840's were joined by a third firm consisting of William A. Noyes, August Flertzheim, and Henry Brugman. Noyes was a skilled mechanic, and both he and Flertzheim had had retailing experience. Brugman supplied the capital for the enterprise. All three firms expanded during the early and mid-1850's. By 1857 Birchard was worth $30,000. Seaman, who had taken on an experienced and wealthy businessman, John Wing, as partner in 1853, was worth $30,000 in 1855. But Noyes, Flertzheim Co., had an even more extensive trade in 1857. All three firms also encountered financial difficulties in the hard times following the Panic of 1857. Birchard came through safely, by drawing on the retail business. Seaman & Wing, whose main function was manufacturing rather than retailing, were hit badly and were forced to ask for an extension of their credit. However, they too survived. Noyes, Flertzheim & Co. had so many monetary problems that the firm was dissolved in 1859. Flertzheim then

---

[52] *Milwaukee Democrat*, Feb. 14, 1844, adv.; *American Freeman*, March 27, 1844, adv.; *Milwaukee Sentinel*, Sept. 14, Dec. 13, 1844, advs.; *Milwaukee Courier*, May 14, 1845, adv.; *MCD, 1847–48*, pp. 22, 30, 76, advs.; D. & B. vol. 36: 52, 61, 91.

[53] *Milwaukee Sentinel*, Sept. 2, 1848, adv.; July 6, 1849; MCSW, Milwaukee County, 1850; D. & B. vol. 36: 11, 52; Buck, 3: 31; Conrad, 2: 388.

became manager of a retail and wholesale furniture store, while Noyes was left to settle up the old business. Yet in 1860 these three (or now rather four) firms still dominated the Milwaukee furniture industry, producing 68 per cent of the value added.[54]

Other cabinetmakers ran small shops and did a limited trade. Some of the more enterprising, such as Nathan Brick, were also involved in the retail trade and were improving their standing. But most had little capital — generally under $1,000 — and a handful of employees. These craftsmen, making furniture, both stock and for the customer trade, and also doing turning and repairing, could not compete effectively against the larger Milwaukee manufacturers and imported merchandise. Their business was therefore restricted.[55] Successful entrepreneurs in the Milwaukee furniture industry needed to have either capital plus manufacturing skill and an early start, or capital plus a retail trade with which to establish customer connections and boost the manufacturing side of the business if necessary.

Other Household-Craft Consumer Industries

The three other branches of the household-craft consumer industries consisted basically of small craftsmen and journeymen supplying a local custom trade and doing repairs. Tinsmiths made kitchen utensils either in their own shops or for the jobbing trade of a drygoods or hardware store. Blacksmiths did a flourishing general repair and service business in the village period. But they declined in relative importance as their function in the urban market was replaced by more specialized artisans such as foundrymen and wheelwrights. The manufacture of confectionery goods depended on the demands of the city population, and was never a well-developed industry when compared to other consumer branches.

AGRICULTURAL INDUSTRIES

The agricultural industries were the weakest group of manufactures in antebellum Milwaukee. A few establishments, of

---

[54] MCSW, Milwaukee County, 1860; D. & B. vol. 36: 11, 52, 91, 220, 223, 305; Buck, 3: 30–32; 4: 95–96, 124–125; Conrad, 2: 388.

[55] MCSW, Milwaukee County, 1850 and 1860; D. & B. vol. 36: 89, 176; Buck, 3: 380–381; 4: 199–203.

which Kirby, Langworthy & Co., was the most notable, made fanning mills, plows, and threshing machines; but their production was limited by comparison with that of firms in Racine and Walworth counties. Wagon and carriage making increased in output, but firms catered to the city rather than to the farm trade. They were usually small, having a capital of less than $1,000 and employing one or two wheelwrights who turned out carriages, buggies, and sleighs on a custom basis and did repairs.[56]

OTHER INDUSTRIES

Foundries and Iron Products

The manufacture of iron and iron products was the only major activity in the other group of manufactures in antebellum Milwaukee, contributing 7.8 per cent of the county's value added in 1850 and 9.9 per cent in 1860. (Table 21 and Table 22.) The iron industry neither processed local resources nor catered to household consumer demands, but rather manufactured producer goods for mills, shops, and railroads. Taking advantage of a lakeshore location to import raw materials and of an urban center to provide the labor force and an initial market, entrepreneurs with capital were able to make Milwaukee the center of the Wisconsin iron industry, commanding 35 per cent of the state production in 1850 and 51 per cent in 1860.

The early iron industry in Milwaukee was run by specialized blacksmiths and machinists who made castings and machinery for local shops, turned iron, and did repairs. By 1839 Loring Doney and Egbert Mosely, the one a practical patternmaker and turner and the other a blacksmith and machinist, had built a small foundry and machine shop on the canal and supplied all kinds of castings. Four years later they had branched out into the manufacture of plows. In the same year, 1843, a second foundry was opened by Bagnall & Sercomb, who, as patternmaker and furnace man respectively, were also prepared to furnish a variety of iron, brass, and stove castings as well as doing turning and

---

[56] MCSW, Milwaukee County, 1850 and 1860; *Milwaukee Sentinel*, Feb. 11, 1840, adv.; Oct. 28, 1858, adv.; *Milwaukee Courier*, Aug. 4, 1841, adv.; *Milwaukee Semi-Weekly Gazette*, Nov. 26, 1845, advs.; Jan. 23, 1846, adv.; *American Freeman*, June 11, 1846, adv.; *Wisconsin Farmer*, 13 (1861), 235; *USDB*, 116–117; Buck, 4: 128–129; D. & B. vol. 36: 96, 208; Conrad, 3: 30.

finishing jobs. When Thomas Turton, an experienced moulder, took over this foundry later in 1843, the character of the enterprise was not altered. In 1844 a third foundry was established by Andrew J. Langworthy and Nelson McCracken, who brought their extensive assortment of patterns and machinery from Rochester, New York. Though these entrepreneurs were experienced in providing machinery for saw- and grist-mills, they also started to manufacture plows.[57]

Milwaukee was probably the best location for foundrymen and machinists settling in frontier Wisconsin. Supplies of iron and coal could be imported by lake from the East, usually from Ohio and Pennsylvania. Wisconsin had no coal resources, and no pig iron was manufactured in the state until the Wisconsin Iron Company started operations at Mayville, Dodge County, in 1849. It was therefore cheaper to be situated in a lakeshore port with reasonable harbor facilities, since the cost of transporting iron and coal by land from the lake would be prohibitive. Then also, Milwaukee, of all the Wisconsin lake towns, had the largest population for supplying a labor force and a central market. By 1843 Milwaukee village already had some 6,000 inhabitants, putting her nearest rival — Racine, with 1,108 inhabitants — in the shade. Four years later, Milwaukee city had a population of 14,067 and Racine city 3,647.[58]

The Milwaukee foundries and machine shops grew in number and size in the late 1840's. In 1847 Decker and Seville built a foundry for the manufacture of saw- and gristmill supplies. Lee and Walton had completed their extensive plant by 1849. At midcentury 104 men were employed in six establishments producing articles worth $96,200. Expansion was even more rapid

[57] *Milwaukee Advertiser,* Aug. 31, Sept. 7, 1839, advs.; *Milwaukee Sentinel,* Apr. 21, 1840, adv.; *Milwaukee Courier,* March 21, June 21, Nov. 15, 1843, advs.; Oct. 23, 1844, adv.; Jan. 21, 1846, adv.; Jan. 20, 1847, adv.; *Milwaukee Semi-Weekly Gazette,* Nov. 26, 1845, adv.; Jan. 23, 1846, adv.; *American Freeman,* Dec. 22, 1846, adv.; *MCD, 1847-48,* pp. 52, 55; Buck, 2: 92, 156, 160, 175, 208; Flower, 190, 1283-1284.

[58] *Racine Advocate,* Sept. 24, 1844; *Milwaukee Sentinel,* July 25, 1849; Robert T. Hilton, "Men of Metal: A History of the Foundry Industry in Wisconsin" (unpublished M.A. thesis, University of Wisconsin, 1952), 7-8; Koss, 161; "Census of Wisconsin from the year 1836 to August, 1860, complied from Official Sources for the *Wisconsin State Journal,*" by H.A. Tenney, *Census of Wisconsin, 1836-1860* (pamphlet, n.d. n.p.).

in the early 1850's. In 1853 the castings and machinery produced were valued at $137,238. Then Turton & Sercomb's Eagle Foundry alone hired between forty-five and fifty hands while the Reliance Works of Decker & Seville employed fifty men. To add a further dimension to the iron industry, the Menominee Furnace of Lee & Walton started manufacturing railroad locomotives. By 1855 Milwaukee's iron products were valued at $532,788.[59]

This notable expansion of the Milwaukee iron industry was centered on the frontier market for steam engines, mill castings, mill machinery, and other miscellaneous machinery. The Reliance Works soon sold its millstones not only to city mills, but also to mills all over Wisconsin and even in Michigan and Iowa. By 1848 Turton & Sercomb were producing steam engines and mill castings for Wisconsin sawmills, especially those in the pineries. They were also selling flour milling equipment throughout southern Wisconsin. At midcentury local newspapers and farming journals were advertising a variety of products, ranging from boilers and steam engines to horse powers, threshing machines, and stoves, made in the various Milwaukee foundries.[60] Then also railroad locomotives and equipment were manufactured by the Menominee Works and in the machine shops of the several railroad companies, though the foundries did not appear to have become heavily involved in the manufacture of rails.[61]

While there was a sellers' market for heavy goods in frontier Wisconsin, iron manufacturers needed to possess adequate capital if they were to stay in business. Both pig iron and coal had to be transported at cost from the East. Wisconsin's local iron resources at Iron Ridge, Dodge County, failed to yield either a steady or a large supply of pig iron despite the efforts of two companies.[62] Then payment for machinery often took at least several

[59] MCSW, Milwaukee County, 1850; Board of Trade, *A.R.*, 1854, pp. 3–4; 1855, pp. 9–10, 11; *Milwaukee Sentinel*, July 16, Sept. 21, 22, 23, 1853; *MCD, 1854–55*, advs.; D. & B. vol. 36: 75; Flower, 1285; Buck, 3: 70–71, 190; J.G. Gregory, 1: 546–547.

[60] *MCD, 1847–48*, p. 55, advs.; *1854–55*, advs.; *1856–57*, p. 284, adv.; *Milwaukee Sentinel*, Apr. 25, 1851; Sept. 22, 23, 1853; *Oshkosh Courier*, Jan. 23, Feb. 27, 1856, advs.; *Oshkosh Democrat*, May 12, 1857, adv.; *Wisconsin Farmer*, 9 (1857), 31, 32, 205, 206; 11 (1859), advs.; D. & B. vol. 36: 137; Buck, 3: 70–71; 4: 92; Flower, 1285.

[61] *Milwaukee Sentinel*, July 16, Sept. 21, 1853; Board of Trade, *A.R.* 1854–1856, *passim; Wisconsin Farmer*, 13 (1861), 235

[62] *Milwaukee Sentinel*, July 25, 1849; Oct. 15, 1853; *Watertown Chronicle*, Aug. 17, 1853, quoting the *Waukesha Press; Watertown Chronicle*, Oct. 19, 1853; *In-*

months and meanwhile the entrepreneur had to keep his works in good running order and pay wages. Most iron founders had enough capital, from $3–5,000, to establish themselves, and most managed to improve their financial standing in the early and middle 1850's. However they did not seem to have the necessary reserves to survive the subsequent depression.

The Milwaukee iron industry was severely crippled by the Panic of 1857 and the nationwide depression. When lumber and flour mill construction ceased, most machinery builders and iron founders not only lost trade but had to shut down. Stone & Stone of the Milwaukee Railroad Steam Engine Company were heavily in debt and closed shop in December, 1857. The boiler makers, Menzel, Cummings & Goodrich assigned their assets in 1858. William Goodnow of the Bay State Iron Company was in financial difficulties. Lee & Walton of the Menominee Locomotive Manufacturing Company were fully mortgaged early in 1858. A. J. Langworthy went out of business in 1859. Decker & Seville were closed out by a sheriff's sale in May, 1861, and I. M. Stowell & Co.'s Foundry was in difficult circumstances early in 1860.[63] The sluggish economic conditions of the late 1850's destroyed firms with insufficient resources and even damaged enterprises with apparently plenty of capital.

There was little sign of recovery by 1860. The census reported that thirteen firms produced only $403,250 worth of machines, castings, engines, wheels, and miscellaneous goods — a product which was well under the capacity seen in the mid-1850's. Although some foundries had resumed their trade, they did so from a position of weakness. Within a few years they either passed into new hands, as, for example, the Reliance Works when it came under the control of E. P. Allis in 1861; or else they retrenched, like I. M. Stowell & Co.[64] All the Milwaukee iron founders had capital before starting their enterprises, and most were experi-

dependent American, March 17, 1854, quoting the Milwaukee Sentinel; WSAS Trans., 4 (1856), 358; Board of Trade, A.R., 1854–1856, passim; Chamber of Commerce, A.R., 1858, passim; State of Wisconsin, Assembly, 7 Legis., 1854 and 10 Legis., 1858, Reports of the State Geologists, pp. 64 and 17.

[63] D. & B. vol. 36: 21, 102, 127, 137, 139, 173, 221; Flower, 1284; The Century Club, 26.

[64] Milwaukee Sentinel, May 27, Aug. 13, adv., 1861; Apr. 29, 1862, adv.; Oct. 12, 1863, adv.; MCSW, Milwaukee County, 1860; D. & B. vol. 36: 102, 173, 221, 321, 326; Hilton, 27–28; Buck, 4: 103–104; Flower, 1284.

enced businessmen, either as blacksmiths, wheelwrights, or iron-workers; but they had to show entrepreneurial initiative and a strong financial standing to survive in a market subject both to general economic fluctuations and frontier instability.

Conclusion

Manufacturing in antebellum Milwaukee County differed significantly from that found in other parts of Wisconsin. One quarter of the state's total industrial output was concentrated in the city. Then too manufacturing was diversified, both in the number of products made and in the relative amounts of their value added. Milwaukee was in fact the Wisconsin urban type of manufacturing, in contrast to other smaller centers whose industrial growth was based either on the natural resources of lumber, agricultural crops, and minerals, or on catering to the service needs of commercial prairie farming. With the exception of lumber, Milwaukee was well placed to process all of Wisconsin's raw materials. In addition the city shops could manufacture domestic consumer goods not only for the people of Milwaukee, but also for other Wisconsin towns. Then also the city was the center of the Wisconsin iron industry. Milwaukee was thus able to combine the advantages of a lakeshore site for communications with those of a large population agglomeration to develop a distinctive type of manufacturing in frontier Wisconsin.

The structure of Milwaukee manufacturing was also remarkable, in that it was a composite of large establishments making goods for a wide market and small shops catering to a very local and often custom trade. The large firms, which tended to be manufactories rather than factories, usually dominated their respective branches of manufacturing because they were able to command adequate capital and because their proprietors were experienced businessmen. Antebellum Milwaukee industrialists could start off as practical mechanics or craftsmen and build up their enterprises if they could survive periodic financial and business crises. And if they already possessed money for investment in plant and machinery and for the purchase either of raw materials or ready-made goods for the retail trade, then they were virtually assured of success.

Certainly some competition was provided by the artisan and his higher-quality goods. But the manufacturer who could employ a sufficient work force to benefit from division of labor or could afford to use machinery commanded the far larger local market for ready-made articles. On a regional scale these industrialists could also sell their goods at a competitive price in many Wisconsin towns, owing to their cheaper production costs and to the lakeside location which conferred transport benefits. Milwaukee was the major urban center both for Wisconsin and for the northern portion of the area west of Lake Michigan. Milwaukee manufacturers suffered direct competition in western-made products only from their Chicago counterparts who sold mainly in the southeastern and southwestern parts of the state. Furthermore, on an even wider scale, some Milwaukee industrialists entered the national market. They processed the resources of the Wisconsin hinterland into commodities such as flour, packed meat, and leather, for which there was a demand in Eastern markets.

Entrepreneurs with money could forge ahead of the craftsmen and practical laborers who had to work their way up with limited assets. For the self-made businessman, even fifteen or twenty years of work might not suffice to accumulate enough capital to weather business crises, contracting credit, the competition of larger concerns with Eastern money and Eastern contacts, and other hazards of the urban manufacturing frontier. Milwaukee's independent craftsmen could and did survive intact, but only on a modest scale and in declining importance.

CHAPTER EIGHT

The Manufacturing Dimensions of Pioneer Wisconsin

By 1860 MANUFACTURING was a salient feature in the economic development of Wisconsin. Although agriculture was still the foundation of the state's economy, and would remain so for the next few decades, enterprises which already produced goods to the value of $30,000,000 could scarcely be called insignificant.[1] Utilizing abundant natural resources and farm outputs and taking advantage of improving transportation routes and technology, Wisconsin enterpreneurs had achieved remarkable progress in the short span of one generation of settlement. To be sure, many manufacturers were essentially craftsmen who responded to and catered to local demands; but already there were indications that some of Wisconsin's industrial operations had much wider significance.

Within Wisconsin, contemporary industrial spokesmen asserted that the importance of developing a manufacturing sector lay in its contribution to making the local economy self-sufficient. They therefore stressed the need to increase production and diversify output. Whether they thought in terms of towns, counties, or even Wisconsin as a whole, few could rise above this parochialism. Yet the major significance of manufacturing growth in pioneer Wisconsin was perhaps not so much the actual amount of goods produced, impressive though that was, but rather that the local economy was rapidly becoming integrated with the regional and

---

[1] The value of the product reported in the manuscript census was $28,596,726. Making allowances for those firms which had an annual value of product under $500, those firms which failed to be counted, and also $127,972 worth of home manufactures, the total would probably approach $30,000,000.

national economies. The pattern of antebellum Wisconsin manufacturing thus becomes remarkable for its character, or its types of activity, and for its structural organization. These were the features of frontier manufacturing which indicated the possibilities of economies of scale and the stages of modernization within industrial growth.

Superficially the industrial profile of Wisconsin in 1860 indicated similarities with that of the larger United States. (Table 23.) Several of the state's leading manufactures also appeared in the nation's list of high-ranking industries. Only in cotton goods, gold mining, and woolen goods was Wisconsin deficient.[2] Certainly Wisconsin's contribution to the national production of any given industry was small — the highest such contribution being made by flour-and-grist milling at 4.9 per cent of the country's value added — but then Wisconsin had only 2.5 per cent of the nation's population, and much of that was but recently settled. However, the degree of comparability between the young state and the country was partly an artifact of the census groupings of manufacturing categories. More important was the manner in which Wisconsin contributed to the national aggregate.

Some two thirds of Wisconsin's manufacturing output came from the processing industries, and of this, lumber planed and sawed and flour-and-grist milling totaled 41.6 per cent. The saw and the millstone were indeed the bases of the state's manufacturing ventures. Brewing, brickmaking, smelting, tanning, barrelmaking, and meatpacking were other less well-developed processing branches which drew on the rich resources of the state as a whole. But abundant natural resources and increased agricultural yields definitely stimulated those industries in which Wisconsin was able to contribute a growing share to the nation's output. Certain of these branches — for example brickmaking and barrelmaking — were oriented to local consumption; but others, such as flour and lumber milling, were already beginning to look to regional and national markets. Meatpacking and brewing were merely emerging, but they too showed signs of becoming important as regional enterprises.

The second-leading group of industries in Wisconsin was the

---

[2] For comparative purposes, the manufacturing figures used here are those reported in the printed census of 1860.

TABLE 23

LEADING INDUSTRIES, UNITED STATES AND WISCONSIN, 1860,
BY VALUE ADDED AND PERCENTAGE CONTRIBUTION TO NATIONAL
AND STATE AGGREGATES

(In Current $000's.)

United States			Wisconsin		
Industry and Rank	Value Added	Per Cent of Total	Industry and Rank	Value Added	Per Cent of Total
1. Cotton	54,671	6.4	1. Lumber	2,505	23.4
2. Lumber	53,570	6.3	2. Flour	1,978	18.5
3. Boots and Shoes	49,191	5.8	3. Liquors	561	5.2
4. Flour	40,191	4.7	4. Agric. Impls.	517	4.8
5. Clothing	36,681	4.3	5. Boots & Shoes	480	4.5
6. Iron	35,689	4.2	6. Carriages	424	4.0
7. Machinery	32,566	3.8	7. Clothing	415	3.9
8. Gold Mining	30,601	3.6	8. Machinery	310	2.9
9. Woolen Goods	25,032	2.9	9. Furniture	274	2.6
10. Carriages	23,654	2.7	10. Cooperage	269	2.5
11. Leather	22,786	2.6	11. Provisions	204	1.9
12. Liquors	20,351	2.4	12. Iron	194	1.8
Aggregate	854,257		Aggregate	10,712	

[SOURCE: *Eighth Census, 1860, Manufactures,* Vol. III, pp. 657–658, 733–742.]

household-craft consumer group, which contributed some 15 per cent of the state's aggregate value added in 1860. These branches of manufacture — clothing, boots and shoes, furniture, tinware, blacksmithing, and confectionery — were important in two opposing ways. Numerous artisans and practical workers in their small shops catered either to local neighborhood needs or to the demands for high-quality, individually styled work. As custom craftsmen they gave the consumer industries the overall characteristic of a traditional prefactory nature. They conformed to the expectations of a frontier economy desirous of self-sufficiency.

However, in the larger towns, and especially in Milwaukee, embryonic factories or manufactories were following in the footsteps of New York, Boston, Philadelphia, and (more appropriately) Cincinnati, and were making cheaper ready-made goods for

popular consumption.[3] These larger firms were organized to benefit from economies of scale. They used machinery and other
technological innovations whenever capital was available. Their
products were not fully competitive with imported ready-made
articles which were retailed in increasing amounts throughout
antebellum Wisconsin, but they were better placed to provide
goods for growing consumer markets in the Middle West than
were the steadily decreasing craftsmen and artisans.

The remaining Wisconsin industries, in the agricultural and
other groups, contributed some 20 per cent of the state's aggregate manufacturing. Most of these branches, like paper manufacture, gas, or wagons and carriages, provided services for local
communities and were therefore extolled as virtuous by contemporary spokesmen. Two branches, however — agricultural implements and iron products, both heavy-goods industries — had
much wider significance. They not only met the machinery needs
of prairie farmers but also serviced the demands of western industries. Centered in the southeastern counties of Wisconsin,
which were well populated and well located in relation to water
transportation and to the Wisconsin-Illinois wheat belt, these
industries took advantage of expanding frontier markets for machinery and castings. They participated in the regional market
economy, but in a westward rather than an eastward direction.
Meeting with competition from older firms in both the East and
the trans-Appalachian West, they had to make technological and
managerial innovations and adaptions; and they were thus the
progenitors of the factory system in Wisconsin. Indeed, these
counties of southeastern Wisconsin were the first areas in the state
to be incorporated into the greater Northeastern manufacturing
belt in the last quarter of the nineteenth century.

The character or type of manufacturing activity in antebellum
Wisconsin illustrated local, regional, and national potentialities
in the pattern of Midwestern industrial development. The structural organization of Wisconsin manufacturing, or the size of the
firms and the resultant scale of organization, was even more
indicative of the changing factors of growth influencing American
industrialization.

---

[3] Rosenberg, 252–253.

In pioneer Wisconsin, manufacturing establishments fell into at least four categories. Household manufacturing existed alongside the craft shop, the mill, and the factory. In terms of both number of establishments and value added by manufacture, craft shops and mills were more representative than were households or factories. Yet within the shops and mills there was a considerable range of scale, and the breakdown in this scale of operation was never really distinct. For example, there were both small and large mills; there were also craft shops which merged into merchant-controlled manufactories and embryonic factories.

The village mill which supplied the neighborhood community with flour or wood for shares, or on a custom basis, was far removed from the Milwaukee flouring mill or the Eau Claire lumber mill which sold a substantial proportion of its products in regional rather than local markets. Likewise, the village cobbler or tailor who often worked on his own or with an apprentice, fashioning footware and clothing to the tastes of his client, was not comparable to the merchant-manufacturer who might employ fifteen or more semiskilled workers to produce ready-made goods for sale in his store. But the difference between the structural forms of the large mill, the large merchant-manufacturers' shop, and the budding factory was marginal. All were backed by adequate capital; most used division of labor, managerial skills, and machinery; all catered to a wide consumer or producer market.

There was indeed a hierarchy of manufacturing firms, but the process of distinguishing the individual stages between each threshold of industrial activity often becomes blurred when factors of production are analyzed. If, however, the two extremes in the range of establishments — namely the owner-operator craft shop or village mill, and the factory or large merchant mill — are juxtaposed, certain elements critical to antebellum industrial progress come into focus. The availability of raw materials was important in determining the type of industrial endeavor; without these, there would have been no manufacturing establishments. But the extent of accessible markets, which in turn was a function of local population agglomeration, transportation routes, capital shortage, technological developments, and limited motive power, was significant in influencing the shape of frontier manufacturing in Wisconsin.

Firm size — at least in the craft-consumer group of industries, and also in some of the processing branches — showed both a notable and a direct relationship to the density of local population. The one-or-two-man shop was frequently found in small towns and villages; the large manufactories were only found in Milwaukee. Medium-sized establishments were often located in smaller cities such as Oshkosh, Racine, and Watertown. However, the one-artisan enterprise was also numerically prominent in Milwaukee and to a lesser extent in the smaller cities. Not surprisingly, the range in the size of operation in the craft industries was most widespread in Milwaukee, which had attained both a local urban and a state threshold, while the smaller communities were more limited in the scale of their craft shops. In certain processing industries the principle of firm size and hinterland thresholds also applies. For example, the custom mill serving community needs was most often located in the village or small town. The larger town mill would buy grain and grind it for export to the nearest market, and supply local needs as well. The city mill, especially one which had access to lake and later to rail transportation, would not only produce for domestic consumption but would also participate in a regional and national trade.

Within this hierarchy, however, there were numerically fewer mills than craft shops, owing to the heavier capital expenditure required to establish a mill. But the number of small mills and craft shops often depended on their ability to compete with ready-made articles and cheaper produce imported from other parts of the country. Here the impact of transportation was significant. Lack of good facilities made gristmills and sawmills, blacksmiths' forges, and tailors' and cobblers' shops necessary institutions in pioneer self-sufficient communities. Manufacturing establishments were therefore both local and numerous until plank roads and railroads opened up the possibilities of purchasing imported articles.

Availability of transport was also notable in extending the potential size of the market for the large processing mill, whose prospect for export eastward was so much greater. To be sure, only the major urban centers could serve as bases for the commercial mill which had built up its output by initially supplying local needs. But those Wisconsin cities located on the Great Lakes

route, for example Milwaukee and Racine, were able to enter
an export-oriented economy as soon as the necessary infrastructure
had been developed. With the relatively rapid spread of railroads through southern Wisconsin in the 1850's, interior communities were also in a position to export surplus processed goods,
especially flour. But they could only achieve this through direct
competition with communities which had already gained an initial advantage. Ports like Milwaukee or Racine, benefiting from
an early start, were devloping economies of scale which aided the
process of centralization in such industries as flour milling, tanning, and meatpacking.

The impact of transportation on those processing industries
in which the raw material was very bulky, for example lumber,
was even more important in influencing structural organization.
The small one-man, owner-operated sawmill, drawing on available timber, generally served the neighborhood market. But
the large lumber enterprises were located in the pineries of northern Wisconsin on navigable waterways. The scale of the firm bore
little relationship to the size of Wisconsin towns. Before processing lumber in any huge quantities it was essential to have an
outlet to regional markets, either through the Great Lakes or by
the tributaries of the Mississippi River. Although there were over
800 miles of railroad by 1860, few were built in northern Wisconsin, and the antebellum lumber industry was still primarily
dependent upon water transportation.

But equally as important as the accessibility of transportation
in explaining the structural form of the lumber industry was the
availability of capital and the business acumen of the entrepreneurs. Wisconsin businessmen could draw on negligible assets
from local banks, but lumbering offered a sound investment opportunity to outside industrialists. Experienced lumbermen from
the Northeast and adjacent regions in Canada were looking for
new forest areas in which to invest their money and managerial
skills. Many antebellum Wisconsin lumber magnates had learned
their business in the East; many had assets, or were able to borrow from relatives and friends or through promotional schemes.
Capital was essential to success. Although a small investment
might suffice to start a lumber operation, the extensive enterprise had to command enough cash for plant, machinery, and

labor, together with reserves for use during slack periods and business crises. The size of the local market had little influence on the growth of the early lumber companies, which rather depended on their ability to survive long enough to establish markets and to gain from long-term sales. This in turn depended on financial resources and managerial skill.

The same factors of transportation, capital, and business experience were operative in shaping the structure of the heavier industries. However, in the case of agricultural implements and iron products, the weighting of these factors was in a different order. In the pioneer agricultural implements industry, entrepreneurial competence was more important than capital, though clearly both were needed for large-scale development. Improved transportation in the form of railroads helped an already established firm. The market for farm machinery in Wisconsin was ubiquitous, but was more heavily concentrated in the wheat belt of southern Wisconsin and northern Illinois. Innovators who were willing to build up a new industry designed to accommodate prairie farming could benefit from a sellers' market. Here it was possible to start on a small scale and work up the ladder of success. Entrepreneurs with capital started on a higher level or threshold. The size of the local urban population had marginal influence on the scale of this branch of manufacturing, which supplied an essentially unagglomerated market. Agricultural implements could be manufactured in most small cities or large towns with access to the wheat-raising counties, provided that a labor force was available. The introduction of quick transport merely enlarged the structure of an industry which had already established its mode of operation.

In the Wisconsin iron industry, capital was the critical element in determining firm size. The industry itself had been attracted to the lakeshore cities, and to Milwaukee in particular, owing to the cheaper water transport for moving raw materials. But capital was essential for investment in plant and machinery, for payment of labor, for the purchase of raw materials, and for reserves upon which to draw during depressed times. The more capital the iron founder possessed, the larger the amount of raw materials he could import from the East, and the larger his output of castings and machinery. Equally, the more capital the iron founder had, the more modern technology he could incorporate in his plant. Again, as in the agricultural implements industry, the improvement of land transportation, in the shape of the railroads, facilitated marketing arrangements and thus added further stimulus to growth; but iron products already sold on a statewide basis prior to the construction of railroads.

The impact of technology and motive power on the scale of antebellum Wisconsin manufacturing is more difficult to ascertain. Most entrepreneurs who used machine technology did so, like the lumbermen, because they had available capital or, like the iron masters, because theirs was an industry whose growth hinged on technological changes. Hence advanced machine methods were directly associated with financial resources and entrepreneurial ability. Technology, then, by itself, appears to have been a secondary rather than a primary condition in shaping the scale of manufacturing growth.

A similar situation holds for the type of motive power employed in manufacturing establishments. Most Wisconsin firms, which used any kind of power other than hand power, were usually dependent on water.[4] Water is both an immobile and a fluctuating source of energy. Wisconsin was fortunately endowed with a well-distributed flow of water, and most entrepreneurs were able to use this cheap, readily available form of power. However many larger firms, either in the processing group or in the heavier branches, gradually decided that they could ill afford to depend completely on power which was subject to seasonal vagaries. Since dependability was an essential criterion in these big enterprises, steam came to be used as a more stable energy source. Few entrepreneurs appear to have been initially aware of the greater profitability to be gained from using steam power; they were more concerned with reliability. Thus the use of new forms of motive power in influencing the scale of operations was secondary to the availability of capital.

The emergence of frontier manufacturing in the mid-nineteenth century, as exemplified by Wisconsin, was a function of two main

[4] It is not possible to provide accurate statistics to support this statement, since many of the returns for motive power in the manuscript census were incomplete. However, working with the partial data in the census and with other qualitative evidence, it is possible to state that water was the main motive power in Wisconsin throughout the antebellum period.

conditions — the supply of raw materials and the range of accessible markets. Plentiful natural resources and bountiful crops enabled and encouraged the growth of industrial activity, but the scale of that activity was then limited or enhanced by the market threshold. The market in turn was a compound of local population agglomeration and transportation routes, which facilitated the export of processed articles and the import of raw materials and ready-made articles. The constraints of capital shortage, entrepreneurial initiative, technological developments, and limited motive power worked within the market framework and were reflected in unit costs. Two major influences — materials and markets — combined to produce a manufacturing economy which emphasized processing goods rather than consumer or heavy goods, and mills and craft shops rather than household or factory organizations. There was a widespread dispersion of activity, focused within a hierarchy of urban centers and a cross section of different stages of industrial growth.

Indeed antebellum Wisconsin industries were a remarkable combination of the traditional and modernizing elements and eras that are often found in industrializing economies. Within the time span of one generation, many Wisconsin manufacturers had passed beyond the autarkic stage typical of young neighborhood communities. As the state moved steadily and distinctly into the market economy, entrepreneurs turned to those industries for which Wisconsin was well endowed, and began to discard those others which could not withstand outside competition.

These trends were to become more marked in the post-Civil War years. Lead mining disappeared, to be replaced by iron mining. The lumber industry would thrive throughout the nineteenth century, but flour milling would fade sooner as new techniques and new areas of supply centralized production in Minnesota. Other processing industries, such as tanning and meatpacking, would also come to concentrate in urban centers outside the state; but brewing would retain a strong foothold in Milwaukee. Among the household-craft-consumer branches of manufacturing only those firms that operated factories could hope to withstand the increasing threat from older established firms whose initial advantages were strengthened by reliable means of transportation. However, the heavy industries, so well located in the lakeshore counties, would continue to thrive, bringing southeastern Wisconsin into the orbit of the Great Lakes manufacturing belt. Pioneer Wisconsin had both shown the possible directions for manufacturing in a national economy and laid the foundations for the state's future industrial growth.

APPENDIX A

The Use of Statistical Information
Provided by the Manuscript Censuses

THE STATISTICS OF MANUFACTURING in Wisconsin, as one branch of the census, were reported at ten-year intervals in the mid-nineteenth century.[1] The Sixth Census of 1840 provided meager and rather inaccurate information about the number of establishments, the capital invested, the number of hands employed, and the value and kind of product. The Seventh Census of 1850 printed aggregate manufacturing outputs by state according to the principal industries, and by county for the categories capital invested, number of hands employed, annual value of product, and value of goods produced in families. The Eighth Census of 1860 reported more detail on a national, state, and county level, giving figures for eight variables: number of establishments; capital invested; cost of raw materials; number of hands employed, both male and female; annual cost of labor; annual value of product; and value of home manufacturing.[2]

The published statistics of manufacturing were thus inadequate for making a thorough analysis of industrial growth on a micro level. It was therefore necessary to obtain more precise and fuller data by using the manuscript census schedules when they were available. "Schedule 5" of the Seventh and Eighth Censuses was devoted to "Products of Industry," and called for information on individual firms, producing articles to the value of at least $500, for fourteen categories: name of the corporation, company or individual; name of business or manufacture; capital invested in real and personal estate in the business; quantity, kind, and value of raw materials; kind of motive power, machinery, structure, or resource; average number of

---

[1] Manufacturing statistics were not included in the census figures taken by state or local officials during the years 1836 to 1860. They were usually concerned with population growth.

[2] *Sixth Census, 1840, Compendium*, 344–353; *Sixth Census, 1840* (as corrected at the Department of State), 460–462; Joseph C.G. Kennedy, "Abstract of the Statistics of Manufactures, According to the Returns of the Seventh Census," *Senate Executive Documents*, 35 Cong. 2 Sess. Doc. 39 (1858–59), *passim*; *Statistical View of the United States: A Compendium of the Seventh Census, 1850*, 331–337; *Eighth Census, 1860, Manufactures*, Vol. 111, 640–658.

male and female hands employed; average monthly cost of male and female labor; and quantity, kind, and value of annual product. "Schedule 4" of the same censuses, devoted to "Products of Agriculture," also reported the value of home-made manufactures.[3] These unpublished returns provided the evidence for a much closer scrutiny of manufacturing developments in Wisconsin.

In order to use this fuller information to best advantage, it was necessary to aggregate the individual figures by categories for each county and by classification for each type of industry, both for Wisconsin as a whole and for the counties separately. Of the fourteen categories available, eight were selected as being more valuable indicators of manufacturing activity.[4] Seven of these were actually recorded in the census, though some acquired a slightly different meaning.

"Number of establishments" was the number of separately capitalized establishments which were clearly individual establishments. "Capital invested" was simply that capital invested in real and personal estate in the business. "Cost of raw materials" included the value of the fuel and the articles used for the production of goods plus the price of transport when movement of materials was involved. The "average number of hands employed," of both sexes, was adjusted to mean the maximum number of workers at any given time during the year. "Wages" were calculated on the basis of the average monthly wage per worker; the "annual value of product" comprised the aggregate value of articles manufactured at the industrial plant, exclusive of the cost of transportation to market. The "value of home manufactures" consisted of all those articles made in the home by members of the family, from raw materials produced largely on the farm where the manufacturing was carried out. "Value added by manufacture" was not recorded in the censuses of manufacture for the years 1850 and 1860, and was computed by subtracting the cost of the materials from the value of the product.[5]

---

[3] For more detailed descriptions of these categories, see *Seventh Census, 1850*, xxiv.

[4] Several categories were not reported fully or were of such a nature as not to lend themselves to ready classification. For example, in about 50 per cent of the returns the category, "kind of motive power, structure or resource," was either not reported or was given as two kinds of power without indicating which was the more important. It was impossible to interpolate for blank spaces since any combination or measure of motive power could have been used. Hence this category could only be used qualitatively in so far as it adds to information available for individual firms from other sources.

[5] For fuller discussions of these categories, see Margaret Walsh, "The Manufacturing Frontier: Pioneer Industry in Antebellum Wisconsin, 1830–1860" (Ph.D. dissertation, University of Wisconsin, 1969), 486–493.

From these eight categories two were chosen for intensive use throughout this study: "value added by manufacture" as a measure of industrial output, and "number of hands employed" as an input measure of resources consumed in the manufacturing process. The construct "value added by manufacture" gives the approximate value created in the process of manufacturing by deducting from the gross product, the cost of materials consumed, the fuel used, and other costs incurred in manufacturing the finished product. It therefore provides the most satisfactory census measure of the relative importance of given industries. As a counterbalance to this output measure, the input measure "number of hands employed" was used to indicate not only the growth of industry in absolute terms, but also the relationship of industry to other gainful occupations.[6] Other categories, such as capital invested or value of product, were used if more detail was needed to illustrate particular points or to give a consistent set of figures.

Not only did the individual firm figures reported in the manuscript census schedules need to be aggregated according to categories of measurement; they also had to be sorted and aggregated according to type of industrial activity, both by state and by county. The printed census of 1840 listed seventy-eight types of manufacture; in 1850 there were ninty-eight broadly defined manufacturing branches; a decade later the number had reached 111.[7] Clearly it was an unmanageable task to sort data into such a large number of classification, and some more practical scheme, suitable to antebellum Midwestern manufacturing, had to be adopted.

Having decided to bypass the 1840 census, which was inaccurate and was taken in a mixed form, and to concentrate on the censuses of 1850 and 1860, a reduction of classifications to twenty-three was achieved. They were as follows:

CODE NUMBER	PRODUCT
01	Lumber (planed and sawed)
02	Flour and Grist Milling
03	Iron Manufactures (foundry, castings, machinery, pig iron, smelting, etc.)
04	Agricultural Implements (plows, fanning mills, reapers, mowers, rakes, etc.)
05	Boots and Shoes

[6] For further details on measuring manufacturing activity, see Walsh, 500–504.

[7] George Tucker, *Progress of the United States* (New York, 1855), 150–151, Appendix, 47; *Seventh Census, 1850,* 929; MCSW, 1850; *Eighth Census, 1860, Manufactures,* Vol. 111, 657–658.

06	Clothing (ready-made, tailored, millinery hats and caps)
07	Wagons and Carriages
08	Furniture (cabinetmakers and carpenters, if, in the case of the latter, the census clearly indicated that furniture rather than house construction was the end product)
09	Blacksmiths
10	Cooperage
11	Liquors (distilled, malt, and rectified)
12	Paper Manufacture and Printing
13	Leather Manufacture (tanning, currying, making harnesses, saddles and trunks)
14	Construction Materials (bricks, shingles, sashes, doors, and blinds; also carpentry when not in category 07)
15	Meatpacking
16	Woolen Manufacture and Woolen Goods
17	Bakery and Food Products
18	Processing Mineral Resources (lime burning, quarrying, smelting, etc.)
19	Tin, Copper, Sheet Iron, and Brass Making
20	Gas
21	Miscellaneous (including daguerreotypes, fishing, dentists, jewelers, basketmakers, picture frames, coffee and spices, pottery, vinegar etc.)
22	Soap and Candles
23	Tobacco Processing

Certain types of manufacturing, such as lumber planed and sawed and flour and grist milling, were placed in a separate classification owing to their importance in the Wisconsin economy. Others were placed in a distinct group to indicate the stage of development in the local economy; for example, blacksmithing and gas. Some kinds of manufactures were combined under the same head because they worked with the same materials; for example, leathergoods or iron products. Other kinds were combined because they made similar products; for example, agricultural implements or construction materials. Still others were placed in the miscellaneous classification either because they occurred infrequently or because they were mainly service functions.

Several of these classifications — furniture, boots and shoes, or flour and meal — are the same as those used by the printed censuses;

but some are combinations of two or three closely allied branches —
for example liquors, which include distilled, malt, and rectified
beverages, and iron, which includes pig, castings, rails, and some
machinery. Some categories are clear and distinct; for example, tobacco and cooperage. Others merge into each other. Blacksmiths were
often wagonmakers; agricultural implements manufacturers often
produced wagons. Planed lumber could easily have been used in
house construction, but not necessarily. The decision to place firms
in one or another classification, if their end product was in ques-
tion, depended on the relative value of their various outputs. If the
value of the product for an establishment was higher for wagonmaking than it was for horseshoeing and repairs, then that establishment belonged to the wagon-and-carriages group rather than to the
blacksmithing group. If a firm made more plows and reapers than
wagons, then it belonged to the agricultural implements branch
rather than to the wagons-and-carriages branch.

Having identified twenty-three classifications it was then necessary
to assign these to groups which showed certain types of industrial
development both in Wisconsin in particular and in the nation as
a whole. Four groups were chosen; namely,

PROCESSING INDUSTRIES
lumber	(01)
flour	(02)
cooperage	(03)
liquors	(04)
leather	(13)
construction materials	(14)
meatpacking	(15)
wool	(16)
minerals	(18)
soap and candles	(22)
tobacco	(23)

HOUSEHOLD-CRAFT CONSUMER INDUSTRIES
boots and shoes	(05)
clothing	(06)
furniture	(08)
blacksmiths	(09)
confectionery	(17)
tin, copper, etc.	(19)

AGRICULTURAL INDUSTRIES
agricultural implements	(04)
wagons and carriages	(07)

OTHER INDUSTRIES

iron	(03)
paper	(12)
gas	(20)
miscellaneous	(21)

The processing group consisted of manufacturing activities in which some natural resource such as minerals, lumber, or farm produce, was refined or processed for the custom trade or for the local or regional trade. These processing branches were often first or primary stage rather than second or secondary stage industries. They made goods either for direct household consumption — for example flour, beer, or packed meat — or for consumption by other industries — for example tanned leather or sawed lumber. The essential element is the first stage or immediate work done on the natural resource. When the second stage of processing is used — for example when tanned leather is turned into harnesses or boots and shoes — the classification of the industry then depends on whether the backward linkage to the raw material is more critical to the existence of the industry than is the forward linkage to the consumer; in other words whether the industry is natural resource or market-oriented.

The household-craft consumer group of industries consists of those branches of manufacturing which fabricated, serviced, and repaired domestic household articles such as clothing, furniture, and kitchen utensils. These activities included a large component of handicrafts where custom work and repairs predominated or where manufacturing consisted of the jobbing trade of a retail store, and also a few manu-factories and factories where division of labor and mechanization of production were being utilized. The key to classifying these indus-tries was their function of catering directly to consumer durable and nondurable needs. The structural form of the establishments was diverse, but the consumer market was basic to all.

The agricultural industries are service industries for the farm sector. They made machinery such as plows, reapers, and fanning mills, for direct use in the production of crops, or wagons and carriages for more indirect transport use by farmers either as consumers or pro-ducers. The last, "other" group included an assortment of manu-facturing branches ranging from the heavy goods industry of iron to the new lighting industry of gas or the miscellaneous branch. This latter branch itself consisted of disparate elements ranging from service activities such as daguerreotypes and dentists to unusual occupations like ice making, glue making, safe making or the manufacture of matches and musical instruments.

Once the 4,459 individual entries for Wisconsin firms in 1850 and 1860 had been sorted and aggregated by categories, classifications, groups, counties, and industries, it seemed pertinent to assess the accuracy of this data. Too often statistics gathered by government officials are regarded as infallible, whereas they often merely provide general guidelines, especially on the local level where they contain gross errors and deficiencies.

The printed manufacturing census material in the mid-nineteenth century was riddled with mistakes and contradictions which are not always apparent. These faults emanated from four sources. In the first place, the census enumerators ignored certain industries, such as meatpacking in 1850, or parts of industries, such as wheelwrights in 1860. In the second place, they underestimated manufacturing capacity by failing to record all establishments. Inadequate counts were taken of many small shops belonging to artisans such as carpenters, tailors, and blacksmiths, and of the jobbing and craft side of retail stores. Seasonal industries — brickmaking, brewing, flour milling, and lumber sawing — were also ignored occasionally. In the third place, the enumerators might have reported wrong information. Although there are no means of ascertaining the efficiency of federal officials in gathering complete data, they were certainly not financially encouraged or even trained to obtain correct information. Poor pay, inattention, and lack of proficiency among the enumerators were responsible for many errors in the collection of manufacturing returns. Then too there was no element of compulsion on manufacturers to reply to the questions of the enumerators in 1840. In the fourth place, the competency of the staff at the census office to combine a column of figures and compile a table was minimal.[8]

The use of the manuscript census schedules eliminated or lessened the fourth possible source of error. The calculator and the computer corrected mathematical mistakes, while alteration of faulty figures and insertion of missing figures modified other errata.[9] On a state

[8] Robert E. Gallman, "Value Added by Agriculture, Mining and Manufacturing in the United States, 1840–1880" (unpublished Ph.D. dissertation, University of Pennsylvania, 1956), passim; Walsh, passim; MCSW, 1850 and 1860; U.S. House Reports, 28 Cong. 1 Sess. (1844), Report 579; U.S. Senate Documents, 28 Cong. 2 Sess. (1844), Doc. 4; 56 Cong. 1 Sess. (1900), Doc. 194 (1898); Carrol D. Wright and William Hunt, "The History and Growth of the United States Census," passim; U.S. Senate Reports, 32 Cong. 1 Sess. (1851), Report 276; Joseph C.G. Kennedy, Review of the Report of the Senate Committee on the Returns of the Seventh Census (Washington, 1852); E.C. Lunt, "History of the United States Census, 1790–1887," American Statistical Association, Publications, 1 (1888), 63–126; Seventh Census, 1850, Compendium, 17–18; Seventh Census, 1850, xv–xxv.

[9] For a discussion of changes made to the figures reported in the manuscript censuses for Wisconsin, see Walsh, 493–500.

TABLE 24

COMPARISON OF MANUSCRIPT AND PRINTED CENSUS,
WISCONSIN, 1850 AND 1860

(In Current $'s.)

	1850		
Category	Manuscript Census	Printed Census	Percentage Change Using the Manuscript Census as a Base.
Capital Invested	$3,421,680	$3,382,148	— 1.16
Number of Hands Employed	6,232	6,089	— 2.29
Value of Product	$8,984,533	$9,293,068	+ 3.43
Value of Home Manufactures	$45,509	$43,624	— 4.14

	1860		
Capital Invested	$17,167,500	$15,831,581	— 7.78
Number of Establishments	3,173	3,064	— 3.44
Number of Hands Employed	17,266	15,414	— 10.73
Cost of Materials	$17,272,709	$17,137,344	— 0.79
Value of Product	$28,596,726	$27,849,467	— 2.61
Value Added by Manufacture	$11,323,017	$10,712,123	— 5.40
Value of Home Manufactures	$128,563	$127,992	— 0.45

[SOURCE: Walsh, pp. 519–526.]

level there was comparatively little difference between the printed and manuscript sets of figures, though the former usually had lower values and thus probably underestimated manufacturing capacity (Table 24.) But on a county or township level, gross inaccuracies were revealed in the printed census, suggesting that for micro analysis these reports are rather unreliable.[10] Yet even the manuscript aggregations could not compensate for the probable underenumeration resulting from administrative deficiencies in census taking.

In conclusion it should be stated that the censuses of manufacturing for Wisconsin in the mid-nineteenth century provided general guidelines for assessing industrial development. In the absence of more reliable and more frequently reported information, they fulfilled a very useful function. But these censuses cannot be regarded as statistical photographs, especially on the local level where they contain numerous errors which can cause misinterpretations. Instead they should be regarded as reasonable approximations to be modified if and as better data become available.

[10] Walsh, 516–531.

APPENDIX B

The Dun and Bradstreet Reports
and Their Value as Historical Source Material

THE BUSINESS NOW KNOWN as Dun & Bradstreet Inc. was originally organized in 1841 by Lewis Tappan, a New York silk merchant.[1] He hoped that his mercantile agency would provide a reliable source of information on entrepreneurs seeking commercial credit. Such information was needed because the general problems and risks involved in granting credit had been aggravated by the disturbed financial conditions following the Panic of 1837.

Originally located in New York, Tappan's agency gathered data from local businessmen. Then gradually branches were opened in other parts of the country. Boston had an office in 1843; Philadelphia in 1845; Baltimore in 1846; Cincinnati in 1849; St. Louis in 1850; Chicago in 1854; and Milwaukee in 1858. Confidential agents, who were usually attorneys, bank clerks, lawyers, merchants, or other men of similar professional standing, were scattered throughout the country and moved westward with the frontier, thus giving indirect evidence of the effective state of the market.[2]

The credit reports sent in to the Mercantile Office by the Wisconsin agents in the 1840's and 1850's followed a similar format. A general one-sentence statement on the firm (which gave its value, its estimated worth in terms of capital invested, real estate held, and personal property, its length of operation, its prospects, and its credit rating) was

---

[1] It should be noted that these are cited as Dun & Bradstreet reports for convenience and ready identification only. The reports were actually created by the predecessor companies of Lewis Tappan & Co., Tappan & Douglass, B. Douglass, or R.G. Dun & Co. The succession of the proprietorship of the Mercantile Agency since 1841 is:

Lewis Tappan & Co.	1841–1849
Tappan & Douglass	1849–1854
B. Douglass	1854–1859
R.G. Dun & Co.	1859–1933
Dun & Bradstreet Inc.	1933–

J.M. Bradstreet & Son's Improved Mercantile Agency was founded in 1853 and was incorporated in 1876 as The Bradstreet Company. In 1933 it merged with R.G. Dun & Co.

[2] *Dun & Bradstreet: The Story of An Idea* (New York, 1968, 2nd printing), 16; scattered references in the reports submitted by the Wisconsin agents.

made twice a year. As information was added over the years it was possible to build up valuable historical material on the stages in the expansion or dissolution of a given enterprise.[3] Occasionally when a subscriber inquired about a particular firm, a special report was made on its business prospects. These special reports might include a character sketch of the proprietor concerned giving age, marital status, nationality or state of birth, if a native-born American, as well as business ability. Sometimes the agent would also note the source of an establishment's capital, the size of its labor force and the general prospects of particular types of business in certain areas.

The Dun & Bradstreet agents' reports thus gave a bountiful supply of descriptive data on manufacturing establishments, but their coverage was neither complete nor comprehensive. For example, information was gathered on eighty-four manufacturing firms in Racine County active some or all of the time from 1846 to 1860. But these firms did not represent a full sample of Racine industrialists and craftsmen in the antebellum years.[4] The firms were only those which were registered with the agency or on which information was actively solicited. The Seventh Census of 1850 listed ninety-nine establishments with an annual value of product of at least $500; the Eighth Census of 1860 named 124 such establishments. For the same years, 1850 and 1860, the firms which appeared to be active in Racine County, according to the Dun & Bradstreet data collected, were twenty-four and fifty-six respectively. There was thus only a certain degree of overlap between the firms recorded in the census schedules and those recorded in the Dun & Bradstreet reports.

Furthermore it was not possible to measure the growth of the reported firms with any degree of statistical accuracy. In some cases the precise age of the entrepreneur would be stated; in others, it would be given within a five-year period or in more general terms: young, middle-aged, or elderly. Again, the financial status of any particular firm might be reported exactly for one year, but in more general terms of small, fair, moderate, or large for other years. Thorough measurement was thus impossible.

---

[3] The manuscript volumes of the Dun & Bradstreet reports for the State of Wisconsin, kept in the Baker Library of the Harvard Business School, run from 1843 to 1883–84. They number sixty in all and contain some 14,735 pages. The reports not only cover manufacturing enterprises, but they also give details of commercial and trading firms, land agents, and banks.

[4] It was not possible to note details on all manufacturing firms in all the sample counties. Information was collected on the main industries and on the important firms in each county, with additional information on other activities as time allowed.

The Dun & Bradstreet agents' reports were a valuable source of qualitative information on the growth of various Wisconsin enterprises. Based on the opinions of contemporary white-collar workers, the reports estimated the character and business acumen of entrepreneurs and stated reasons for the success or failure of certain firms. These reports were of major importance because they supplied annual evidence of development, thus providing regular data on firms for which business records are frequently unavailable.

BIBLIOGRAPHY

UNPUBLISHED PRIMARY SOURCES

Archival Materials, Business Papers, Personal Papers, Manuscript Censuses, and Miscellany

Apart from the handwritten Dun & Bradstreet commercial credit rating reports at the Baker Library of the Harvard Business School, and the miscellaneous business and personal papers of J.I. Case and J.I. Case & Co., at the J.I. Case Co., Racine, Wisconsin, the unpublished primary sources are located either in the State Historical Society of Wisconsin, Madison, or in one of the area research centers run in co-operation with the State Historical Society.

There is a lamentable lack of business papers for early Wisconsin history. Existing records are piecemeal and usually poor in quality. The most valuable sources are the federal manuscript censuses for the state of Wisconsin, 1850 and 1860, Schedule 5, Products of Industry, and the Dun & Bradstreet commercial credit rating reports. The papers of Richard E. Ela, Racine County manufacturer of agricultural implements, and the papers of Orrin H. Ingram, Chippewa Valley lumberman, are also useful.

Less valuable collections include the Joseph Bennett papers, pertaining to lead smelting; the Jerome I. Case miscellaneous business papers, concerning the agricultural implements business; the George W. Esterly papers, relating to farm machinery; the early Henry E. Knapp papers, dealing with lumbering in northwestern Wisconsin; the Harrison Ludington papers, dealing with lumbering in Milwaukee and northeastern Wisconsin; the Henry Neidecken papers, records of stationers and blank-book manufacturers; and the papers of John H. Rountree, concerning lead mining.

There are many other small collections or diaries which contain scattered information; for example, the Thomas J. & Henry J. Bailey records, the John Bryon correspondence, the Lathrop Burgess account book and diary, the James C. Campbell diaries, the Carson & Eaton Lumber Co. account book, the Enoch Chase reminiscences, the Eau Claire Lumber Co. records, the early records of the Menasha Wooden Ware Corporation, the Milwaukee Grain Exchange Collection, the Olin Nelson reminiscences, the Lydia Petit manuscript in Racine, the William W. Wright reminiscences, and the file of biographical sketches prepared for, but not used in, the *Dictionary of Wisconsin Biography*.

Two additional sources of a different nature are the maps of the changing county boundaries of Wisconsin, 1840–1860, and the papers of two Wisconsin historians of the late nineteenth and early twentieth centuries. The maps, based on the *Origin and Legislative History of County Boundaries in Wisconsin* (Wisconsin Historical Records Survey, 1942), and the State of Wisconsin, *General Laws,* were drawn for Andrew H. Clark of the Geography Department of the University of Wisconsin. Copies have been deposited in the State Historical Society of Wisconsin. The historians, Publius V. Lawson of Winnebago County and Eugene W. Leach of Racine County, both left numerous papers and notes containing information not printed in their published works.

For a detailed guide to the archival collections of the State Historical Society of Wisconsin, see:

Delgado, David J. *Guide to Wisconsin State Archives.* Madison, State Historical Society of Wisconsin, 1966.

For full guides to the manuscript collections of the State Historical Society of Wisconsin, see:

Smith, Alice E. *Guide to the Manuscripts of the Wisconsin Historical Society.* Madison, State Historical Society of Wisconsin, 1944.

Harper, Josephine L. and Smith, Sharon C. *Guide to Manuscripts of the State Historical Society of Wisconsin, Supplement Number One.* Madison, State Historical Society of Wisconsin, 1957.

Harper, Josephine L. *Guide to Manuscripts of the State Historical Society of Wisconsin, Supplement Number Two.* Madison, State Historical Society of Wisconsin, 1966.

PUBLISHED PRIMARY SOURCES

[A.] *Publications of the Federal Government*

The most important publications of the federal government for this study are the decennial census reports.

United States. *Sixth Census, 1840.* Washington, 1841.

————. *Sixth Census, 1840, Compendium.* Washington, 1841.

————. *Abstract of the Seventh Census.* Washington, 1853.

————. *Seventh Census, 1850.* J.D.B. De Bow, Superintendent, Washington, 1853.

————. *Statistical View of the United States. A Compendium of the Seventh Census.* J.D.B. De Bow, Superintendent, Washington, 1854.

————. *Eighth Census, Preliminary Report.* J.C.G. Kennedy, Washington, 1862.

————. *Eighth Census, 1860.* J.C.G. Kennedy, Superintendent. Vol. I. *Population.* Washington, 1864.

Vol. II. *Agriculture.* Washington, 1864.

Vol. III. *Manufactures.* Washington, 1865.

—————.*Ninth Census, 1870.* Compiled under the direction of the Secretary of the Interior by Francis A. Walker, Washington, 1872.

Vol. I. *The Statistics of Population.*

Vol. II. *The Statistics of Wealth and Industry.*

—————. *Ninth Census, 1870. A Compendium.* Francis A. Walker, Superintendent of the Census, Washington, 1872.

—————. *Tenth Census, 1880.* Washington, 1887.

Vol. XVI. *Reports On The Water Powers Of The United States.*

—————. *Twelfth Census, 1900.* William B. Merriam, Director, Washington, 1902.

Vol. VII. *Manufactures, Part 1, United States by Industries.*

—————. *Thirteenth Census, 1910.* Washington, 1912.

Vol. IX. *Manufactures, 1909, Reports by States, with Statistics for Principal Cities.*

Other publications of the federal government, mainly relating to the taking of the censuses, are also helpful.

Cram, Thomas J. "Internal Improvements in the Territory of Wisconsin." *Senate Documents.* 26 Congress. 1 Session. Document 40 (1840). Serial 357.

Owen, David D. "Report of a Geological Exploration of part of Iowa, Wisconsin and Illinois." *Senate Reports.* 28 Congress. 1 Session. Report 407 (1844). Serial 437.

Blair and Rives. "Report of the Select Committee on Statistics. Last Census Errors." *House Reports.* 28 Congress. 1 Session. Report 580 (1844). Serial 447.

"Memorial of the American Statistical Association Praying for the Adoption of Measures for the Correction of Errors in the Returns of the Sixth Census." *Senate Documents.* 28 Congress. 2 Session. Document 5 (1844). Serial 449.

"Statistics of the Agriculture and Manufactures, Domestic Trade, Currency and Banks of the United States." *Senate Documents.* 28 Congress. 2 Session. Document 21 (1844). Serial 450.

Owen, David D. "Report of a Geological Reconnaissance of the Chippewa Lead District of Wisconsin." *Senate Executive Documents.* 30 Congress. 1 Session. Document 57 (1847). Serial 509.

Capen, Nahu, and Chickering. "Letter Concerning the Census of 1849." *Senate Miscellaneous Documents.* 30 Congress. 2 Session. Document 64 (1849). Serial 533.

Andrews, Israel D. "Report of the Trade and Commerce of the British and North American Colonies and upon the Trade of the Great

Lakes and Rivers." *Senate Documents.* 32 Congress. 1 Session. Document 112 (1853). Serial 622.

"Report of the Select Committee to Whom Was Referred for Revision the Plan for the Publications of the Returns of the Census, as Exemplified in Relation to the State of Maryland." *Senate Reports.* 32 Congress. 1 Session. Report 276 (1851). Serial 631.

De Bow, J.D.B., Superintendent of the Census. "Report on Work of the Census of 1850." Contained in a letter from the Secretary of the Interior. *Senate Executive Documents.* 33 Congress. 1 Session. Document 9 (1853). Serial 694.

Kennedy, Joseph C.G. "Abstract of the Statistics of Manufactures According to the Returns of the Seventh Census. Condensed from the Digest under the Direction of the Secretary of the Interior in Conformity with the First Section of the Act of June 12, 1858." *Senate Executive Documents.* 35 Congress. 2 Session. Document 39 (1858–59). Serial 984.

Kennedy, Joseph C.G. "Preliminary Report on the Eighth Census, 1860." *House Executive Documents.* 37 Congress. 2 Session. Document 116 (1862). Serial 1137.

Wright, Carroll D. "A Permanent Census Bureau." *Senate Executive Documents.* 52 Congress. 1 Session. Document 1 (1892). Serial 2892.

Tunnell, George G. "Report to the Bureau of Statistics on Lake Commerce." *House Documents.* 55 Congress. 2 Session. Document 277 (1898). Serial 3679.

Wright, Carroll D. "The History and Growth of the United States' Census." *Senate Documents.* 56 Congress. 1 Session. Document 194 (1899). Serial 3856.

[B.] *State Government Publications*

The annual *Journals* of the House and the Council of the Territory of Wisconsin, and of the Assembly and the Senate of the State of Wisconsin, provide the outline of the legislative history of bills and resolutions; but they do not record the contents of the proposed legislation or the debates. The more useful sources of data herein are the appendices, which give official reports and committee investigations.

State of New York. *Census of the State of New York for 1855.* Albany, 1857.

State of Wisconsin. *Journal of the Assembly,* 1848–1865. Madison, 1849–1866.

————. *Journal of the Senate,* 1848–1865. Madison, 1849–1866.

————. *Messages of the Governor,* 1848–1865. Madison. Published in both the House and Senate *Journals* and in pamphlet form.
Territory of Wisconsin. *Journal of the Council,* 1836–1847. Madison, 1837–1848.
————. *Journal of the House,* 1836–1848. Madison, 1837–1849.

[C.] *Newspapers and Periodicals*

Advertisements in the local newspapers of the sample counties frequently reveal information on manufacturing growth in Wisconsin. Sometimes editorial comments or feature articles also give historical sketches of business firms. The periodicals usually offer more general information on economic conditions. The following newspapers and periodicals were read in whole or in part for the periods cited.

Burlington Gazette. Burlington. 1859–1860.

De Bow's Commercial Review of the South and West. New Orleans. Vols. 1–34. 1846–1864.

Eau Claire Free Press. Eau Claire. 1858–1861.

Fisher's National Magazine and Industrial Record. New York. 1845–1846.

Fort Atkinson Standard. Fort Atkinson. 1859–1861.

Grant County Herald. Lancaster. 1843–1849, 1850, 1859–1861.

Grant County Witness. Platteville. 1859–1861.

Hunt's Merchants' Magazine and Commercial Review. New York. Vols. 1–53. 1839–1865.

Independent American. Platteville. 1845–1849, 1851–1857.

Menasha Advocate. Menasha. 1854–1856.

Menasha Conservator. Menasha. 1856–1860.

Milwaukee Advertiser. Milwaukee. 1837–1841. (Incomplete.)

Milwaukee Commercial Herald. Milwaukee. 1843–1844.

Milwaukee Courier. Milwaukee. 1841–1847.

Milwaukee Daily Commercial Advertiser. Milwaukee. 1850.

Milwaukee Democrat. Milwaukee. 1843–1844.

Milwaukee Journal. Milwaukee. 1841–1842.

Milwaukee Semi-Weekly Gazette. Milwaukee. 1845–1846.

Milwaukee Sentinel. Milwaukee. 1838–1862.

Neenah and Menasha Examiner. Neenah. 1856.

Niles' National Register. Philadelphia. Vols. 48–75. 1835–1849.

Oshkosh Courier. Oshkosh. 1853, 1854–1861.

Oshkosh Democrat. Oshkosh. 1849–1850, 1850–1853; scattered editions 1855, 1857.

Platteville Examiner. Platteville. 1858.

Racine Advocate. Racine. 1842–1847, 1848–1849, 1851–1854, 1855–1861.

Racine Argus. Racine. 1838.

Rock River Pilot. Watertown. 1847–1848.

Watertown Chronicle. Watertown. 1847–1855.

Watertown Democrat. Watertown. 1854–1861.

Weekly Jeffersonian. Jefferson. 1853–1860.

Weekly Manufacturer. Menasha. 1861–1862.

Weekly Northwestern. Oshkosh. 1860.

Western Journal and Civilian. St. Louis. Vols. 1–15. 1848–1856.

Wisconsin Chief. Fort Atkinson. 1859–1861.

Wisconsin Farmer and Northwestern Cultivator. Racine, Dubuque, Janesville, and Madison. 1849–1865.

Wisconsin Free Democrat. Milwaukee and Prairieville. 1845–1846.

Wisconsin Miscellaneous Papers. Microfilm. (Includes *Northern Badger.* Platteville. 1840 and 1841; *Omro Republican.* Omro. 1858. *Winnebago Telegraph.* Oshkosh. 1850, and *Wisconsin Whig.* Platteville. 1842.)

Wisconsin State Agricultural Society. *Transactions,* 1851–1868.

A comprehensive guide to Wisconsin newspapers is given by:

Oehlerts, Donald E. *Guide to Wisconsin Newspapers.* Madison. State Historical Society of Wisconsin, 1958.

[D.] *City Directories and Reports of Boards of Trade*

Milwaukee Board of Trade. *Annual Report* of the Commerce, Manufactures, Banking, Business and the Railroad System of the City of Milwaukee. Milwaukee, 1854–1857.

Milwaukee Business Directories. Milwaukee. 1858, 1862, and 1863.

Milwaukee Chamber of Commerce. *Annual Report* of the Trade and Commerce Together with the General Business of the City of Milwaukee. Milwaukee. 1858–1865.

Milwaukee City Directories. Milwaukee. 1847–1848, 1848–1849, 1851–1852, 1854–1855, 1857–1858, 1858, 1859–1860, 1860–1861, 1862, 1863, and 1865.

Oshkosh City Directory for the Year 1857. Oshkosh. 1857.

Racine City Directory, 1858–59. Racine. 1859.

Racine Register, Business Directory and Advertiser, 1850. Racine. 1850.

Wisconsin State Directories. Madison, 1853; Milwaukee, 1857–1858, 1858, and 1858–1859.

[E.] *Contemporary Articles and Books*

Chapman, S. *Handbook of Wisconsin.* Milwaukee, S. Chapman, 1855.

Curtiss, Daniel S. *Western Portraiture and Emigrants' Guide.* New York, J.H. Colton, 1852.

De Bow, J.D.B. *Industrial Resources of the Southern and Western States.* 3 Vols. New Orleans, De Bow's Review, 1852–1853.

Decker and Goodwin, eds. *The Village of Menasha: Its Location, History and Advantages.* Menasha, D.C. Felton, 1857.

Dwinnell, S.A. *Wisconsin As It Was And As It Is, 1836–1866.* Milwaukee, 1867.

Finney and Davis, *History of Oshkosh.* Oshkosh, 1867.

Gregory, John. *Industrial Resources of Wisconsin.* Milwaukee, Starrs' Book and Job Printing Office, 1855.

Kennedy, Joseph C.G. *Progress of Statistics. Read before the American Geographical and Statistical Society at the Annual Meeting in New York, Dec. 1, 1859.* New York, J.F. Trow, 1861.

––––––. *Review of the Report of the Senate Committee on the Returns of the Seventh Census.* Washington, Gideon & Co., 1852.

Lapham, Increase A. *A Geographical and Topographical Description of Wisconsin.* Milwaukee, P.C. Hale, 1844.

Milwaukee in 1860: A Glance At Its Business Houses. Milwaukee, 1860.

Mitchell, Martin, and Joseph Osborne. *Geographical and Statistical History of the County of Winnebago, with Interesting Incidents Among the Aboriginal and Pioneer Settlers.* Oshkosh, Mitchell and Martin, 1856.

Peto, S. Morton. *The Resources and Prospects of America.* London, Strahan Publishers, 1866.

Quiner, E.B. *City of Watertown, Wisconsin: Its Manufacturing and Railroad Advantages and Business Statistics.* Watertown, Published by order of the City Council, 1856.

Ritchie, James S. *Wisconsin and Its Resources, with Lake Superior, Its Commerce and Navigation.* Chicago, Keen and Lee, 1857.

Ross, James. *Wisconsin and Her Resources for Remunerating Capital and Supporting Labor.* Madison, 1871.

Smith, William R. *The History of Wisconsin.* 3 Vols. Madison, B. Brown, 1854.

The Emigrant's Instructor on Wisconsin and the Western States of America. Liverpool, British Temperance Emigration Society, Second Edition, Enlarged, 1844.

Tucker, George. *Progress of the United States, in Population and Wealth, in Fifty Years, as Exhibited by the Decennial Census From*

1790 to 1840; with an Appendix Containing An Abstract of the Census of 1850. New York, Press of Hunt's Merchants' Magazine, 1855. (Reprinted Economic Classics, New York, Augustus Kelley, 1964.)

Wheeler, Andrew C. *The Chronicles of Milwaukee: Being a Narrative of the Town from its Earliest Period to the Present.* Milwaukee, Jermain and Brightman, 1861.

Whitney, Thomas. "An Address. At the Opening of the New Chamber of Commerce Rooms in the City of Milwaukee, Feb. 3, 1863." Milwaukee, 1863, in *Milwaukee Pamphlets,* Vol. 4.

SECONDARY SOURCES

[A.] *Books*

Aiken, Andrew J. and Lewis A. Proctor, eds. *Men of Progress: Wisconsin.* Milwaukee, Evening Wisconsin Co., 1897.

Anderson, Theodore A. *A Century of Banking in Wisconsin.* Madison, State Historical Society of Wisconsin, 1954.

Anderson, W.J. and Julius Blayer, eds. *Milwaukee's Great Industries: A Compilation of Facts.* Milwaukee, Association for the Advancement of Milwaukee, 1892.

Ardrey, R.L. *American Agricultural Implements.* Chicago, published by the author, 1894.

Atherton, Lewis E. *The Pioneer Merchant in Mid-America.* Columbia, University of Missouri Studies, Vol. 45, No. 2, 1939.

Bailey, William F., ed. *History of Eau Claire County, Wisconsin, Past and Present.* Chicago, C.F. Cooper & Co., 1914.

Barland, Lois. *Sawdust City: A History of Eau Claire, Wisconsin, from the Earliest Times to 1910.* Stevens Point, Wisconsin, Worzalla Publ. Co., 1960.

Barton, Elmer E. *Industrial History of Milwaukee, the Commercial, Manufacturing and Railway Metropolis of the North West.* Milwaukee, E.E. Barton, 1886.

Belcher, Wyatt B. *The Economic Rivalry Between St. Louis and Chicago, 1850–1880.* New York, Columbia University Studies in History, Economics, and Public Law, No. 529, 1947.

Berry, Brian J.L. *Geography of Market Centers and Retail Distribution.* Englewood Cliffs, New Jersey, Prentice-Hall, 1967.

————, and Allan Pred. *Central Place Studies: A Bibliography of Theory and Applications.* (*Including a Supplement Through 1964.*) Philadelphia, Regional Science Institute, 1965.

Berry, Thomas S. *Western Prices Before 1861: A Study in the Cin-*

cinnati Market. Cambridge, Harvard University Economic Studies, Vol. 74, 1943.

Billington, Ray A. *Westward Expansion: A History of the American Frontier.* New York, McMillan Co., 2nd edition, 1960.

Bishop, John L. *A History of American Manufactures from 1608– 1860.* Philadelphia, Edward Young & Co., 3rd edition, 1868.

Bruce, William G. *Builders of Milwaukee.* Milwaukee, Bruce Publ. Co., 1946.

————. *History of Milwaukee City and County.* 3 Vols. Chicago, 1922.

Buck, James S. *Pioneer History of Milwaukee.* 4 Vols. Milwaukee, Milwaukee News Co., 1876–1886.

Buley, R. Carlyle. *The Old Northwest: Pioneer Period 1815–1840.* 2 Vols. Indianapolis, Indiana Historical Society, 1950.

Bundy, Charles S. *Early Days in the Chippewa Valley.* Menominee, Wisconsin, Flint-Douglas, 1916.

Campbell, Henry C. *et al. Wisconsin in Three Centuries, 1634–1905.* 4 Vols. New York, The Century History Company, 1906.

Carter, Margaret S. *New Diggings on the Fever, 1824–1869.* Benton, Wisconsin, privately printed, 1959.

Cary, John W. *The Organization and History of the Chicago, Milwaukee and St. Paul Railway Company.* Milwaukee, Press of Cramer, Aikens & Cramer, 1893.

Chamberlin, Thomas C. *Geology of Wisconsin, 1873–1879.* 4 Vols. Madison, Published under the direction of the Chief Geologist by the Commissioners of Public Printing, 1877–1883.

Chippewa County, Wisconsin, Past and Present. 2 Vols. Chicago, S.J. Clarke Publ. Co., 1913.

Christaller, Walter. *Central Places in Southern Germany.* (Trans. C.W. Baskin.) Englewood Cliffs, New Jersey, Prentice-Hall, Inc., 1966.

Clark, John G. *The Grain Trade in the Old Northwest.* Urbana, University of Ilinois Press, 1966.

Clark, Victor S. *The History of Manufactures in the United States.* 3 Vols. New York, Peter Smith, 1929 edition (reprint).

Cochran, Thomas C. *The Pabst Brewing Company: The History of an American Business.* New York, New York University Press, 1948.

Cole, Arthur H. *Wholesale Commodity Prices in the United States, 1700–1861.* 2 Vols. Cambridge, Harvard University Press, 1938.

Commemorative Biographical Record of the Counties of Rock, Green, Grant, Iowa and Lafayette. Chicago, J.H. Beers & Co., 1901.

Commemorative Biographical Record of the Fox River Valley Coun-

ties of Brown, Outagamie and Winnebago. Chicago, J.H. Beers & Co., 1895.

Commemorative Biographical Record of the Prominent and Representative Men of Racine and Kenosha Counties. Chicago, J.H. Beers & Co., 1906.

Conrad, Howard L., ed. *History of Milwaukee from Its First Settlement to the Year 1895.* 3 Vols. Chicago, American Biographical Publ. Co., 1895.

Crockett, Norman L. *The Woolen Industry Of The Midwest.* Lexington, University Press of Kentucky, 1970.

Cunningham, Gustav A. *History of Neenah.* Neenah, Gazette Printing Estab., 1878.

Current, Richard N. *Pine Logs and Politics: A Life of Philetus Sawyer, 1816–1900.* Madison, State Historical Society of Wisconsin, 1950.

Curti, Merle, *et al. The Making of an American Community: A Case Study of Democracy in a Frontier County.* Stanford, Stanford University Press, 1959.

Danhof, Clarence H. *Change in Agriculture: The Northern United States, 1820–1870.* Cambridge, Harvard University Press, 1969.

Derleth, August. *The Milwaukee Road: Its First Hundred Years.* New York, Creative Age Press, 1948.

Dictionary of Wisconsin Biography. Madison, State Historical Society of Wisconsin, 1960.

Duckett, Kenneth W. *Frontiersman of Fortune: Moses M. Strong.* Madison, State Historical Society of Wisconsin, 1951.

Easum, Chester V. *The Americanization of Carl Schurz.* Chicago, University of Chicago Press, 1929.

Fisher, Marvin. *Workshops in the Wilderness: The European Response to American Industrialization, 1830–1860.* New York, Oxford University Press, 1967.

Fishlow, Albert. *American Railroads and The Transformation of the Ante-bellum Economy.* Cambridge, Harvard University Press, 1965.

Fite, Emerson. *Social and Industrial Conditions in the North during the Civil War.* New York, McMillan Company, 1910.

Flower, Frank A., ed. *History of Milwaukee, Wisconsin.* Chicago, Western Historical Company, 1881.

Fogel, Robert W. *Railroads and American Growth: Essays in Econometric History.* Baltimore, Johns Hopkins Press, 1964.

Forrester, George, ed. *Historical and Biographical Album of the Chippewa Valley, Wisconsin.* Chicago, A. Warner, 1892.

Fries, Robert F. *Empire in Pine: The Story of Lumbering in Wisconsin, 1830–1900*. Madison, State Historical Society of Wisconsin, 1951.

Gara, Larry. *Westernized Yankee: The Story of Cyrus Woodman*. Madison, State Historical Society of Wisconsin, 1956.

Gates, Paul W. *The Farmers' Age: Agriculture, 1815–1860*. (Vol. 3, Economic History of the United States.) New York, Holt, Rinehart & Winston, 1960.

————. *The Wisconsin Pine Lands of Cornell University: A Study in Land Policy and Absentee Ownership*. Ithaca, Cornell University Press, 1943.

Geist, Walter. *Allis Chalmers: A Brief History of 103 Years of Production*. New York, Newcomen Society in North America, 1950.

Gephart, William F. *Transportation and Industrial Development in the Middle West*. New York, Columbia University Studies in History, Economics and Public Law, No. 34, 1909.

Glaab, Charles N., and Lawrence H. Larsen. *Factories in the Valley: Neenah-Menasha, 1870–1910*. Madison, State Historical Society of Wisconsin, 1969.

Grant, Ulysses Sherman. *Report of the Lead and Zinc Deposits of Wisconsin*. (Wisconsin Geological and Natural History Survey, Bulletin No. 14, Economic Series, No. 9.) Madison, University of Wisconsin, 1906.

Greenhut, Melvin L. *Plant Location in Theory and in Practice: The Economics of Space*. Chapel Hill, University of North Carolina Press, 1956.

Gregory, John G. *History of Milwaukee, Wisconsin*. 4 Vols. Chicago, S.J. Clarke Publ. Co., 1931.

————. (Ed.) *Southeastern Wisconsin: A History of Old Milwaukee County*. 4 Vols. Chicago, S.J. Clarke Publ. Co., 1932.

Habakkuk, H. J. *American and British Technology in the Nineteenth Century*. Cambridge, Cambridge University Press, 1962.

Haggett, Peter. *Locational Analysis in Human Geography*. London, Edward Arnold Publishers Ltd., 1965.

Hamming, Edward. *The Port of Milwaukee*. Rock Island, Illinois, Augustana College Library Publications Number 25, 1953.

Hanna, Frank A. *The Compilation of Manufacturing Statistics*. Washington, United States Department of Commerce, 1959.

Harney, Richard J. *History of Winnebago County, Wisconsin, and Early History of the Northwest*. Oshkosh, Allen and Hicks, 1880.

Hibbard, Benjamin H. *A History of the Public Land Policies*. New York, The McMillan Company, 1924.

————. *The History of Agriculture in Dane County, Wisconsin.* (Bulletin of the University of Wisconsin No. 101, Economics and Political Science Series, Vol. 1, No. 2.) Madison, University of Wisconsin, 1904.

Hidy, Ralph, *et al. Timber and the Weyerhauser Story.* New York, McMillan and Co., 1963.

Hindle, Brooke. *Technology In Early America. Needs and Opportunities For Study.* Chapel Hill, University of North Carolina Press, 1966.

History of Grant County, Wisconsin. Chicago, Western Historical Company, 1881.

History of Jefferson County, Wisconsin. Chicago, Western Historical Company, 1879.

History of Northern Wisconsin. Chicago, Western Historical Company, 1881.

History of Racine and Kenosha Counties, Wisconsin. Chicago, Western Historical Company, 1879.

Holbrook, Stewart H. *Machines of Plenty: Pioneering in Western Agriculture.* New York, McMillan Company, 1955.

Holford, Castello N. *History of Grant County, Wisconsin.* Lancaster, Wisconsin, 1900.

Holt, W. Stull. *The Bureau of the Census: Its History, Activities and Organization.* (Institute for Government Research, Service Monographs of the United States Government No. 53.) Washington, 1929.

Hoover, Edgar M. *The Location of Economic Activity.* New York, McGraw Hill, 1948.

Hotchkiss, George W. *History of the Lumber and Forest Industry of the Northwest.* Chicago, G. W. Hotchkiss & Co., 1898.

Howard Publishing Company, *A History of the Wisconsin Paper Industry.* Chicago, 1948.

Hunt, Robert S. *Law and Locomotives: The Impact of the Railroad on Wisconsin Law in the Nineteenth Century.* Madison, State Historical Society of Wisconsin, 1958.

Hunter, Louis C. *Studies in the Economic History of the Ohio Valley: Seasonal Aspects of Industry and Commerce before the Age of Big Business.* Northampton, Massachusetts, Smith College Studies in History, No. 19, 1935.

Hurst, J. Willard. *Law and Economic Growth: The Legal History of the Lumber Industry in Wisconsin, 1836–1915.* Cambridge, Belknap Press of Harvard University Press, 1964.

Hutchinson, William T. *Cyrus Hall McCormick.* 2 Vols. New York, The Century Company, 1935.

Ingram, Orrin H. *Letters of a Pioneer: Early Lumbering Days.* Eau Claire, Wisconsin. 1916.

Isard, Walter. *Location and Space Economy: A General Theory Relating to Industrial Location, Market Areas, Land Use, Trade and Urban Structure.* New York, John Wiley & Sons, 1956.

Jones, Fred M. *Middlemen In the Domestic Trade Of the United States, 1800–1860.* (Illinois Studies in the Social Sciences, Vol. 21, No. 3.) Urbana, University of Illinois Press, 1937. (Johnson Reprints, 1968.)

Kaysen, James P. *The Railroads of Wisconsin, 1827–1937.* Boston, Railway and Locomotive Historical Society, 1937.

Korman, Gerd. *Industrialization, Immigrants and Americanizers: The View from Milwaukee, 1866–1921.* Madison, State Historical Society of Wisconsin, 1967.

Koss, Rudolph A. *Milwaukee* (Trans. Hans Ibsen.) Milwaukee, 1871.

Krueger, Leonard B. *History of Commercial Banking in Wisconsin.* Madison, University of Wisconsin Studies in Social Sciences and History, No. 18, 1933.

Kuehnl, George J. *The Wisconsin Business Corporation.* Madison, University of Wisconsin Press, 1959.

Kuhlmann, Charles B. *The Development of the Flour Milling Industry in the United States.* Boston, Houghton, Mifflin Company, 1929.

Lake, James A. *Law and Mineral Wealth: The Legal Profile of the Wisconsin Mining Industry.* Madison, University of Wisconsin Press, 1962.

Lampard, Eric E. *The Rise of the Dairy Industry in Wisconsin: A Study in Agricultural Change, 1820–1920.* Madison, State Historical Society of Wisconsin, 1963.

Larson, Agnes M. *History of the White Pine Industry in Minnesota.* Minneapolis, University of Minnesota Press, 1949.

Larson, Henrietta M. *The Wheat Market and the Farmer in Minnesota, 1858–1900.* New York, Columbia University Studies in History, Economics and Public Law, No. 122, 1926.

Larson, Lawrence M. *A Financial and Administrative History of Milwaukee.* (University of Wisconsin Bulletin No. 242, Economics and Political Science Series, 4, No. 2.) Madison, University of Wisconsin, 1908.

Lawson, Publius V., ed. *History of Winnebago County, Wisconsin: Its Cities, Towns, Resources and People.* 2 Vols. Chicago, 1908.

Lebergott, Stanley. *Manpower in Economic Growth: The American Record Since 1800.* New York, McGraw-Hill, 1964.

Lee, Judson F. *Transportation as a Factor in the Development of Northern Illinois Previous to 1860.* (University of Chicago Libraries Reprint from the Illinois Historical Journal, 10.) Chicago, 1917.

Leech, Harper, and John C. Carroll. *Armour and His Times.* New York, Appleton-Century Company, 1938.

Leiby, James. *Carrol Wright and Labor Reform: The Origin of Labor Statistics.* Cambridge, Harvard University Press, 1960.

Lippincott, Isaac. *A History of Manufacturing in the Ohio Valley to the Year 1860.* New York, Knickerbocker Press, 1914.

Litterer, Oscar. *Where Does Small Business Obtain its Capital.* Minneapolis, 1948.

Losch, August. *The Economics of Location.* (Trans. William H. Woglum.) New York, Science Editions, 1967.

Martin, Roy L. *History of the Wisconsin Central.* Boston, Railway and Locomotive Historical Society, Bulletin No. 54, 1941.

Memorial and Genealogical Record of Dodge and Jefferson Counties, Wisconsin. Chicago, Goodspeed Bros., 1894.

Merk, Frederick. *Economic History of Wisconsin During the Civil War Decade.* Madison, State Historical Society of Wisconsin, 1916.

Milwaukee: A Souvenir Of The Exposition, State Fair and Saengerfest. Milwaukee, Caspar and Zahn, 1886.

Miner, H. A. *Memorial of Elisha Dickinson Smith, 1827–1899.* Madison, 1903.

Mortenson, W. P., et al. *Wisconsin Farm Prices, 1841–1933.* (Wisconsin Agricultural Experiment Station Bulletin No. 119.) Madison, 1933.

National Bureau of Economic Research. *Output, Employment and Productivity in the United States After 1800.* New York, Princeton University Studies in Income and Wealth, No. 30, 1966.

————. *Trends in the American Economy in the Nineteenth Century.* Princeton, Princeton University Studies in Income and Wealth, No. 24, 1960.

Norris, James D. *Frontier Iron: The Maramec Iron Works, 1826–1876.* Madison, State Historical Society of Wisconsin, 1964.

North, Douglass C. *The Economic Growth of the United States, 1790–1860.* Englewood Cliffs, New Jersey, Prentice-Hall, 1961.

Perloff, Harvey S., et al. *Regions, Resources and Economic Growth.* Baltimore, Johns Hopkins Press, 1960.

Portrait and Biographical Album of Racine and Kenosha Counties, Wisconsin. Chicago, Lake City Publishing Company, 1892.

Portrait and Biographical Record of Walworth and Jefferson Counties. Chicago, Lake City Publishing Company, 1894.

Pred, Allan. *The Spatial Dynamics of United States Urban Industrial Growth, 1800–1914.* Cambridge, M.I.T. Press, 1966.

Quaife, Milo M. *Wisconsin: Its History and Its People, 1634–1924.* 4 Vols. Chicago, S. J. Clarke Publ. Co., 1924.

Randall, Thomas E. *History of the Chippewa Valley.* Eau Claire, Eau Claire Free Press, 1875.

Reynolds, Arthur R. *The Daniel Shaw Lumber Company: A Case Study of the Wisconsin Lumbering Frontier.* New York, New York University Press, 1957.

Riley, Elmer A. *The Industrial Development of Chicago and Vicinity Prior to 1880.* Chicago, McElroy Publishing Co., 1911.

Rogin, Leo. *The Introduction of Farm Machinery in its Relation to the Productivity of Labor in the Agriculture of the United States during the Nineteenth Century.* Berkeley, University of California Publications in Economics, Vol. 9, 1931.

Rosenberg, Nathan, ed. *The American System of Manufactures: The Report of the Committee On the Machinery Of the United States, 1855, and The Special Reports of George Wallis and Joseph Whitworth, 1854.* Edinburgh, University of Edinburgh Press, 1969.

Russell, Austin H. *The Milwaukee Story.* Milwaukee, Milwaukee Journal, 1946.

Sankey, Alice. *Racine, the Belle City.* Racine, Western Printing and Lithographical Co., n.d.

Schafer, Joseph. *A History of Agriculture in Wisconsin.* (Wisconsin Domesday Book, General Studies, 1.) Madison, State Historical Society of Wisconsin, 1922.

————. *Four Wisconsin Counties: Prairie and Forest.* (Wisconsin Domesday Book, General Studies, 2.) Madison, State Historical Society of Wisconsin, 1927.

————. *The Wisconsin Lead Region.* (Wisconsin Domesday Book, General Studies, 3.) Madison, State Historical Society of Wisconsin, 1932.

————. *The Winnebago-Horicon Basin.* (Wisconsin Domesday Book, General Studies, 4.) Madison, State Historical Society of Wisconsin, 1937.

Smith, Alice E. *James Duane Doty, Frontier Promoter.* Madison, State Historical Society of Wisconsin, 1954.

————. *George Smith's Money: A Scottish Investor in America.* Madison, State Historical Society of Wisconsin, 1966.

————. *Millstone and Saw: The Origins of Neenah-Menasha.* Madison, State Historical Society of Wisconsin, 1966.

Smith, Leonard S. *The Water Powers of Wisconsin.* (Wisconsin Geo-

248 THE MANUFACTURING FRONTIER

logical and Natural History Survey, Bulletin No. 20, Economics
Series No. 13.) Madison, Published by the State, 1908.

Smith, Walter B. and Arthur H. Cole. *Fluctuations in American Business, 1790-1860.* Cambridge, Harvard University Press, 1935.

Steen, Herman. *Flour Milling in America.* Minneapolis, T.S. Denison & Co. Inc., 1963.

Stephenson, Isaac. *Recollections of a Long Life, 1829-1915.* Chicago privately printed, 1915.

Still, Bayrd. *Milwaukee: The History of a City.* Madison, State Historical Society of Wisconsin, 1965. 2nd printing.

Stone, Fanny S., ed. *Racine, Belle City of the Lakes, and Racine County, Wisconsin.* Chicago, S.J. Clarke Publ. Co., 1916.

Strassmann, W. Paul. *Risk and Technological Innovation: American Manufacturing Methods during the Nineteenth Century.* Ithaca, Cornell University Press, 1959.

Strong, Moses M. *History of the Territory of Wisconsin from 1836-1848.* Madison, Published by authority of the State, 1885.

Swank, James M. *The Ironworks Of The United States.* Philadelphia, J.D. Chandler, 1876.

Taylor, George R. *The Transportation Revolution, 1815-1860.* (Vol. 4, Economic History of the United States.) New York, Rinehart, 1951.

Temin, Peter. *Iron and Steel in Nineteenth Century America: An Economic Inquiry.* Cambridge, M.I.T. Press, 1964.

The Century Club of Business in Milwaukee. Milwaukee, Sentinel Press, 1966.

Thernstrom, Stephen. *Poverty and Progress: Social Mobility in a Nineteenth Century City.* Cambridge, Harvard University Press, 1964.

Thompson, John G. *The Rise and Decline of the Wheat Growing Industry in Wisconsin.* Madison, University of Wisconsin Economics and Political Science Series, Bulletin Vol. 5, No. 3, 1909.

Todd, Arthur Cecil. *The Cornish Miner in America: The Contribution to the Mining History of the United States by Emigrant Cornish Miners — The Men Called Cousin Jacks.* Glendale, California, The Arthur H. Clark Co., 1967.

Truesdell, Leon E. *The Development of Punch Card Tabulation in the Bureau of the Census, 1890-1940.* Washington, Bureau of the Census, 1965.

Tryon, Rolla M. *Household Manufactures in the United States, 1640-1860: A Study in Industrial History.* Chicago, University of Chicago Press, 1917.

Turner, Frederick J. *The Frontier in American History.* New York, H. Holt and Co., 1921.

Uber, Harvey A. *Environmental Factors in the Development of Wisconsin.* Milwaukee, Marquette University Press, 1937.

United States Biographical Dictionary and Portrait Gallery of Eminent and Self-Made Men. Wisconsin volume. Chicago, 1877.

Usher, Ellis B. *Wisconsin: Its Story and Biography, 1848–1913.* 8 Vols. Chicago, Lewis Publ. Co., 1914.

Wade, Richard C. *The Urban Frontier: The Rise of Western Cities, 1790–1830.* Cambridge, Harvard University Press, 1959.

Waltrous, Jerome Anthony (Ed.) *Memoirs of Milwaukee County.* 2 Vols. Madison, Western Historical Association, 1909.

Warren, George F. and Frank A. Pearson. *Gold and Prices.* New York, John Wiley & Sons, 1935.

————. *Wholesale Prices for 213 Years, 1720–1932.* (Cornell University Agricultural Experimental Station, Memoir No. 142.) Ithaca, 1942.

Weber, Alfred. *Theory of the Location of Industries.* Trans. C.J. Friedrich. Chicago, University of Chicago Press, 1929.

Wells, Robert W. *This Is Milwaukee.* New York, Doubleday & Co. Inc., 1970.

Whitbeck, Ray H. *Industries of Wisconsin and their Geographic Basis.* Madison, University of Wisconsin Geological and Natural History Survey Bulletin, No. 26, 1913.

————. *The Geography and Economic Development of Southeastern Wisconsin.* Madison, University of Wisconsin Geological and Natural History Survey Bulletin No. 58, Educational Series No. 6, 1921.

————. *The Geography of the Fox Winnebago Valley.* Madison, University of Wisconsin, Geological and Natural History Survey, No. 42, 1915.

Wik, Reynold M. *Steam Power on the American Farm.* Philadelphia, University of Pennsylvania Press, 1953.

Wisconsin Historical Records Survey. *Origin and Legislative History of County Boundaries in Wisconsin.* Madison, 1942.

Wisconsin State Highway Commission. *A History of Wisconsin Highway Development, 1835–1945.* Madison, compiled and edited by the Highway Planning Survey, 1947.

Works Project Administration, Writers' Program. *Milwaukee: History of Milwaukee County.* Milwaukee, Milwaukee Public Library, 1947. Typewritten.

Wright, James E. *The Galena Lead District, Federal Policy and*

Practice, 1824–1847. Madison, State Historical Society for the Department of History of the University of Wisconsin, 1966.

[B.] *Articles and Pamphlets*

The files of the Wisconsin Academy of Science, Arts, and Letters *Transactions*; the Wisconsin Historical *Collections*; the Wisconsin Historical *Proceedings*; and the *Wisconsin Magazine of History* contain many accounts, both secondary and primary, which were of use in this study. Where used they are cited fully in the relevant footnote. They are not cited individually in the bibliography. The following other articles and pamphlets were also of value.

Alexander, John W., and James B. Lindberg. "Measurements of Manufacturing, Coefficients of Correlations." *Journal of Regional Science,* 3 (1961), 71–81.

Allis Chalmers. *A Story of Men and a Great Industrial Era, 1847–1947.* Milwaukee, Allis Chalmers Manufacturing Company, 1947.

Atherton, Lewis T. "Early Western Mercantile Advertising." *Business History Society Bulletin,* 12 (1938), 52–57.

Bateman, Fred, James D. Foust, and Thomas J. Weiss. "Large Scale Manufacturing in the South and West, 1850–1860." *Business History Review,* 45 (1971), 1–17.

Berry, Brian J.L., and William L. Garrison. "The Functional Bases of the Central Pace Hierarchy." *Economic Geography,* 34 (1958), 145–154.

Blumin, Stuart. "The Historical Study of Vertical Mobility." *Historical Methods Newsletter,* 1 (1968), 1–13.

Bullock, Charles J. "Wage Statistics and the Federal Census." *The Federal Census Critical Essays,* American Economic Association, New Series, Number 2 (1889), 343–368.

Case, J.I., Company. *Serving Farmers Since 1842.* Racine, Wisconsin, J.I. Case Company, 1948.

Census of Wisconsin, 1836–1880. Compiled pamphlet, n.p.n.d.

Clark, James I. *Edward P. Allis, Pioneer Industrialist.* (Men of Wisconsin, No. 4.) Madison, State Historical Society of Wisconsin, 1958.

David, Paul A. "The Mechanization of Reaping in the Antebellum Midwest." *Industrialization in Two Systems,* Henry Rosofsky, ed. New York, Wiley, 1966.

Dun and Bradstreet. *The Story of an Idea.* New York, Dun and Bradstreet, 2nd printing, 1968.

Easterlin, Richard A. "Estimates of Manufacturing Activity." *Population Redistribution and Economic Growth in the United States,* Vol. 1, E.S. Lee, *et al.* Philadelphia, American Philosophical Society, 1957, 635–701.

Gould, Peter R. "Man Against His Eenvironment: A Game Theoretic Framework." Association of American Geographers, *Annals*, 53 (1963), 290–297.

Green, F.H.W. "Community of Interest Areas: Notes on the Hierarchy of Central Places and their Hinterlands." *Economic Geography*, 34 (1958), 210–222.

Guttman, Herbert G. "The Reality Of the Rags-To-Riches 'Myth': The Case of Paterson, New Jersey Locomotive, Iron and Machinery Manufacturers, 1830–1880." *Nineteenth Century Cities: Essays In The New Urban History*, Stephan Thernstrom and Richard Sennett, eds. New Haven, Yale University Press, 1969, pp. 98–124.

Hunter, Louis C. "Factors in the Early Pittsburgh Iron Industry." *Facts and Factors in Economic History: Essays in Honor of E.F. Gay*. Cambridge, Harvard University Press, 1932, pp. 424–445.

Isard, Walter. "Game Theory, Location Theory and Industrial Agglomeration." *Papers and Proceedings of the Regional Science Association*, 18 (1967), 1–12.

Kohlmeyer, Frederick W. "Northern Pine Lumbermen: A Study in Origins and Migrations." *Journal of Economic History*, 16 (1956), 529–538.

Leach, Eugene W. "Foundations for a Great City Were Laid by Sturdy Pioneers of Racine in 1834–40." Pamphlet combined from articles written for the *Racine Times-Call*, 1925, n.p. n.d.

————. "Pioneer Facts and Folks." Pamphlet compiled from articles written for the *Racine Journal News*, 1926, n.p. n.d.

Lunt, E.C. "History of the United States' Census, 1790–1887." American Statistical Association, *Publications*, 1 (1888), 63–97.

Newman, J. Wilson. "Dun and Bradstreet, Established in 1841 for the Promotion and Protection of Trade." Newcomen Society in North America *Addresses*, 15, No. 5 (1956), 5–32.

North, Douglass C. "Industrialization in the United States." *Cambridge Economic History of Europe*, Vol. 6, Pt. 2, Cambridge, Cambridge University Press, 1965, 673–705.

————. "Location Theory and Regional Economic Growth", *Journal of Political Economy*, 62 (1955), 243–258.

North, S.N.D. "Manufactures in the Federal Census." *The Federal Census: Critical Essays*. American Economic Association, New Series, Number 2 (1889), 257–303.

Perloff, Harvey S. and Lowdon Wingo, Jr. "Natural Resources Endowment and Regional Economic Growth." *Natural Resources and Economic Growth*. Joseph J. Spengler, ed. Washington, Resources

For the Future, Inc., 1961.

Peterson, William J. "The Lead Traffic on the Upper Mississippi, 1823–1848." *Mississippi Valley Historical Review,* 17 (1930), 72–97.

Poulson, Barry W. "Estimates of the Value of Manufacturing Output in the Early Nineteenth Century." *Journal of Economic History,* 29 (1969), 521–525.

Pred, Allan. "Behavior and Location — Foundations for a Geographic and Dynamic Location Theory." *Lund Studies in Geography,* Series B. Human Geography, 7 (1967).

Racine Centennial Book Committee. *Racine Centennial, 1848–1948.* Racine, 1949.

Racine, Wisconsin, and its Manufacturing Interests, 1834–1888. Racine Times Publishing Company, 1888.

Roth, Filibert. *On the Forestry Conditions of Northern Wisconsin.* Madison, University of Wisconsin Geological and Natural History Survey, Bulletin No. 1, Economic Series No. 1, 1898.

Severson, Robert W. "The American Manufacturing Frontier, 1870–1940." *Business History Review,* 34 (1960), 356–372.

Smith, D.M. "A Theoretical Framework for Geographical Studies of Industrial Location." *Economic Geography,* 42 (1966), 95–113.

Stevens, Benjamin H. "An Application of Game Theory to a Problem in Location Strategy." *Papers and Proceedings of the Regional Science Association,* 7 (1961), 143–157.

Still, Bayrd. "Patterns of Mid-Nineteenth Century Urbanization in the Middle West." *Mississippi Valley Historical Review,* 28 (1941), 187–206.

Swichkow, Louis J. "The Jewish Community of Milwaukee, Wisconsin, 1860–1870." *Publications of the American Jewish Historical Society,* 47 (1957), 34–58.

Temin, Peter. "Steam and Waterpower in the Early Nineteenth Century." *Journal of Economic History,* 26 (1966), 187–205.

Thwaites, Reuben G. "Winnebago County." Originally written for the *Oshkosh Times. Wisconsin Local History,* Vol. 5, No. 7, Madison, n.d.

Wolpert, Julian. "The Decision Process in Spatial Context." American Association of Geographers, *Annals,* 54 (1964), 537–558.

Wooster, Harvey A. "A Forgotten Factor in American Industrial History." *American Economic Review,* 26 (1926), 14–27.

————. "Manufacturer and Artisan, 1790–1840." *Journal of Political Economy,* 34 (1926), 61–77.

Wright, Carroll D. "Problems of the Census." *Journal of Social Science,* 23 (1887), 1–20.

[C.] *Theses and Dissertations*

There is an abundance of information on Wisconsin economic history in these unpublished sources, most of which are in the Memorial Library of the University of Wisconsin. The quality of the material varies considerably, but some is useful.

Atwood, Marion J. "Economic Conditions of Wisconsin at the Outbreak of the Civil War." Unpublished B.A. thesis, University of Wisconsin, 1910.

Bartz, Melvin E. "Origin and Development of the Paper Industry in the Fox River Valley, Wisconsin." Unpublished M.A. thesis, State University of Iowa, 1940.

Bemis, Florence I. "The Beginnings of Winnebago County." Unpublished Ph.B. thesis, University of Wisconsin, 1906.

Blackburn, Arthur W. "Some Social and Economic Factors in the Development of Racine County." Unpublished B.A. thesis, University of Wisconsin, 1901.

Bolton, William L. "The Plank Roads of Wisconsin." Unpublished B.L. thesis, University of Wisconsin, 1897.

Borak, Arthur. "The Financial History of the Chicago, Milwaukee and St. Paul Company." Unpublished Ph.D. dissertation, University of Minnesota, 1929.

Branch, Maurice L. "The Paper Industry in the Lake States Region, 1834–1937." Unpublished Ph.D. dissertation, University of Wisconsin, 1954.

Brown, Richard L. "An Economic Base Study of Racine, Wisconsin." Unpublished M.S. thesis, University of Wisconsin, 1953.

Canuteson, Richard L. "The Railroad Development of Northern Wisconsin." Unpublished M.A. thesis, University of Wisconsin, 1930.

Collar, William. "The Utilization of Whitney Rapids: From Sawmill to Paper Company, 1831–1908." Unpublished M.S. thesis, Wisconsin State University at La Crosse, 1967.

Derby, William E. "A History of the Port of Milwaukee." Unpublished Ph.D. dissertation, University of Wisconsin, 1963.

Dykstra, Daniel J. "Law and the Lumber Industry, 1861–1881." Unpublished S.J.D. thesis, University of Wisconsin, 1950.

Elliot, Frank N. "The Causes and Growth of Railroad Regulation in Wisconsin, 1848–1876." Unpublished Ph.D. dissertation, University of Wisconsin, 1956.

Fischer, Duane D. "The Disposal of Federal Lands in the Eau Claire Land District of Wisconsin, 1848–1925." Unpublished M.S. thesis, University of Wisconsin, 1961.

Flippo, Forest D. "The McCormick Reaper and the Development of the United States' Wheat Production in the Ante-Bellum Years." Unpublished M.S. thesis, University of Wisconsin, 1964.

Gallman, Robert E. "Value Added by Agriculture, Mining and Manufacturing in the United States, 1840–1880." Unpublished Ph.D. dissertation, University of Pennsylvania, 1956.

Gebhard, Cornelia. "The Development of Railroads in Wisconsin from 1850–1865." Unpublished B.A. thesis, University of Wisconsin, 1917.

Hadley, Ella J. "Transportation and Travel on Wisconsin Wagon Roads, 1848–1860." Unpublished B.A. thesis, University of Wisconsin, 1919.

Hendry, Melvin A. "Methods Used in the Census and the Annual Survey of Manufactures and Their Effects on the Character of the Data." Unpublished M.A. thesis, Howard University, 1953.

Henseler, Alice M. "A History of Racine County, Wisconsin, 1835–1880." Unpublished M.A. thesis, University of Wisconsin, 1966.

Herrman, William H. "Wisconsin and the California Gold Rush." Unpublished M.A. thesis, University of Wisconsin, 1940.

Heyer, Clair B. "How Reliable Is Census Data? An Evaluation of Manuscript Census Reports As Source Material for Historical Research in a Study of One Iowa Township." Unpublished thesis, Northern Illinois University, n.d.

Hilton, Robert T. "Men of Metal: A History of the Foundry Industry in Wisconsin." Unpublished M.S. thesis, University of Wisconsin, 1952.

Karn, Edwin D. "Road Making in Wisconsin Territory." Unpublished M.A. thesis, University of Wisconsin, 1959.

Kleven, Bernhardt J. "The Wisconsin Lumber Industry." Unpublished Ph.D. dissertation, University of Minnesota, 1941.

Korn, Bernhard C. "Eber Brock Ward: Pathfinder of American Industry." Unpublished Ph.D. dissertation, Marquette University, Milwaukee, 1942.

————. "The Story of Bay View." Unpublished M.A. thesis, Marquette University, Milwaukee, 1935.

Landaal, Bernice P. "Early Lumbering Communities in Northern Wisconsin." Unpublished M.Phil. thesis, University of Wisconsin, 1934.

Lander, Ernest McP., Jr. "Manufacturing in Ante-bellum South Carolina." Unpublished Ph.D. dissertation, University of North Carolina, 1950.

Legler, Peter F. "Josiah A. Noonan: A Story of Promotion and Excoriation in the Old Northwest." Unpublished M.A. thesis, University of Wisconsin, 1954.

Leonard, David. "A Biography of Alexander Mitchell, 1817–1887." Unpublished M.S. thesis, University of Wisconsin, 1951.

Licking, Ralph H. "Geographic Factors Influencing the Lumber Trade in the Great Lakes Region." Unpublished M.A. thesis, University of Wisconsin, 1926.

Linley, Victor. "A Brief History of the Lumber Industry in the Chippewa Valley." Unpublished B.A. thesis, University of Wisconsin, 1925.

Loft, Genivera E. "The Evolution of the Wood-Working Industries of Wisconsin." Unpublished M.A. thesis, University of Wisconsin, 1916.

McCluggage, Robert W. "The Fox-Wisconsin Waterway, 1836–1872." Unpublished Ph.D. dissertation, University of Wisconsin, 1954.

Margosian, Michael N. "Town Promotion in Early-Day Racine." Unpublished M.S. thesis, University of Wisconsin, Milwaukee, 1966.

Marquette, Clare L. "The Business Activities of C.C. Washburn." Unpublished Ph.D. dissertation, University of Wisconsin, 1940.

Miller, Willard F. "A History of Eau Claire During the Civil War." Unpublished M.S. thesis, University of Wisconsin, 1954.

Neu, Irene D. "Land Credit in Frontier Wisconsin." Unpublished M.A. thesis, Cornell University, 1945.

Neuhaus, Alma J. "History of the Roads of Wisconsin." Unpublished Ph.D. thesis, University of Wisconsin, 1904.

Odle, Thomas D. "The American Grain Trade of the Great Lakes, 1825–1873." Unpublished Ph.D. dissertation, University of Michigan, 1952.

Phelan, Sister Mary L. "The Origins and Development of the Lumbering and Woodworking Industries in the Vicinity of Oshkosh, Wisconsin, 1830–1880: A Study in the Use and Exploitation of the Wolf River Pinery." Unpublished M.A. thesis, Catholic University of America, 1954.

Read, Mary J. "A Population Study of the Driftless Hill Land During the Pioneer Period, 1832–1860." Unpublished Ph.D. dissertation, University of Wisconsin, 1941.

Rice, Herbert W. "The Early History of the Chicago, Milwaukee and St. Paul Company." Unpublished Ph.D. dissertation, University of Iowa, 1939.

Rodewald John W. "Railroad Development in Wisconsin, 1850–1865." Unpublished M.Phil. thesis, University of Wisconsin, 1911.

Schefft, Charles E. "The Tanning Industry in Wisconsin: A History of its Frontier Origins and its Development." Unpublished M.A. thesis, University of Wisconsin, 1938.

Simpson, Olive M. "Transportation in the Early Lead Mining Region of Wisconsin." Unpublished B.A. thesis, University of Wisconsin, 1912.

Taylor, John W. "Reservation and Leasing of the Salines, Lead and Copper Mines of the Public Domain." Unpublished Ph.D. dissertation, University of Chicago, 1930.

Twining, Charles E. "Lumbering and the Chippewa River." Unpublished M.S. thesis, University of Wisconsin, 1963.

Vaughan, Thomas J. "Life of the Wisconsin Lumberjack, 1850–1880." Unpublished M.S. thesis, University of Wisconsin, 1951.

Whitaker, James W. "Wisconsin Land Speculation, 1830–1860: Case Studies of Small Scale Speculators." Unpublished M.S. thesis, University of Wisconsin, 1962.

For a guide to theses and dissertations on Wisconsin subjects see:

State Historical Society of Wisconsin and the University of Wisconsin Extension Division. *A Guide to Theses on Wisconsin Subjects*. Madison, 1964.

State Historical Society of Wisconsin and the University of Wisconsin Extension Division. *A Guide to Theses on Wisconsin Subjects: A Supplement*. Madison, 1966.

INDEX